ACT® MATH PREP

The Staff of The Princeton Review

PrincetonReview.com

Penguin
Random
House

The Princeton Review

The Princeton Review
110 East 42nd Street, 7th Floor
New York, NY 10017
Email: editorialsupport@review.com

Published in the United States by Penguin Random House LLC,
New York.

Some of the content in ACT Math Prep has previously
appeared in Math and Science Workout for the ACT, 4th
Edition published as a trade paperback by Random House, an
imprint and division of Penguin Random House LLC, in 2019.

Terms of Service: The Princeton Review Online Companion
Tools ("Student Tools") for retail books are available for only
the two most recent editions of that book. Student Tools
may be activated only once per eligible book purchased for
a total of 24 months of access. Activation of Student Tools
more than once per book is in direct violation of these Terms
of Service and may result in discontinuation of access to
Student Tools Services.

ISBN: 978-0-525-57035-6
eBook ISBN: 978-0-525-57039-4
ISSN: 2691-7130

ACT is a registered trademark of ACT, Inc.

The Princeton Review is not affiliated with Princeton University.

The material in this book is up-to-date at the time of publication.
However, changes may have been instituted by the testing
body in the test after this book was published.

If there are any important late-breaking developments,
changes, or corrections to the materials in this book, we will
post that information online in the Student Tools. Register
your book and check your Student Tools to see if there are
any updates posted there.

Editor: Chris Chimera
Production Editors: Liz Dacey, Kathy G. Carter
Production Artists: Gabriel Berlin and Jason Ullmeyer

Printed in the United States of America.

10 9 8 7 6 5 4 3 2 1

The Princeton Review Publishing Team
Rob Franek, Editor-in-Chief
David Soto, Senior Director, Data Operations
Stephen Koch, Senior Manager, Data Operations
Deborah Weber, Director of Production
Jason Ullmeyer, Production Design Manager
Jennifer Chapman, Senior Production Artist
Selena Coppock, Director of Editorial
Orion McBean, Senior Editor
Aaron Riccio, Senior Editor
Meave Shelton, Senior Editor
Chris Chimera, Editor
Patricia Murphy, Editor
Laura Rose, Editor
Alexa Schmitt Bugler, Editorial Assistant

Penguin Random House Publishing Team
Tom Russell, VP, Publisher
Alison Stoltzfus, Senior Director, Publishing
Brett Wright, Senior Editor
Emily Hoffman, Assistant Managing Editor
Ellen Reed, Production Manager
Suzanne Lee, Designer
Eugenia Lo, Publishing Assistant

Acknowledgments

Special thanks to Nicole Cosme, Stacey Cowap, Lori DesRochers, Spencer LeDoux, Aaron Lindh, Scott O'Neal, Jacob Schiff, and James Williams for their work in creating this title.

—Amy Minster
Content Director, High School Programs

Thanks for Gabriel Berlin, Jason Ullmeyer, Kathy Carter, and Liz Dacey for their hard work and careful attention to every page in the production of this book.

Special thanks to Adam Robinson, who conceived of and perfected the Joe Bloggs approach to standardized tests, and many of the other successful techniques used by The Princeton Review.

Contents

Get More (Free) Content
at PrincetonReview.com/prep

As easy as 1•2•3

1 Go to PrincetonReview.com/prep or scan the **QR code** and enter the following ISBN for your book:

9780525570356

2 Answer a few simple questions to set up an exclusive Princeton Review account. *(If you already have one, you can just log in.)*

3 Enjoy access to your **FREE** content!

Once you've registered, you can...

- Get our take on any recent or pending updates to the ACT

- Take a full-length practice ACT

- Get valuable advice about the college application process, including tips for writing a great essay and where to apply for financial aid

- If you're still choosing between colleges, use our searchable rankings of *The Best 388 Colleges* to find out more information about your dream school.

- Check to see if there have been any corrections or updates to this edition

Need to report a potential **content** issue?

Contact **EditorialSupport@review.com** and include:

- full title of the book
- ISBN
- page number

Need to report a **technical** issue?

Contact **TPRStudentTech@review.com** and provide:

- your full name
- email address used to register the book
- full book title and ISBN
- Operating system (Mac/PC) and browser (Chrome, Firefox, Safari, etc.)

Look For These Icons Throughout The Book

 **PROVEN TECHNIQUES**

 APPLIED STRATEGIES

 MORE GREAT BOOKS

 ONLINE ARTICLES

CONSIDERING AN ACT® PREP COURSE?

Pick the Option That's Right For You

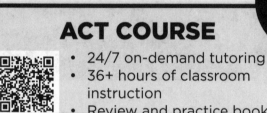

Part I
Orientation

Chapter 1
All About the ACT

WELCOME

The ACT can be an important part of college admissions. Many schools require or recommend their applicants submit either SAT or ACT scores. It's worth keeping in mind, though, that the importance of these tests will vary among the many colleges and universities in the United States. If you haven't already, make sure to research whether the ACT is required or recommended for admission to the schools you plan to apply to.

During the COVID-19 pandemic, many schools went test-optional to account for the numerous students whose SAT and ACT tests were canceled. Some of those schools have returned to requiring test scores, while others have not yet but still may. For the most up-to-date information on the schools you are interested in, check out their admissions websites.

Even if ACT scores are optional, you may still want to submit them if you think your great ACT scores will boost your chances of acceptance. Furthermore, ACT scores are often used for scholarships, so it can be worth putting time into preparing for the test if you can save a good amount on your college education in return.

When colleges require standardized test scores, they will accept either SAT or ACT scores. The expert advice of The Princeton Review is to take whichever test you do better on and focus your efforts on preparing for that one.

Because you bought this book, we assume you've already made the decision to boost your ACT score. This book provides a strategic and efficient way to improve your scores, specifically on the Math test. For a more thorough review of content and exhaustive practice, we recommend purchasing the latest editions of *ACT Prep* and our *ACT Practice Questions* book.

For more on admissions, see The Princeton Review's *The Best 388 Colleges* or visit our website, PrincetonReview.com.

FUN FACTS ABOUT THE ACT

The ACT Math test is nothing like the math tests you take in school. All of the content review and strategies we teach in the following lessons are based on the specific structure and format of the ACT. Before you can beat a test, you have to know how it's built.

If you feel like you need help with English, Reading, or Science, please see our companion books: *ACT English Prep*, *ACT Reading Prep*, and *ACT Science Prep*.

Structure

The ACT is made up of four multiple-choice tests and an optional Writing test.

The five tests are always given in the same order.

English	Math	Reading	Science	Writing
45 minutes	60 minutes	35 minutes	35 minutes	40 minutes
75 questions	60 questions	40 questions	40 questions	1 essay

Scoring

When students and schools talk about ACT scores, they mean the composite score, a range of 1–36. The composite is an average of the four multiple-choice tests, each scored on the same 1–36 scale. If you take the Writing test, you'll also receive an additional Writing score on a scale of 2–12. The Writing score is an average of four 2–12 subscores: Ideas and Analysis, Development and Support, Organization, and Language Use and Conventions. Neither the Writing test score nor the combined English plus Writing English Language Arts score affects the composite. Be sure to check ACT's website to determine whether your target schools want you to take the ACT Writing test.

Students also receive subscores in addition to their (1–36) composite ACT score. These indicators are designed to measure student performance and predict career readiness, as well as competency in STEM (Science, Technology, Engineering, Mathematics) and English language arts. ACT believes that these additional scores will give students better insight into their strengths and how those strengths can be harnessed for success in college and beyond. In addition to the 1–36 score for each of the tests and their composite score, students now see score breakdowns in the following categories:

- **STEM score.** This score will show you how well you did on the Math and Science portions of the test.
- **Progress Toward Career Readiness indicator.** The ACT would have you believe this indicator measures how prepared you are for a career, but really it just measures how prepared you are to take yet another test: the ACT National Career Readiness Certificate™.
- **English Language Arts score.** If you take the Writing test, this score will give you a combined score for the English, Reading, and Writing tests.
- **Text Complexity Progress indicator.** This score will tell you how well you fared on those hard passages throughout the test.

There is also a section on the score report that breaks each section down into categories and tells you both how many questions there were in each category and how many of them you got correct. Some of these categories can be useful in helping you know what you need to study: for example, if you missed a lot of questions in the "Geometry" category, you should brush up your geometry skills. But if you did poorly in the "Integration of Knowledge and Ideas" category, it's not quite as obvious what you need to study. Don't worry about these scores though—they're there because they align with federal academic standards, and school districts that use the ACT for standardized testing for all juniors want those scores, but colleges don't typically look at them for admissions purposes.

It's All About the Composite

Whether you look at your score online or wait to get it in the mail, the biggest number on the page is always the composite. While admissions offices will certainly see the individual scores of all five tests (and their subscores), schools will use the composite to evaluate your application, and that's why, in the end, it's the only one that matters.

The composite is an average: let the full weight of that sink in. Do you need to bring up all four scores equally to raise your composite? Do you need to be a superstar in all four tests? Should you focus more on your weaknesses than your strengths? No, no, and absolutely not. The best way to improve your composite is not to shore up your weaknesses but exploit your strengths as much as possible.

> To improve your ACT score, use your strengths to lift the composite score as high as possible.

You don't need to be a rock star on all four tests. Identify two, maybe three tests, and focus on raising those scores as much as you can to raise your composite. Work on your weakest scores to keep them from pulling you down. Think of it this way: if you had only one hour to devote to practice the week before the ACT, spend that hour on your best subjects.

Single-Section Tests and Superscoring

The people who write the ACT have announced their intention to allow students to take one, two, or three individual sections in a day—that is, you will not have to take the entire test in one single day. However, before using this option, you will need to take a full ACT. Also, single-section tests are offered only on computer.

Unfortunately, plans to offer single-section retesting were delayed by the COVID-19 pandemic, and as of the publication of this book, a date for the rollout has not been announced. We encourage you to check the ACT website, www.act.org, for the most up-to-date information about the availability of single-section retesting when it is eventually offered.

One piece of good news is that ACT has begun Superscoring. If you take the ACT more than once, ACT will automatically take your highest English, Math, Reading, and Science scores and average them together to calculate a new "Superscore" composite.

Sounds great, right? We think it is—this gives you the opportunity to show your best ACT score to schools. Now, colleges and universities still have the option of whether to accept the Superscore, but for the schools that let you Superscore, this is all positive for you.

> Single-section testing is great, but research your goal schools' testing policies before relying on it!

Of course, you might have grabbed this book because you've already decided to focus on improving a single test for your superscore. So, let's move on so we can dive into the good stuff!

Math Score

Many students find Math scores the easiest to improve. A strategic review of the rules and formulas, coupled with rigorous practice, can add several points. In order to most effectively raise your Math score, focus on mastering the Big Impact skills and topics. These are strategies to help you tackle the most commonly covered Math content in a strategic and efficient way.

Time

How often do you take a final exam in school that gives you *at most* a minute per question? Probably never. The ACT isn't a school test, and you can't approach it as if it is. While speed and accuracy depend on individual skills and grasp of content, almost all students struggle to finish the Math test on time. The more you treat this test the same way you would a school final, the less likely you are to finish, much less finish with the greatest accuracy. All of The Princeton Review's strategies are based on this time crunch. There's a difference between knowing *how* to do a question under the best of circumstance and getting it *right* with a ticking clock and glowering proctor in the room.

Crack It Open

For more comprehensive review and practice for the ACT, pick up a copy of *ACT Premium Prep*, which includes sample questions and guidance for each of the tests on the exam.

Chapter 2
How to Approach the ACT Online Test

In this chapter, you'll learn what to expect on the ACT Online Test, including how to apply its computer-based features and our strategies to the question types in each section—English, Math, Reading, Science, and Writing. If your ACT will be pencil-and-paper, skip this chapter.

At the time of this book's printing, the option to take the ACT online at a testing center was postponed. ACT also plans to offer at-home online testing, although an exact rollout date has not yet been announced. For up-to-date news on both options, check the ACT website.

WHAT IS THE ACT ONLINE TEST?

The ACT Online Test is the ACT that you take on a computer, rather than with a pencil and paper. Despite the name, you can't take the ACT from the comfort of your own home; instead, you'll have to go to a testing center (possibly your high school) and take the test on one of the center's computers.

The ACT Online Test has the same overall structure, timing, and number of questions as the pencil-and-paper ACT. The scoring, score range, and scoring method are also the same. If the ACT Online Test is basically the same as the pencil-and-paper ACT, who would take the ACT Online Test?

WHO TAKES THE ACT ONLINE TEST?

ACT has been offering versions of the ACT on computer since about 2016. The first students to take the ACT on the computer were students taking the test at school. Schools and school districts decided whether to give the test on the computer.

As of September 2018, all students taking the ACT outside of the United States take the test on a computer (except for those students with accommodations requiring the use of a traditional pencil-and-paper test).

ACT has indicated that eventually students in the United States will have the option of taking the ACT Online Test instead of the traditional pencil-and-paper version. Students choosing this option will get their scores in about two to three business days (e.g., take the test on Saturday, have your score the next Wednesday). However, at the time of this printing, no specific timeline was available.

Single-Section Retesting is an incredible option for students. However, colleges still have the option to accept or not accept these new scores. Research your target schools early so you know your options!

Single-Section Retesting

If you are happy with the score you receive from a single test administration, you will still have the option to send just that score to colleges. If your score in one section is not as high as you'd like, you will eventually have a chance to correct that. Students who have already taken the full ACT may choose to take one, two, or three sections again using Single-Section Retesting. ACT will then produce a "superscore" consisting of your best results in all tests (English, Math, Reading, Science, and Writing (if you took it)). Note that not all colleges accept a superscored ACT, so do your research before taking advantage of this option.

ACT ONLINE TEST FEATURES

So, besides the obvious fact that it's taken on a computer, what are the differences between taking the ACT on the computer and taking it on paper? Let's start with what you can't do on the ACT Online Test. You can't "write" on the screen in a freehand way. You're limited in how you're able to mark the answer choices, and each question appears on its own screen (so you can't see multiple questions at one glance). You will also be given a small "whiteboard" and dry erase pen with which to make notes and do work.

So, what features does the ACT Online Test have?

- Timer
  - You can hide the timer by clicking on it.
  - There is a 5-minute warning toward the end of each test. There is no audible signal at the 5-minute warning, only a small indicator in the upper-right corner of the screen.
- Nav tool
  - You can use this tool to navigate directly to any question in the section.
  - The Nav tool blocks the current question when opened.
  - It also shows what questions you have flagged and/or left blank.
  - You can flag questions in this menu.
- Question numbers at the bottom of the screen
  - You can click on these numbers to navigate directly to any question in the section.
  - These numbers also indicate whether a question has been flagged and/or left blank.
- Flag tool
  - You can flag a question on the question screen itself or by using the Nav tool.
  - Flagging a question has no effect besides marking the question for your own purposes.
- Answer Eliminator
  - Answer choices can be "crossed-off" on-screen.
  - An answer choice that's been eliminated cannot be chosen and must be "un-crossed-off" first by clicking the answer choice.
- Magnifier
  - You can use this to magnify specific parts of the screen.
- Line Mask
  - This tool covers part of the screen. There is an adjustable window you can use to limit what you can see.
  - This is an excellent tool if you need an aid to help you focus on specific parts of the text or figure.
  - However, not everyone will find this tool useful, so do not feel obligated to use it!
  - Note that you cannot highlight the text in the window of the Line Mask.
- Answer Mask
  - This tool hides the answer choices of a question.
  - Answers can be revealed one at a time.
- Screen Zoom
  - This tool changes the zoom of the entire screen (as opposed to the magnifier, which magnifies only one part of the screen).
  - Your screen zoom setting will remain the same from question to question.
- Highlighter
  - You can use this tool to highlight parts of passage text, question text, or answer text.
  - You cannot highlight within figures.
  - If you highlight in a passage with multiple questions, your highlights will only show up on that question. (In other words, if you highlight, for example, question 1 of a Reading passage, questions 2–10 of that same passage will not show those highlights.)
  - Turning off the highlighter tool removes your highlights.

- Shortcuts:

Keybind	Function	Keybind	Function
Ctrl + H	Toggle Help	Ctrl + Enter	Answer Question
Ctrl + F	Flag Item	Alt + M	Toggle Magnifier
Ctrl + I	Item Navigation	Alt + H	Toggle Highlighter
Alt + P	Previous Question	Alt + E	Toggle Answer Eliminator
Alt + N	Next Question	Alt + A	Toggle Answer Masking
A-E or 1-5	Select Alternative	Alt + L	Toggle Line Masking

- The Writing test is typed, rather than written by hand.

You will also be given a small "whiteboard" and dry erase pen with which to make notes and do work.

HOW TO APPROACH THE ACT ONLINE TEST

The strategies mentioned in this chapter are thoroughly discussed in our comprehensive guide, *ACT Prep*, so be sure to pick up a copy of that book if you have not already done so. These approaches were created in reference to the pencil-and-paper format, but they still apply to the ACT Online Test with some adjustments. This chapter assumes your familiarity with these strategies and will show you how to make the best use of them given the tools available in the computer-based format.

You will also want to incorporate some computer-based practice into your prep plan. ACT's website has practice sections for each of the four multiple-choice parts of the test and for the essay. We recommend that you do those sections toward the end of your preparation (and close to your test date) to give yourself an opportunity to practice what you've learned on a platform similar to the one you'll be using on the day of the test.

> **Remember!**
> Your goal is to get the best possible score on the ACT. ACT's goal is to assign a number to you that (supposedly) means something to colleges. Focus on your goal!

If you are planning to take the ACT online, you should practice as if you're doing all your work on the computer, even when you're working in a physical book. Use a highlighter, but don't use the highlighter on any figures (as the ACT Online Test won't let you do so). Use your pencil to eliminate answer choices and have a separate sheet of paper or a whiteboard to do any work you need to do, instead of writing on the problem itself.

Also, remember that our approaches work. Don't get misled by ACT's instructions on the day of the test—their way of approaching the test won't give you the best results!

Overall

Your Personal Order of Difficulty (POOD) and Pacing goals will be the same on the ACT Online Test as on the pencil-and-paper version. Because it is easy to change your answers, put in your Letter of the Day (LOTD) when skipping a Later or Never question. Use the Flag tool on the Later questions so you can jump back easily (using either the navigation bar at the bottom of the screen or the Nav tool).

Process of Elimination (POE) is still a vital approach. On both the paper-and-pencil ACT and the ACT Online Test, there are more wrong answers than correct ones. Eliminating one you know are wrong helps you to save time, avoid trap answers, and make a better guess if you have to. On the ACT Online Test, you cannot write on the test, but you can use the Highlighter tool. Turn on these tools (and the Line Mask, if desired) at the beginning of the English section and use them throughout.

ENGLISH

The Basic Approaches to both Proofreader and Editor questions are the same on the computerized and the paper versions of the ACT. When you decide to skip a question to come back to it Later (for example, a question asking for the introduction to the topic of the passage before you've read any part of the passage), flag the question so you can easily jump back to it before moving on to the next passage. When you have five minutes remaining, flag your current question and use the Nav tool to make sure you've put in your LOTD for any questions that you haven't done, then return to your spot and work until time runs out.

For a comprehensive review of all sections of the ACT and the strategies mentioned throughout this chapter, check out our book, *ACT Prep*.

When you work Proofreader questions, you can use the Highlighter tool to help you focus on the key parts of the text. Let's see an example:

Sneaking down the corridor, the agent, taking

care not to alert the guards, spotting the locked door.

- ○ **A.** NO CHANGE
- ○ **B.** spot
- ○ **C.** are spotting
- ○ **D.** spots

Use the tools available to help you focus on the key portions of the text. Practice with a highlighter when you're working on paper (instead of underlining with your pencil).

Here's How to Crack It

Verbs are changing in the answer choices, so the question is testing subject/verb agreement. The verb must be consistent with the subject. *The agent* is the subject; highlight it:

Sneaking down the corridor, the agent, taking

care not to alert the guards, spotting the locked door.

- ○ **A.** NO CHANGE
- ○ **B.** spot
- ○ **C.** are spotting
- ○ **D.** spots

The agent is singular, so the verb must be singular. Eliminate (B) and (C), as both are plural. *Spotting* cannot be the main verb of a sentence, so eliminate (A). The correct answer is (D).

Similarly, the Highlighter tool is helpful on Editor questions. Use the tool on both the passage and the question to help you focus on the relevant parts of each.

As it's name suggests, the Indian fantail is not native to North America. In fact, its establishment here was quite accidental. In 1926, the San Diego Zoo acquired four pythons from India for its reptile exhibit. The long trip from India required, that, the pythons be provided with food for the journey, and a group of unfortunate fantails was shipped for just that purpose. Two lucky fantails survived, and their beautiful appearance caused the San Diego Zoo to keep and breed them for the public to see. Eventually, some of the animals escaped captivity and developed populations in the wild, all thanks to those two birds!

Given that all the choices are true, which one provides the most relevant and specific information at this point in the essay?
- **A.** NO CHANGE
- **B.** and they have quite an appetite.
- **C.** because no one wanted them to starve.
- **D.** and they are quite picky in what they'll eat.

Here's How to Crack It

The question asks for the *most relevant and specific information*. Highlight those words in the question. The first sentence of the paragraph focuses on the *Indian fantail,* and the sentence after the underlined portion discusses *(t)wo lucky fantails.* The final sentence discusses *the animals* that escaped. Highlight these words in the paragraph.

Your screen should look like this:

As it's name suggests, the Indian fantail is not native to North America. In fact, its establishment here was quite accidental. In 1926, the San Diego Zoo acquired four pythons from India for its reptile exhibit. The long trip from India required, that, the pythons be provided with food for the journey, and a group of unfortunate fantails was shipped for just that purpose. Two lucky fantails survived, and their beautiful appearance caused the San Diego Zoo to keep and breed them for the public to see. Eventually, some of the animals escaped captivity and developed populations in the wild, all thanks to those two birds!

Given that all the choices are true, which one provides the most relevant and specific information at this point in the essay?
- **A.** NO CHANGE
- **B.** and they have quite an appetite.
- **C.** because no one wanted them to starve.
- **D.** and they are quite picky in what they'll eat.

Use POE, focusing on whether the choice is consistent with the highlights in the passage. The sentence as written discusses *a group of unfortunate fantails*; keep (A). Choices (B), (C), and (D) do not talk about the Indian fantail; instead, they focus on the pythons. This is inconsistent with the goal of the sentence and the content of the paragraph; eliminate those answers. The correct answer is (A).

Finally, you can't write in the passage, so you'll need to approach the Vertical Line Test slightly differently. On the paper-and-pencil ACT, you would use this strategy for questions about punctuation, drawing a vertical line where the punctuation breaks up the ideas in the text. On the computerized ACT, you should use the whiteboard to handle these questions.

I'm not searching for a ghost or yeti, my phantom is the Indian fantail. These beautiful creatures are members of the pigeon family, but you could not tell that by looking at them.

- **A.** NO CHANGE
- **B.** yeti: my phantom
- **C.** yeti my phantom
- **D.** yeti, since this

Here's How to Crack It

Punctuation is changing in the answer choices, so the question is testing STOP and GO punctuation. There is Half-Stop punctuation in (B), so use the Vertical Line Test. You cannot draw a line in the text, so draw a "t" on your whiteboard, with "yeti" in the bottom-left and "my" in the bottom-right:

Read each part of the sentence and determine whether it is complete or incomplete. *I'm not searching for a ghost or yeti* is a complete idea; write "C" in the upper-left of the "t." *My phantom is the Indian fantail* is also a complete idea; write "C" (for "complete") in the upper-right of the "t." Your board should look like this:

Eliminate any answer that cannot link two complete ideas. Both (A) and (C) use GO punctuation, which cannot link complete ideas; eliminate (A) and (C). Choice (D) adds *since*, which makes the idea to the right of the line incomplete. However, *since* is used to show time or causation, which does not work in the context of the sentence. Eliminate (D). The correct answer is (B).

MATH

First off, you'll still need to bring your calculator to the ACT Online Test—which is a good thing! You're already comfortable with your personal calculator, so there will be one less thing to worry about on the day of the test.

> **Write it down!**
>
> It is tempting to do all your work in your head. Don't fall into this trap! It's easier to make mistakes when you're not writing down your work, and you'll often have to "go back" if you don't have something written down. Use your whiteboard!

When choosing questions to do Later, flag the question so you can easily navigate back to it after doing your Now questions. Do put in your LOTD when doing so; you don't want to accidently leave a question blank! When you get the five-minute warning, finish the question you're working on, flag it (so you can find your spot easily), then put in your LOTD for every unanswered question. Then you can go back to working until time runs out.

Use the Highlighter tool to highlight what the question is actually asking, especially in Word Problems. Of course, you'll want to use your whiteboard when working the steps of a math problem (don't do the work in your head!).

ACT Online Geometry Basic Approach

Because you can't write on the screen, the Basic Approach for Geometry questions needs a few slight tweaks:

1. Draw the figure on your whiteboard (copy if it's provided; draw it yourself otherwise). If the figure would be better drawn differently from the way ACT has drawn it (for instance, a similar triangles question), redraw the figure in a way that will help you answer the question.

2. Label the figure you drew on your whiteboard with the information from both ACT's figure and the question.

3. Write down any formulas you need and fill in the information you know.

Let's see how that works on a question.

In the figure below, triangle *ABC* is similar to triangle *DEF*. What is the length of *EF* ?

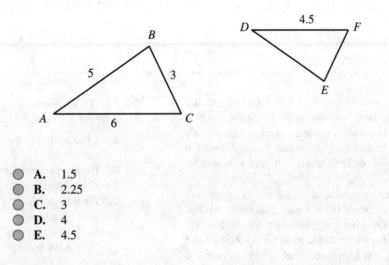

- **A.** 1.5
- **B.** 2.25
- **C.** 3
- **D.** 4
- **E.** 4.5

Here's How to Crack It

The question asks for the length of *EF*, so highlight that in the question. Follow the Geometry Basic Approach. Start by drawing the figure on your whiteboard. Because the triangles are similar, redraw triangle *DEF* to be oriented the same way as *ABC*. Label your figure with the given information.

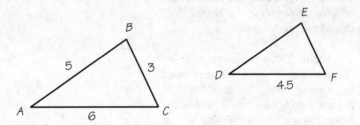

Write down the equation you need and fill in the necessary information. *AC* corresponds to *DF*, and *BC* corresponds to *EF*. Set up a proportion: $\dfrac{AC}{DF} = \dfrac{BC}{EF}$. Fill in the information from your figure: $\dfrac{6}{4.5} = \dfrac{3}{x}$, where x is equal to *EF*. Cross-multiply to get $6x = 3(4.5)$, or $6x = 13.5$. Divide both sides by 6 to get $x = 2.25$. The correct answer is (B).

READING

First off, there are a few differences between the pencil-and-paper ACT and the ACT Online Test. In the ACT Online Test, there are no line references; rather, the relevant part of the text is highlighted. The passage will also "jump" to the highlighted text if it's off the screen when you go to that question. This may disorient you at first: be prepared for this to happen.

Let's see an example.

...protested every step. We could still run, but, Hook worried, for how long? In a cross-country race, only a team's top five runners score, and we weren't those five. Our job was to finish ahead of as many of our rival teams' top fives as we could.

Leah was a senior that year, my freshman year. All season, she'd been counting down to this last race, praying her body wouldn't say *No*. She and I joked that we needed to go to the Knee Store and pick out new knees, ones that wouldn't crack and pop and burn all the time. It was hard to watch a teammate in that much pain, but Leah was a trooper, never slacking from workouts, never stopping to walk, never losing sight of the next person in front of her to catch.

The crack of the starter's pistol sent us surging out of that little crop of trees and onto the race course. I hollered, "See you at the Knee Store!" Behind me, she laughed.

The pack stayed tight through the first quarter-mile, and I was surrounded by so many bodies I couldn't think. I just ran, putting one foot in front of the other, trying not to fall. Trying to look beyond the jostling mass surrounding me, I could barely...

The narrator's references to the Knee Store primarily serve to suggest that:

- **A.** Leah wishes to buy better knee supports.
- **B.** the narrator and Leah use humor to cope with their pain.
- **C.** the narrator desires to learn more about her injury.
- **D.** Leah's injuries, unlike the narrator's, have become unbearable.

> Reading on a computer screen can be disorienting. Practice by reading articles or other passages on the computer when possible.

Here's How to Crack It

The question asks what the *references to the Knee Store...suggest*. The references to the *Knee Store* are highlighted in the text. Note that the text has shifted down to the highlighted portions. The window indicates that Leah and the narrator *joked that we needed to go to the Knee Store*. Leah *laughed* after the narrator referred to the Knee Store. Therefore, the answer should be consistent with joking and laughing. Choice (A) takes the reference too literally; eliminate (A). "Humor" is consistent with the text's references to *joked* and *laughed*; keep (B). There's no indication of the narrator's goal to *learn more about her injury*, nor does the text support the idea that Leah's injuries *have become unbearable*, eliminate (C) and (D). The correct answer is (B).

When you have five minutes remaining, flag your current question and use the Nav tool to make sure you've put in your LOTD for any questions that you haven't done. Then return to your spot and work until time runs out. If you've just started or finished a passage, click through the questions to look for Easy to Find questions in the remaining time, and don't forget to put in your LOTD for any question you don't answer!

The biggest difference between the ACT Online Test and the paper-and-pencil ACT is that you can only see one question on the screen at a time. Rather than looking over the questions at a glance, you must click from question to question. This feature means that the Reading Basic Approach (covered below) needs to be modified in order to be as time efficient as possible.

ACT Online Reading Basic Approach

1. **Preview**

   Read only the blurb—do not go through and map the questions. Instead, write the question numbers on your whiteboard to prepare to Work the Passage.

2. **Work the Passage**

   This step is *even more* optional on the ACT Online Test than on the pencil-and-paper ACT. You haven't mapped the questions, and your highlights only show up on one question. If you do decide to Work the Passage, ensure that you're getting through the passage in 2–3 minutes. More likely, you'll find it best to just skip this step and move on to the questions after reading the blurb and setting up your whiteboard.

   > You don't get points for reading—only for answering questions correctly. Determine whether Working the Passage helps you answer questions correctly and quickly.

3. **Select and Understand a Question**

   When Selecting a Question, if a question is Easy to Find (a portion of the text is highlighted or you Worked the Passage and know where in the passage the content you need is), do it Now. Understand the question, then move on to Step 4. If the question is not Easy to Find (in other words, you don't immediately know where in the passage to go), write down the question's lead words on your whiteboard next to the question number. Include EXCEPT/LEAST/NOT if the question includes those words. If there are no lead words, flag the question.

   After you do all the questions with highlights, then Work the Passage, scanning actively for your lead words. Once you find a lead word, do the corresponding question. After answering the questions with lead words, finish with the flagged questions.

4. **Read What You Need**

   Find the 5–10 lines you need to answer the question. Remember that only the quotation will be highlighted—the answer is not necessarily highlighted. You must read the lines before and after the highlighted portion to ensure that you find the correct answer to the question. If you find the Line Mask tool helpful, use it to frame your window.

5. **Predict the Correct Answer**

    As you read, look for evidence for the answer to the question in your window and highlight it using the highlighter tool. (You can highlight text that ACT has already highlighted—the color will change to "your" highlighting color.) As always, base your prediction on the words in the passage as much as possible.

6. **Use POE**

    Use the Answer Eliminator tool to narrow the answer choices down to one answer. If the question is an EXCEPT/LEAST/NOT question, instead write ABCD on your whiteboard and mark each answer T or F for True or False (or Y or N for Yes or No) and choose the odd one out.

Dual Reading Approach

The questions for Dual Reading passages are grouped with the questions about Passage A, then those about Passage B, then those about both passages. Each question should be labeled with an indicator for the passage the question refers to. Work each passage separately, answering all the Passage A questions you plan to answer before moving onto the Passage B questions.

You should also write down the Golden Thread of each passage on your whiteboard—either after Working the Passage or after finishing the questions on that passage. That will aid you in answering the questions about both passages.

SCIENCE

The overall approach to the Science test is the same on the ACT Online Test as it is on the traditional pencil-and-paper version. There are a few small adjustments to make, but the overall strategy remains the same.

The Flag tool is very important when identifying Later passages and questions. On a Later passage, flag the first question, then put your LOTD for every question on the passage. Make a note on your whiteboard of the first question in the passage so you can easily jump back to the passage.

When working a Now passage, you may still encounter a Later question. For these stand-alone Later questions, flag the question but don't put in your LOTD. When you get to the end of a passage, check the bar at the bottom of the screen to make sure you have answered every question up to that point.

Science Basic Approach

There are a few small changes to the Science approach when taking the ACT Online Test.

1. **Work the Figures**

    You can't highlight the figures. Experiment with taking quick notes about the variables, units, and trends on your whiteboard and determine whether it helps you find the needed information quickly.

2. **Work the Questions**

Highlight the words and phrases from the figures in the question to help guide you to the relevant information.

3. **Work the Answers**

Use the Answer Eliminator tool to work POE on answer choices with multiple parts.

Let's look at an example.

A block is placed on a frictionless horizontal surface at point Q. The block is pushed with a plunger and given initial velocity v along the horizontal surface. At point R, the block slides up a ramp with coefficient of friction f to a maximum distance L along the ramp. The distance between points Q and R is 1.0 m.

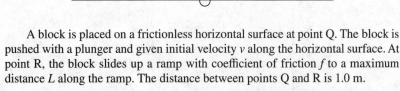

Figure 1

Figure 2, below, shows how L varies with v for different f on a ramp with $\theta = 20°$. Figure 3 (on the following page) shows how L varies with v for different θ on a ramp with $f = 0.1$.

Scrolling Passages
Most passages in Science will require scrolling down to see all the figures. Look for a scroll bar for every passage!

Key	
Marker	f
□	0.15
○	0.30
△	0.60
×	0.90

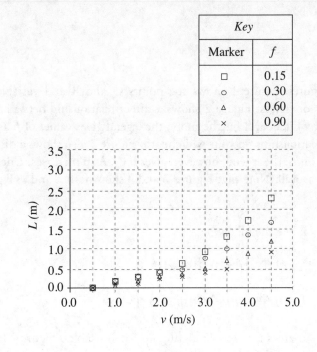

Figure 2

Key	
Marker	θ(°)
▲	15
∗	30
◇	45
●	60

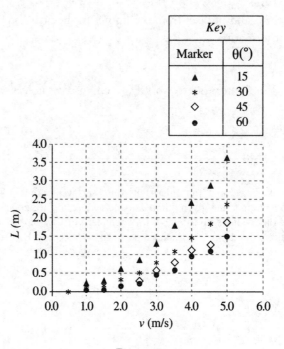

Figure 3

If $f = 0.90$ for the sliding block and $v = 5.5$ m/s, L will most likely be closest to which of the following?

- **A.** 0.3 m
- **B.** 0.7 m
- **C.** 1.5 m
- **D.** 3.0 m

Here's How to Crack It

Start by Working the Figures. Figure 1 shows the points Q and R and variables L and θ, but there are no numbers or trends. Figure 2 shows a direct relationship between L (m) and v (m/s); mark this on your whiteboard. Furthermore, the legend gives values of f; as f increases, L decreases. Mark these relationships on your whiteboard. Figure 3 also shows a direct relationship between L (m) and v (m/s); the legend, however, gives θ (°). As θ increases, L decreases. Put these on your whiteboard as well. Note that Figures 2 and 3 show both L and v; Figure 2 has f, whereas Figure 3 has θ.

Your whiteboard should look like the following:

Figure 2: L (m) ↑ v (m/s) ↑ and f ↑ L ↓

Figure 3: L (m) ↑ v (m/s) ↑ and θ ↑ L ↓

The question refers to the variables f, v, and L; highlight those variables. Figure 2 has all three variables. The highest value of v given in the figure is 4.5, so start there and use the trend to make a prediction about a v of 5.5. At $v = 4.5$ and $f = 0.90$, L is approximately 0.9. The trend is increasing, so a v of 5.5 must result in an L value of greater than 0.9; eliminate (A) and (B).

An *L* value of 3.0 would be higher than any value already in Figure 2, and extending the trend for the line created by the $f = 0.90$ marks would not result in *L* increasing to 3.0 by the time *v* reaches 5.5; eliminate (D). Although you can't physically extend the line because it's on a computer screen, it may be a good idea to use your finger to trace where you would draw on the screen. The correct answer is (C).

You'll still approach the passage that's all or mostly text as if it is a Reading passage. Unlike in Reading, you will want to Map the Questions during the Preview step, as there will not be a group of questions about each passage like there is in the Dual Reading passage. Instead, the questions will not be asked in any particular order, so use your whiteboard to map out which scientist(s) or experiment(s) each question refers to. As with the other sections, at the five-minute warning, flag your question, put in your LOTD on any unanswered question, then keep working until time runs out.

WRITING

As you have probably guessed, you'll be typing the Writing test on the ACT Online Test. But before we get to writing the essay, there are a few minor points to note about the format of this test on the computer.

First, you won't be able to highlight when Working the Prompt or Perspectives, so be sure to write notes on your whiteboard. Second, ACT has given the prompt and perspectives on one screen, then repeated them on the screen that contains a text box. Feel free to do your work on the screen within the text box. If you're used to making your essay outlines on a computer, you can use the text box to do so here, as long as you remember to delete any notes before the section comes to an end.

When writing the essay, all the same points apply to both the pencil-and-paper and online tests (have a clear thesis, make and organize your arguments in a way that is easy to follow, etc.). When you have 5 minutes left, quickly type up a conclusion paragraph (if you haven't already), then go back and finish up your body paragraph ideas. It's more important to have a conclusion than it is to have perfect body paragraphs. Finally, spend a minute or two at the end to quickly fix any obvious typos or grammatical issues.

When you practice the Writing test at home, type your essay in a word processing program instead of writing it by hand. Be sure to turn off spell check, as the ACT does not provide it, so you don't want to rely on it.

That's it! Everything you've learned for the pencil-and-paper ACT can be applied to the ACT Online Test with a few small tweaks. You've got this!

Chapter 3
ACT Strategies and the Math Test

ACT TEST-TAKING STRATEGIES

You will raise your ACT score by working smarter, not harder, and a smart test-taker is a strategic test-taker. You will target specific content to review, you will apply an effective and efficient approach, and you will employ the common sense that frequently deserts many others when they pick up a number 2 pencil.

Each test on the ACT demands a different approach, and even the most universal strategies vary in their applications. In the chapters that follow, we'll discuss these terms in greater detail customized to Math.

Personal Order of Difficulty (POOD)

If time is going to run out, would you rather it run out on the most difficult questions or on the easiest questions? Of course you want it to run out on the points you are less likely to get right. The trick is to find all of the easiest questions and get them done first.

The Best Way to Bubble In

Work one page at a time, circling your answers right on the booklet. Transfer a page's worth of answers to the answer sheet. It's better to stay focused on working questions rather than disrupt your concentration to find where you left off on the answer sheet. You'll be more accurate at both tasks. Do not wait to the end, however, to transfer all the answers of that test on your answer sheet. Go one page at a time.

Now

Does a question look okay? Do you know how to do it? Do it *Now*.

Later

Does a question make you go, "hmm"? If you can't find a way to get your pencil moving right away, consider leaving it and coming back *Later*. Circle the question number (or flag the question on the computer) for easy reference to return.

Never

Test-taker, know thyself. Know the topics that are most difficult for you, and learn the signs that flash danger. Don't waste time on questions you should *Never* do. Instead, use your Letter of the Day and use more time to answer the Now and Later questions accurately.

Letter of the Day (LOTD)   Just because you don't *work* a question doesn't mean you don't *answer* it. There is no penalty for wrong answers on the ACT, so you should never leave any blanks on your answer sheet. When you guess on Never questions, pick your favorite two-letter combo of answers and stick with it. For example, always choose A/F or C/H. If you're consistent, you're statistically more likely to pick up more points.

Note: if you are taking the ACT on a computer, all of the questions will have answer choices A, B, C, and D (or A, B, C, D, and E on the Math test). On the paper-and-pencil ACT, every other question will have answer choices F, G, H, and J (or F, G, H, J, and K on the Math test).

Process of Elimination (POE)

In a perfect world, you'll know how to work all of your Now and Later questions, quickly and accurately, circling the correct answer among the choices. The ACT is *not* a perfect world. But even with a ticking clock and a number 2 pencil in your sweaty hand, wrong answers can be obvious. POE can be a great Plan B on Math when you're stuck. But even when you can't narrow the answers to only one, using POE to get rid of at least one or two wrong answers will substantially increase your odds of getting a question right. Whenever you know an answer is wrong, physically cross it out with your pencil or use the Answer Eliminator on the computer.

The Power of POE
Very often, the quickest way to the correct answer is to eliminate the wrong answer choices rather than focusing on finding the right one.

Pacing

The ACT may be designed for you to run out of time, but you can't rush through it as quickly as possible. All you'll do is make careless errors on easy questions you should get right and spend way too much time on difficult ones you're unlikely to get right.

To hit your target score, you have to know how many raw points you need. Once you have determined this score, you can use the entire time allotted where it will do the most good. Go slowly enough to avoid careless errors on Now questions, but go quickly enough to get to as many Later questions as you need to hit your goal.

On each test of the ACT, the number of correct answers converts to a scaled score of 1–36. ACT works hard to adjust the scale of each test at each administration as necessary to make all scaled scores comparable, smoothing out any differences in level of difficulty across test dates. Thus, there is no truth to any one test date being "easier" than the others, but you can expect to see slight variations in the scale from test to test.

This is the scale from the 2021-2022 free test that ACT makes available on its website, ACT.org. We're going to use it to explain how to pick a target score and pace yourself.

Math Pacing

Scaled Score	Raw Score	Scaled Score	Raw Score	Scaled Score	Raw Score
36	58–60	27	41–43	18	24–25
35	56–57	26	39–40	17	21–23
34	54–55	25	37–38	16	17–20
33	53	24	35–36	15	13–16
32	51–52	23	33–34	14	10–12
31	49–50	22	31–32	13	8–9
30	48	21	30	12	6–7
29	46–47	20	28–29	11	5
28	44–45	19	26–27	10	4

Our advice is to add 5 questions to your targeted raw score. You have a cushion to get a few wrong—nobody's perfect—and you're likely to pick up at least a few points from your LOTDs. Track your progress on practice tests to pinpoint your target score.

Let's say your goal on Math is a 26. Find 26 under the scaled score column, and you'll see that you need 39–40 raw points. Take all 60 minutes and work 45 questions, using your Letter of the Day on 15 Never questions. With 60 minutes to work on just 45 questions, you'll raise your accuracy on the Now and Later questions. You may get a few wrong, but you're also likely to pick up a few points in your LOTDs, and you should hit your target score of 26. Spend more time to do fewer questions, and you'll raise your accuracy.

Here's another way to think about pacing. Let's say your goal is to move from a 26 to a 29. How many more raw points do you need? As few as six. Do you think you could find six careless errors on your last practice test that you *should* have gotten right?

Be Ruthless

The worst mistake a test-taker can make is to throw good time after bad. You read a question and don't understand it, so you read it again. And again. If you stare at it really hard, you know you're going to just *see* it. And you can't move on, because really, after spending all that time, it would be a waste not to keep at it, right? Actually, that way of thinking couldn't be more wrong.

You can't let one tough question drag you down. Instead, the best way to improve your ACT score is to follow our advice.

1. Use the techniques and strategies in the lessons to work efficiently and accurately through all your Now and Later questions.
2. Know your Never questions and use your LOTD.
3. Know when to move on. Use POE and guess from what's left.

ALL ABOUT THE MATH TEST

In some ways, the Math test of the ACT is the content-heaviest of all the tests. In other words, there are many questions on the Math that test concepts similar to those you've learned in your Math classes. In fact, ACT makes a big deal about how "curricular" the exam is, claiming that the Math test is "designed to assess the mathematical skills students have typically acquired in courses taken up to the beginning of grade 12." They even go so far as to offer a list of how the topics will break down in any given administration.

Preparing for Higher Math (34–36 questions)

- Number & Quantity (4–6 questions)

- Algebra (7–9 questions)

- Functions (7–9 questions)

- Geometry (7–9 questions)

- Statistics and Probability (5–7 questions)

Integrating Essential Skills (24–26 questions)—This is what the ACT calls the Math you learned before high school, including percentages, rates, proportions, and much of geometry.

Modeling (15+ questions)—This is what the ACT calls Word Problem questions that make math out of situations. These questions are also counted in the above.

As with all things ACT, however, these distinctions may not mean a ton to you, the test-taker. Nor should they. At best, this list should help to drive home one main point:

> The Math test of the ACT is roughly half Algebra and half Geometry.

While there's really no substitute for a solid and complete knowledge of Math fundamentals (and not-so-fundamentals), there are a number of ways you can still get a really great Math score by being a smart test-taker.

In the next four chapters, you'll examine some of the specific ways you can improve your scores in Algebra and Geometry. As you move through these chapters, keep an eye on the question number. ACT Math is the one section that is in a rough Order of Difficulty, so the question numbers offer a decent gauge of how difficult ACT considers certain concepts and types of Word Problems.

For the algebra questions on the test, there will be some that fall more in the elementary algebra realm and some that are more advanced. Many will be Plug and Chug questions (more on these in the next chapter), and others will be in the form of word problems. So you've got a lot of algebra questions to tackle on any given Math test. It's probably a good idea to comb the test looking for the most straightforward pre-algebra questions first, and then to track down the medium ones, then the harder ones, right? No way! That would be a tremendous waste of time, and even a nearly impossible task—what are the distinctions among those categories anyway? The next two chapters will give you tools to handle all kinds of algebra questions.

Crack It Open

For more comprehensive review and practice for the ACT, pick up a copy of *ACT Premium Prep*, which includes sample questions and guidance for each of the tests on the exam.

Test Tip

The ACT Math test is in a rough Order of Difficulty. Keep an eye on the question numbers!

Part II
Big Impact

Chapter 4
Plugging In

ALGEBRA

For our money, it's best to think of Algebra questions (and really all Math questions) as broken down into two categories: *Plug and Chug* and *Word Problems*. Plug and Chug questions are short questions that test basic rules, formulas, or terms. Word Problems are longer and place the math content in the context of a real-life setting. Many of the Math skills you use in these questions will be the same, but each will require a slightly different approach, for the obvious reason that Word Problems require that you deal with, well, words.

But let's start with a nice, straightforward, Plug and Chug question:

MADSPM
(Multiply/Add, Divide/Subtract, Power/Multiply)

When you *multiply* two like bases, you *add* their exponents.

$$\text{e.g., } x^2 \times x^3 = x^5$$

When you *divide* two like bases, you *subtract* their exponents.

$$\text{e.g., } \frac{x^5}{x^3} = x^2$$

When you raise a base to a *power*, you *multiply* the exponents.

$$\text{e.g., } \left(x^2\right)^3 = x^6$$

25. The expression $-4y^2\left(9y^7 - 3y^5\right)$ is equivalent to:

   A. $-36y^9 + 12y^7$

   B. $-36y^9 - 12y^7$

   C. $-36y^{14} + 12y^{10}$

   D. $-36y^{14} - 12y^{10}$

   E. $-24y^4$

Here's How to Crack It

The question asks for an equivalent expression to the one given. Sure, there are words in this question, but all it's really asking you to do is to match up the expression in the question with one of the expressions in the answer choices. Remember to distribute and use MADSPM.

Let's see how this works with the equation given in question 25.

$$-4y^2(9y^7 - 3y^5) = y^2(-36y^7 + 12y^5)$$
$$= -36y^9 + 12y^7$$

This matches up with (A). If you worked through this question and got one of the other answer choices, think about what you may have done wrong. If you chose (B), you may have forgotten to distribute the negative sign when you multiplied the −4. If you chose (C), you may have multiplied the exponents rather than adding them together. If you chose (D), you may have multiplied the exponents and forgotten to distribute the negative. If you chose (E), you may have forgotten that like bases with different exponents cannot be combined by addition or subtraction.

Whatever the case may be, don't sell these questions short. Even though they don't take as long, they're worth just as much as the "harder" questions. Recall from Chapter 2 how few questions you really need to pull up your math score. Make sure you work carefully on all your Now and Later questions. There is no partial credit on the ACT, so a careless error leaves you with an answer just as wrong as a random guess.

Fixing a few careless math errors can improve your ACT Math score significantly by ensuring that you get all the points on questions you know how to do.

Let's take a look at another question.

43. $4x^2 + 20x + 24$ is equivalent to:
- **A.** $(4x + 4)(x + 6)$
- **B.** $(4x - 4)(x - 6)$
- **C.** $(4x + 24)(x - 1)$
- **D.** $2(2x - 4)(x - 3)$
- **E.** $2(2x + 4)(x + 3)$

This one looks a lot like question 25, but the math is a good deal more difficult. In fact, even if you're pretty good at factoring quadratic equations, you might still find this one to be a bit of an issue. If you can do the factoring quickly and accurately, great, but if not, help is on the way!

PLUGGING IN

What is it about Algebra that makes some people nervous? Well, for one thing, with Algebra inevitably comes *variables*. You probably remember first hearing about these things in sixth or seventh grade and thinking to yourself how much easier life was when math was just plain numbers.

Here's the good news. Many of the algebra questions on the ACT, even the most complex, can be solved with what we like to call *Plugging In*. What Plugging In enables you to do is to solve difficult variable questions using basic arithmetic.

First, you'll need to identify whether you can use Plugging In.

Plug It In
A content-based approach to math questions isn't always necessary! Simply plug in to find the correct answer.

Use Plugging In when

• there are variables in the answer choices

• there are variables in the question

• the question is dealing with fractions, percents, or other relational numbers

Here's How to Crack It

Plugging In works with both Word Problems and Plug and Chug questions. The previous question 43 asks for an equivalent form of an expression. This question may look like it requires a "content-based" approach, but see how much easier it is if you plug in.

First, plug in a number for the variable. The best numbers to plug in are usually small and easy to deal with: numbers such as 2, 5, and 10. Try 2 in this question. If $x = 2$,

$$4(2)^2 + 20(2) + 24 = 4(4) + 20(2) + 24$$
$$= 16 + 40 + 24$$
$$= 56 + 24$$
$$= 80$$

So if you plug in 2 everywhere there's an x, the expression gives you 80. Now, since the question is merely asking for an equivalent expression, the correct answer will also equal 80 when 2 is plugged in for x. Therefore, 80 is our *target answer*. Finally, plug 2 into each of the answer choices and eliminate every answer that doesn't result in 80.

43. $4(2)^2 + 20(2) + 24$ is equivalent to $\boxed{80}$.

~~A.~~ $(4(2) + 4)((2) + 6) = (12)(8) = 96$
~~B.~~ $(4(2) - 4)((2) - 6) = (4)(-4) = -16$
~~C.~~ $(4(2) - 24)((2) - 1) = (-16)(1) = -16$
~~D.~~ $2(2(2) - 4)((2) - 3) = 2(0)(-1) = 0$
E. $2(2(2) + 4)((2) + 3) = 2(8)(5) = 80$

The only one that matches up is (E), the correct answer. No quadratic formula or difficult factoring required!

Let's review the steps:

> Once you've determined that you can plug in, follow these steps.
>
> 1. Plug in an easy-to-use value for your variable or variables.
>
> 2. Work the information in the question using the numbers you've plugged in to find a *target answer*.
>
> 3. Plug the variables into the answer choices and eliminate every answer that does not match up with the target.
>
> 4. Make sure you check all the answer choices. If more than one answer choice works, plug in a new set of numbers and try again until only one number works.

Let's try another one.

28. As part of an analysis to determine how summer vacations affect students' retention of school materials, scientists conducted an experiment. As shown in the chart below, they showed the time, d days, since the student had finished and the number of facts, f, that the student remembered from the previous year.

d	1	3	5	7	9
f	96	72	48	24	0

Which of the following equations represents all the data found in this study?

F. $f = 9 - d$
G. $f = 3(9 - d)$
H. $f = 3d + 3$
J. $f = 3(36 - 4d)$
K. $f = 96d$

Here's How to Crack It

The question asks for an equation to represent the data in the table. This question looks very different from the previous one, but notice that the two questions share some important features. Most importantly, both have variables in the answer choices.

This question is much bulkier than the previous question, though, and in many ways more intimidating. This is because it's a *Word Problem*. As we mentioned earlier in this chapter, even though Word Problems often use the same mathematical concepts as plug-and-chug questions, they ask about them in much more convoluted ways. Here's a simple Basic Approach for dealing with Word Problems.

When dealing with Word Problems on the ACT Math test

1. **Know the question.** Read the whole question before calculating anything, and underline the actual question.

2. **Let the answers help.** Look for clues on how to solve and ways to use POE (Process of Elimination).

3. **Break the question into bite-sized pieces.** Watch out for tricky phrasing.

Use these steps to solve this question.

1. **Know the question**. You need to find an equation that can accommodate all of the information in the table for *d* and *f*. The actual question in this question is below the chart. How much of the other stuff do you need? Not much.
2. **Let the answers help.** Remember how important the answers have been in what you've done so far in this chapter. If there are variables in those answer choices, you can usually plug in. You have variables in these answer choices, so plan to plug in here.
3. **Break the question into bite-sized pieces.** You know you need an equation that will work for all the points in this chart. Pick one set of points that will be easy to test, and then a second set to confirm your answers. Go easy on yourself! There's no reason to pick the biggest numbers. First, try the point to the far right of the chart: $d = 9, f = 0$. You want an equation that will work for these points, so try the answers:

   F. $0 = 9 - 9$
   G. $0 = 3(9 - 9)$
   ~~H.~~ $0 = 3(9) + 3$
   J. $0 = 3(36 - 4(9))$
   ~~K.~~ $0 = 96(99)$

Okay, you've eliminated two of the answer choices. Now try another set of points: $d = 7, f = 24$.

   ~~F.~~ $24 = 9 - 7$
   ~~G.~~ $24 = 3(9 - 7)$
   ~~H.~~ $f = 3d + 3$
   J. $24 = 3(36 - 4(7))$
   ~~K.~~ $f = 96d$

Only one remains, and your best answer is (J). All using basic arithmetic in the formulas provided.

A NOTE ON PLUGGING IN

Plugging In is not the only way to solve the questions above, and it may feel weird using this method instead of trying to do these questions "the real way." You may have even found that you knew how to work algebraically with the variables in questions we've identified as Plugging In questions. If you can do that, you're already on your way to a great Math score.

But think about it this way. We've already said that ACT doesn't give any partial credit. So, do you think doing it "the real way" gets you any extra points? It doesn't: on the ACT, a right answer is a right answer, no matter how you get it. "The real way" is great, but unfortunately, it's often a lot more complex and offers more opportunities for you to make careless errors.

The biggest problem with doing things the real way, though, is that it essentially requires you to invent a new approach for every question. This can be time-consuming and unreliable. Instead, notice what we've given you here: a powerful, time-saving strategy that will work toward getting you the right answer on any number of questions. You may have heard the saying, "Give a man a fish and you've fed him for a day, but teach a man to fish and you've fed him for a lifetime." Now, don't worry, our delusions of grandeur are not quite so extreme, but Plugging In is useful in a similar way. Rather than giving you a detailed description of how to create formulas and work through them for questions that won't themselves ever appear on an ACT again, we're giving you a strategy that will help you to recognize and work through a number of similar questions in future ACTs.

Try this strategy on your own in the drill that concludes this chapter. Make sure to master the easy and medium ones before tackling the hard ones. You may just be surprised how much easier a hard question can be when you use this strategy! We'll give you a related strategy in the next chapter, and then a chance to do more even more algebra practice with Plugging In.

PLUGGING IN DRILL

Easy

5. Points A, B, and C lie on a line in that order, as shown below. The ratio of the length of $\overline{AB}$ to the length of $\overline{AC}$ is 7 to 10. What is the ratio of the length of $\overline{AB}$ to the length of $\overline{BC}$, if it can be determined?

```
A           B    C
```

- **A.** 3:7
- **B.** 3:17
- **C.** 7:3
- **D.** 7:17
- **E.** Cannot be determined from the given information

9. Which of the following expressions is equivalent to

$$(3x^2 - 2x + 4) + (2x - 1) - (x^2 - 3x + 2)\ ?$$

- **A.** $x^2 - 2x + 3$
- **B.** $x^2 + 2x - 1$
- **C.** $2x^2 - 3x - 5$
- **D.** $2x^2 - 3x - 1$
- **E.** $2x^2 + 3x + 1$

14. The following statements are true of the players of a game that uses cards numbered 1–10.

  I. George has none of the same cards as Ian.
  II. George has all the cards that Fiona has.
  III. Ian has all the cards that Hailey has.

Which of the following statements *must* be true?

- **F.** George has none of the cards that Fiona has.
- **G.** Hailey has none of the cards that Fiona has.
- **H.** George has all the cards that Hailey has.
- **J.** Ian has all the cards that George has.
- **K.** Hailey has all the cards that Fiona has.

16. Which of the following expressions is equivalent to $\dfrac{p^2 - 3p}{2p} + \dfrac{1}{p^2}$?

  F. $\dfrac{p^2 - 3p + 1}{2p^3}$

  G. $\dfrac{2p^2}{p^3 - 3p^2 + 2}$

  H. $\dfrac{p^3 - 3p^2 + 2}{2p^2}$

  J. $\dfrac{p - 3p^2}{p^3 + 4}$

  K. $\dfrac{2 - p^2}{p^2 + p - 2}$

20. The students in a math class are asked to determine the equation of an unknown linear function, f. The teacher tells the class that the output of the function is 7 when the input is 4. The teacher also says that the output of the function is 28 when the input is 16. Which of the following equations correctly expresses the function f, where x is the input and $f(x)$ is the output?

  F. $f(x) = \dfrac{4}{7}x + \dfrac{33}{7}$

  G. $f(x) = x + 3$

  H. $f(x) = x + 12$

  J. $f(x) = \dfrac{4}{7}x$

  K. $f(x) = \dfrac{7}{4}x$

Medium

24. A salesman earns $600 per week in base salary. For each successful sale, he receives $125 in commission. Which of the following represents the amount of money, in dollars, the salesman earns in a given week in which he makes s successful sales?

  F. $725s$
  G. $125s - 600$
  H. $600s + 125$
  J. $600 - 125s$
  K. $600 + 125s$

27. The expression $(n^2 - 6n + 5)(n + 4)$ is equivalent to:

  A. $n^3 - 2n^2 - 19n + 20$
  B. $n^3 - n^2 + 9n + 20$
  C. $n^3 - 2n^2 - 7n + 20$
  D. $n^3 + 2n^2 - 24n + 20$
  E. $n^3 - 2n^2 - 29n + 20$

32. If $f(a) = a^2 + 3$ and $g(a) = 3a - 1$, which of the following is an expression for $g(f(a))$?

    F. $a^2 + 3a + 2$

    G. $3a^2 - 3$

    H. $-a^2 + 3a - 2$

    J. $3a^2 + 9a - 3$

    K. $3a^2 + 8$

37. Which of the following expressions is equivalent to $(y - 4)^{-50}$?

    A. $-50y + 200$

    B. $-y^{50} + 4^{50}$

    C. $\dfrac{1}{(-4y)^{50}}$

    D. $\dfrac{1}{(y-4)^{50}}$

    E. $\dfrac{1}{y^{50}} - \dfrac{1}{4^{50}}$

40. In a professional sports league consisting of x teams, y represents the number of teams that qualify for the playoffs in a given season. Which of the following could be used to determine the fraction of teams that does NOT make the playoffs in a given season?

    F. $\dfrac{x - y}{x}$

    G. $\dfrac{y - x}{x}$

    H. $\dfrac{y}{x}$

    J. $\dfrac{x - y}{y}$

    K. $\dfrac{x + y}{x}$

Hard

41. For positive real numbers x, y, and z such that $3x = 4y$ and $\frac{2}{3}y = \frac{1}{3}z$, which of the following inequalities is true?

A. $x < y < z$
B. $x < z < y$
C. $y < x < z$
D. $y < z < x$
E. $z < y < x$

46. If $x > y$, then $-|y - x|$ is equivalent to which of the following?

F. $\sqrt{y - x}$
G. $x - y$
H. $|y - x|$
J. $-(x - y)$
K. $|x - y|$

47. What is the LEAST possible integer value of $a + b$, if $6 < b < a$?

A. 9
B. 11
C. 13
D. 14
E. 15

48. If $-1 < x < 0$, then which of the following must be true?

F. $0^x > 0$

G. $-\dfrac{1}{x} > 1$

H. $x + \dfrac{1}{x} = 0$

J. $\dfrac{1}{x} > 0$

K. $x^0 < 0$

59. Consider all pairs of positive integers a and b whose sum is 6. For how many values of a does $a^b = b^a$?

A. None
B. 1
C. 2
D. 3
E. 6

PLUGGING IN DRILL ANSWER KEY

Easy	Medium	Hard
5. C	24. K	41. C
9. E	27. A	46. J
14. G	32. K	47. C
16. H	37. D	48. G
20. K	40. F	59. D

PLUGGING IN DRILL EXPLANATIONS

Easy

5. **C** The question asks for the ratio of $\overline{AB}$ to $\overline{BC}$. Since the question gives the ratio of $\overline{AB}$ to $\overline{AC}$, plug in values for those lengths to determine whether it is possible to solve for the desired ratio. The ratio numbers themselves would work well. Label $\overline{AB}$ as 7 and label $\overline{AC}$ as 10. In this case, $\overline{BC}$ would equal 10 − 7 or 3, making the ratio of $\overline{AB} : \overline{BC}$ equal to 7:3. This matches (C). However, because *Cannot be determined* is an option, plug in different values for $\overline{AB}$ and $\overline{AC}$ to determine whether 7:3 is the answer no matter what values are used. Choose different values that also have a ratio of 7:10 such as $\overline{AB}$ = 14 and $\overline{AC}$ = 20. In this case, $\overline{BC}$ = 20 − 14 = 6. This makes the ratio of $\overline{AB} : \overline{BC}$ equal to 14:6 or 7:3. This confirms that plugging in different values will still result in the same answer. The correct answer is (C).

9. **E** The question asks for an equivalent form of an expression. There are variables in the answer choices, so plug in. Make x = 2. The expression becomes $[3(2^2) − 2(2) + 4] + [2(2) − 1] − [(2^2) − 3(2) + 2]$. Simplify to $[3(4) − 4 + 4] + (4 − 1) − (4 − 6 + 2)$. Simplify further to $(12 − 4 + 4) + 3 − 0$ and finally to $12 + 3$, which equals 15. This is the target value; circle it. Now plug x = 2 into each of the answer choices to see which one matches the target value. Choice (A) becomes $2^2 − 2(2) + 3 = 4 − 4 + 3 = 3$. This does not match the target value. Eliminate (A). Choice (B) becomes $2^2 + 2(2) − 1 = 4 + 4 − 1 = 7$. Eliminate (B). Choice (C) becomes $2(2)^2 − 3(2) − 5 = 2(4) − 6 − 5 = −3$. Eliminate (C). Choice (D) becomes $2(2)^2 − 3(2) − 1 = 2(4) − 6 − 1 = 1$. Eliminate (D). Only (E) remains, but check it just in case. Choice (E) becomes $2(2^2) + 3(2) + 1 = 2(4) + 6 + 1 = 8 + 6 + 1 = 15$. This matches the target value. The correct answer is (E).

14. **G** The question asks which of the statements in the answer choices *must* be true, given the three Roman numeral statements about the cards each player has. A good way to tackle this question would be to plug in different sets of cards that adhere to the Roman numeral statements until four answer choices can be proven false, making the remaining answer the one that must be true. First, give each player a selection of cards. Following statement (I), give George cards 1, 2, 3, 4, and 5 and give Ian cards 6, 7, 8, 9, and 10. Eliminate (J), which says Ian and George have the same cards. Then, following statement (II), give Fiona cards 1, 2, 3, 4, and 5. Eliminate (F), which says Fiona and George have none of the same cards. Finally, following statement (III), give Hailey cards 6, 7, 8, 9, 10 as well. Eliminate (H) and (K), which say that George and Fiona have the same cards as Hailey. The correct answer is (G).

16. **H** The question asks for an equivalent form of an expression. There are variables in the answer choices, so plug in. Make p = 2. The expression becomes $\dfrac{2^2 − 3(2)}{2(2)} + \dfrac{1}{2^2}$ or $\dfrac{4 − 6}{4} + \dfrac{1}{4}$. This simplifies to $−\dfrac{2}{4} + \dfrac{1}{4}$, which equals $−\dfrac{1}{4}$. This is the target value; circle it. Now plug p = 2 into each of the answer choices

to see which one matches the target value. Choice (F) becomes $\dfrac{2^2-3(2)+1}{2(2)^3}$. This simplifies to

$\dfrac{4-6+1}{2(8)}=-\dfrac{1}{16}$. This does not match the target, so eliminate (F). Choice (G) becomes $\dfrac{2(2)^2}{2^3-3(2)^2+2}$.

This simplifies to $\dfrac{2(4)}{8-3(4)+2}=\dfrac{8}{-2}=-4$. This does not match the target, so eliminate (G). Choice

(H) becomes $\dfrac{2^3-3(2)^2+2}{2(2)^2}$. This simplifies to $\dfrac{8-3(4)+2}{2(4)}=\dfrac{8-12+2}{8}=\dfrac{-2}{8}=-\dfrac{1}{4}$. This matches

the target. Keep (H) but check the rest of the answers just in case. Choice (J) becomes $\dfrac{2-3(2)^2}{2^3+4}$.

This simplifies to $\dfrac{2-3(4)}{8+4}=\dfrac{2-12}{12}=\dfrac{-10}{12}=-\dfrac{5}{6}$. This does not match the target, so eliminate (J).

Choice (K) becomes $\dfrac{2-2^2}{2^2+2-2}$. This simplifies to $\dfrac{2-4}{4+0}=\dfrac{-2}{4}=-\dfrac{1}{2}$. This does not match the target,

so eliminate (K). The correct answer is (H).

20. **K** The question asks for an equation expressing the function f, where x is the input and $f(x)$ is the output.

Since the question gives actual numbers for the input and output, plug those numbers in to determine

which equation is correct. The teacher first tells the class that when the input x is 4, the output $f(x)$ is 7.

Choice (F) becomes $7=\dfrac{4}{7}(4)+\dfrac{33}{7}$ or $7=\dfrac{16}{7}+\dfrac{33}{7}$. This simplifies to $7=\dfrac{49}{7}$ or 7 = 7. This is true,

so keep (F) but check the rest because the correct answer must work for both pairs of numbers. Choice

(G) becomes 7 = 4 + 3, so keep (G). Choice (H) becomes 7 = 3 + 12. This is not true, so eliminate (H).

Choice (J) becomes $7=\dfrac{4}{7}(4)$ or $7=\dfrac{16}{7}$. Eliminate (J). Choice (K) becomes $7=\dfrac{7}{4}(4)$ or 7 = 7, so

keep (K). The teacher also tells the class that when the input x is 16, the output $f(x)$ is 28, so plug those

numbers into each remaining answer choice. Choice (F) becomes $28=\dfrac{4}{7}(16)+\dfrac{33}{7}$ or $28=\dfrac{64}{7}+\dfrac{33}{7}$.

This simplifies to $28=\dfrac{97}{7}$. This is not true, so eliminate (F). Choice (G) becomes 28 = 16 + 3 or

28 = 19. Eliminate (G). Choice (K) becomes $28=\dfrac{7}{4}(16)$ or $28=\dfrac{112}{4}$, which simplifies to 28 = 28.

This is true. The correct answer is (K).

Medium

24. K The question asks for the amount of money the salesman earns if he makes s successful sales. There are variables in the answer choices, so plug in. Make $s = 2$. Translate the English to math in this word problem in bite-sized pieces. The question states that the salesman makes $600 in base salary and an additional $125 per sale. If $s = 2$, the salesman would earn $600 + $125(2) = $600 + $250 = $850. This is the target value; circle it. Now plug $s = 2$ into each of the answer choices to see which one matches the target value. Choice (F) becomes 725(2) = 1,450. This does not match the target, so eliminate (F). Choice (G) becomes 125(2) − 600 = 250 − 600 = −350. Eliminate (G). Choice (H) becomes 600(2) + 125 = 1,200 + 125 = 1,325. Eliminate (H). Choice (J) becomes 600 − 125(2) = 600 − 250 = 350. Eliminate (J). Choice (K) becomes 600 + 125(2) = 600 + 250 = 850. This matches the target. The correct answer is (K).

27. A The question asks for an equivalent form of an expression. There are variables in the answer choices, so plug in. Make $n = 2$. The expression becomes $[2^2 − 6(2) + 5](2 + 4)$. This simplifies to $[4 − 12 + 5](6) = (−3)(6) = −18$. This is the target value; circle it. Now plug $n = 2$ into each of the answer choices to see which one matches the target value. Choice (A) becomes $2^3 − 2(2)^2 − 19(2) + 20$. This simplifies to $8 − 2(4) − 38 + 20 = 8 − 8 − 38 + 20 = −18$. This matches the target. Keep (A), but check the rest to make sure. Choice (B) becomes $2^3 − 2^2 + 9(2) + 20 = 8 − 4 + 18 + 20 = 42$. This does not match the target. Eliminate (B). Choice (C) becomes $2^3 − 2(2)^2 − 7(2) + 20 = 8 − 2(4) − 14 + 20 = 6$. Eliminate (C). Choice (D) becomes $2^3 + 2(2)^2 − 24(2) + 20 = 8 + 2(4) − 48 + 20 = −12$. Eliminate (D). Choice (E) becomes $2^3 − 2(2)^2 − 29(2) + 20 = 8 − 2(4) − 58 + 20 = −38$. Eliminate (E). The correct answer is (A).

32. K The question asks for the value of a compound function. In function notation, the number inside the parentheses is the x-value that goes into the function, and the value that comes out of the function is the y-value. There are variables in the answer choices, so plug in. Plug $a = 2$ into the f function to get $f(2) = 2^2 + 3$ or $f(2) = 4 + 3 = 7$. Since $f(a)$ is the input of the g function and $f(2) = 7$, substitute 7 as the input of the g function: $g(7) = 3(7) − 1 = 21 − 1 = 20$. This is the target value; circle it. Now plug $a = 2$ into each of the answer choices to see which one matches the target value. Choice (F) becomes $2^2 + 3(2) + 2 = 4 + 6 + 2 = 12$. This does not match the target value. Eliminate (F). Choice (G) becomes $3(2^2) − 3 = 3(4) − 3 = 12 − 3 = 9$. Eliminate (G). Choice (H) becomes $−2^2 + 3(2) − 2 = −4 + 6 − 2 = 0$. Eliminate (H). Choice (J) becomes $3(2^2) + 9(2) − 3 = 3(4) + 18 − 3 = 12 + 18 − 3 = 27$. Eliminate (J). Only (K) remains, but check it just in case. Choice (K) becomes $3(2^2) + 8 = 3(4) + 8 = 12 + 8 = 20$. This matches the target value. The correct answer is (K).

37. D The question asks for an equivalent form of an expression. There are variables in the answer choices, so plug in. Because most numbers raised to the power of −50 would be difficult to calculate, choose a number for y that makes the expression easy to calculate, such as $y = 5$. In this case, the expression becomes $(5 − 4)^{−50}$ or $(1)^{−50}$, which is easy to calculate because 1 raised to any power equals 1. This is the target value; circle it. Now plug $y = 5$ into each of the answer choices to see which one matches the target value. Choice (A) becomes $-50(5) + 200$ or $-250 + 200 = -50$. This does not match the target, so eliminate (A). Choice (B) becomes $-(5)^{50} + 4^{50}$. This is difficult to calculate, so ballpark. The first part will be a very large negative number and the second part will be a positive number that is not as large. The result of adding those will be a negative number, so eliminate (B). Choice (C) becomes $\dfrac{1}{(-4 \times 5)^{50}}$ or $\dfrac{1}{(-20)^{50}}$. This will result in a very small number, not 1. Eliminate (C). Choice (D) becomes $\dfrac{1}{(5-4)^{50}} = \dfrac{1}{1^{50}} = \dfrac{1}{1} = 1$. Keep (D), but check (E) just in case. Choice (E) becomes $\dfrac{1}{5^{50}} - \dfrac{1}{4^{50}}$. This is difficult to calculate, but the first part will be a very small number and the second part will be a number that is not as small. The result of subtracting those will be a negative number, so eliminate (E). The correct answer is (D).

40. **F** The question asks for an expression that could be used to determine the fraction of teams that does NOT make the playoffs. There are variables in the answer choices, so plug in. Note that x must be greater than y because it would be impossible for more teams to qualify for the playoffs than there are teams in the entire league. Make $x = 5$ and $y = 2$. Thus, there are 5 teams and 2 qualify for the playoffs. The number of teams that do NOT qualify must be $5 - 2 = 3$, so the fraction of teams that do NOT qualify is $\dfrac{3}{5}$. This is the target value; circle it. Now plug $x = 5$ and $y = 2$ into each of the answer choices to see which one matches the target value. Choice (F) becomes $\dfrac{5-2}{5} = \dfrac{3}{5}$. This matches the target value, so keep (F) but check the other answers to make sure. Choice (G) becomes $\dfrac{2-5}{5} = -\dfrac{3}{5}$. This does not match the target value. Eliminate (G). Choice (H) becomes $\dfrac{2}{5}$. Eliminate (H). Choice (J) becomes $\dfrac{5-2}{2} = \dfrac{3}{2}$. Eliminate (J). Choice (K) becomes $\dfrac{5+2}{5} = \dfrac{7}{5}$. Eliminate (K). The correct answer is (F).

Hard

41. C   The question asks which of the inequalities listed is true, given certain relationships among variables. There are variables in the answer choices, so plug in. Because there are fractions in the question, a multiple of those fractions' denominators is a good number to plug in. Make $y = 6$. Now solve for x and z using the given equations. $3x = 4y$ becomes $3x = 4(6)$ or $3x = 24$ or $x = 8$. The second equation, $\frac{2}{3}y = \frac{1}{3}z$, becomes $\frac{2}{3}(6) = \frac{1}{3}z$ or $4 = \frac{z}{3}$. Therefore, $z = 12$. Put these values in order from least to greatest: $y = 6$, $x = 8$, and $z = 12$. Thus, $y < x < z$. The correct answer is (C).

46. J   The question asks for an equivalent form of an expression. There are variables in the answer choices, so plug in. Because it is given that $x > y$, select values that fit that requirement. Make $x = 3$ and $y = 2$. The given expression $-|y - x|$ becomes $-|2 - 3|$ then $-|-1|$ or -1. This is the target value; circle it. Now plug $x = 3$ and $y = 2$ into each of the answer choices to see which one matches the target value. Choice (F) is not a possible match for the target value because the square root of any number will not be negative. Eliminate (F). Choice (G) becomes $3 - 2 = 1$. This does not match the target value. Eliminate (G). Choice (H) is not a possible match for the target value because the absolute value of any number will not be negative. Eliminate (H). Choice (J) becomes $-(3 - 2)$ or -1. This matches the target value, so keep (J) but check (K) just in case. Choice (K) cannot match the target for the same reason that (H) cannot, so eliminate (K). The correct answer is (J).

47. C   The question asks for the least possible integer value of $a + b$ given that $6 < b < a$. Because a and b are each greater than 6, it would be impossible for $a + b$ to be less than or equal to $6 + 6 = 12$. Eliminate (A) and (B) for that reason. The next least value is 13, so plug in values for a and b to see if this is a possible sum. There is no requirement that a and b are integers, so plug in $b = 6.1$. The sum becomes $a + 6.1 = 13$. Subtract 6.1 from both sides of the equation to get $a = 6.9$. These numbers fit the conditions of the question: $6 < 6.1 < 6.9$. Because no smaller answer choice is possible and $6.1 + 6.9 = 13$, stop here. The correct answer is (C).

48. G   The question asks which expression must be true given a range of values for x. There are variables in the answer choices, so plug in. Since it is given that $-1 < x < 0$, make $x = -\frac{1}{2}$. Plug this into each answer choice to determine which one gives a true statement. Choice (F) becomes $0^{-\left(\frac{1}{2}\right)} > 0$. This is not true because raising 0 to a negative power results in a denominator of zero, which is undefined. Eliminate (F). Choice (G) becomes $-\frac{1}{\left(-\frac{1}{2}\right)} > 1$ or $2 > 1$. This is true. Keep (G), but check the remaining answers just in case. Choice (H) becomes $-\dfrac{1}{2} + \dfrac{1}{\left(-\dfrac{1}{2}\right)} = 0$ or $-\dfrac{1}{2} - 2 = 0$. This

becomes $-\dfrac{1}{2} - \dfrac{4}{2} = 0$ or $-\dfrac{5}{2} = 0$. This is not true. Eliminate (H). Choice (J) becomes $\dfrac{1}{\left(-\dfrac{1}{2}\right)} > 0$

or $-2 > 0$. This is not true. Eliminate (J). Choice (K) becomes $\left(-\dfrac{1}{2}\right)^{0} < 0$ or $1 < 0$. This is not true.

Eliminate (K). The correct answer is (G).

59. **D**   The question asks how many values of a satisfy the given conditions. Plug in, considering the limited number of values for a and b that fit the conditions. Both a and b must be positive integers and $a + b = 6$. List out all the possible values for a and b. $a = 1$, $b = 5$; $a = 2$, $b = 4$; $a = 3$, $b = 3$; $a = 4$, $b = 2$; $a = 5$, $b = 1$. Now count how many of these pairs make it true that $a^b = b^a$. With the first pair, $1^5 = 5^1$ is not true because $1 \neq 5$. With the second pair, $2^4 = 4^2$ is true because $16 = 16$. With the third pair, $3^3 = 3^3$ is true because $27 = 27$. With the fourth pair, $4^2 = 2^4$ is true because $16 = 16$. With the fifth and final pair, $5^1 = 1^5$ is not true because $5 \neq 1$. There are no other values to consider. Therefore, three possible values of a satisfy the conditions of the question: $a = 2$, $a = 3$, and $a = 4$. The correct answer is (D).

Chapter 5
Plugging In the
Answers

PLUGGING IN THE ANSWERS

In the previous chapter, we showed you how to plug in your own numbers to make algebra questions easier to deal with. Now, what happens when you don't have the hallmarks of easy Plugging In questions: variables in the answer choices or in the question? Like question 45:

---

45. A high-school basketball player has shot 170 free throws and has made 100 of those free throws. Starting now, if she makes each free throw she attempts, what is the *least* number of free throws she must attempt in order to raise her free-throw percentage to at least 70% ?

   A. 19
   B. 20
   C. 63
   D. 64
   E. 70

In this question, there are no variables anywhere to be seen. Still, you're going to need to put together some kind of equation or something that will enable you to answer the question. For this one, you can *Plug In the Answers* (PITA).

Care for Some PITA?
Note that the PITA strategy is slightly different from just Plugging In. With PITA, you're specifically using the answer choices.

PITA when

- the question asks for a specific amount. Look for "How many?" or "How much?" or "What is the value of?"

- there are no variables in the answer choices

Question 45 is a Word Problem, so let's go through the steps:

1. **Know the question.** You need to figure out how many additional free throws this player will need to have a free-throw percentage of 70%. Also, when ACT italicizes or capitalizes a word, pay special attention. In this case, they've italicized the word *least*. Keep this in mind; it tells you that a number of the answer choices may work, but the correct one will be the *least* of these. The phrase "What is the least number?" is the kind of very specific question that usually makes for a good PITA question.

2. **Let the answers help.** There are no variables in these answer choices, and that coupled with the fact that it asks for a specific value is a good indication that you'll be using these answer choices to PITA. Notice the answer choices are listed in ascending order, which means it might be smart to start with the middle choice. That way you can eliminate answers that are too high or too low.

3. **Break the question into bite-sized pieces.** With many PITA questions, it can help to create columns, building on the information given in the answer choices and the question. Start with the question that's being asked: you've already got five possible answers to that question.

45. A high-school basketball player has shot 170 free throws and has made 100 of those free throws. Starting now, if she makes each free throw she attempts, what is the *least* number of free throws she must attempt in order to raise her free-throw percentage to at least 70% ?

	Free-throws	Total free-throws	Total completed	Percentage free-throws
A.	19			
B.	20			
C.	63	233	163	69.9%
D.	64			
E.	70			

Here's How to Crack It

As (C) has shown, 63 additional free throws raises the percentage to only 69.9%. You know this is wrong because you want to raise it to 70%. Therefore, since (C) gives a value that is too small, (A) and (B) must be too small as well. Try (D).

Your best answer here is (D) because it produces a free-throw percentage of 70.1%. Choice (E) will produce a percentage greater than 70% as well, but remember, this question is asking for the *least*.

45. A high-school basketball player has shot 170 free throws and has made 100 of those free throws. Starting now, if she makes each free throw she attempts, what is the *least* number of free throws she must attempt in order to raise her free-throw percentage to at least 70% ?

	Free-throws	Total free-throws	Total completed	Percentage free-throws
A.	~~19~~			
B.	~~20~~			
C.	~~63~~	233	163	69.9%
D.	64	234	164	70.1%
E.	70			

Let's review what you've learned about this type of question so far.

When you've identified a question as a PITA question, do the following:

- Start with the middle answer choice. This can help with POE.

- Label your answer choices—they answer the question you underlined in the question.

- When you find the correct answer, stop! But make sure you're answering the right question.

- Make sure you account for all the relevant information. PITA is most effective in simplifying difficult Word Problems, but make sure you've got everything you need!

Let's try another question.

18. The product of two distinct integers is 192. If the sum of those same two integers is 28, what is the value of the larger of the two integers?

   F. 18
   G. 16
   H. 12
   J. 10
   K. 8

Here's How to Crack It
Let's go through the steps.

1. **Know the question.** "What is the value of the larger of the two integers?" The key word here is *larger*. The numbers in the answer choices will be possibilities for this *larger* value. Notice this is asking for a specific value, which means you can use PITA.

2. **Let the answers help.** You've got a list of non-variable answers in ascending order. Each one offers a possible answer to the specific question posed in the question. Use PITA, and use the answers to work backward through the question.

3. **Break the question into bite-sized pieces.** Even though this is a short question, there's a lot of information here, so you should use columns to help keep all the information straight. The question says that the *sum* of the two integers is 28, so start there. Begin with (C) to help with POE.

18. The product of two distinct integers is 192. If the sum of those same two integers is 28, <u>what is the value of the larger of the two integers?</u>

Larger integer	Smaller integer	(Larger × Smaller) = 192?
F. 18		
G. 16		
H. 12	16	CAN'T WORK
J. 10		
K. 8		

You can eliminate (H) right off the bat. Just from what you've found, 12 can't be the *larger* integer if 16 is the *smaller* integer. You will therefore need a number larger than 12, so you can eliminate (J) and (K) as well. Try (G).

18. The product of two distinct integers is 192. If the sum of those same two integers is 28, <u>what is the value of the larger of the two integers?</u>

Larger integer	Smaller integer	(Larger × Smaller) = 192?
F. 18		
G. 16	12	16 × 12 = 192 Yes!
~~**H.** 12~~	~~16~~	~~CAN'T WORK~~
~~**J.** 10~~		
~~**K.** 8~~		

Choice (G) works, so you can stop there. Notice how PITA and Plugging In have enabled you to do these questions quickly and accurately without getting bogged down in generating difficult algebraic formulas.

———————○———————

A NOTE ON PLUGGING IN THE ANSWERS

Just as we noted at the end of the Plugging In chapter, using PITA may not come naturally to you at first. Especially if you are great at algebra, you may not see the value of doing it this way. But just as with Plugging In questions, doing algebra questions "the real way" instead of with PITA can slow you down and give you more opportunities to make careless mistakes. ACT questions are often written so that if you write your own equation, you'll end up solving for the wrong thing. Why waste your time with that? Practice using the answers whenever possible to increase your efficiency and accuracy. The following drill gives you a chance to get started mastering this awesome tool.

PLUGGING IN THE ANSWERS DRILL

Easy

2. If $\dfrac{3n}{4} - 7 = 2$, then $n =$

   F. -9

   G. $-\dfrac{7}{3}$

   H. $\dfrac{7}{3}$

   J. 9

   K. 12

6. Liz rented a car for a business trip with a rental agreement that included a \$20.00 charge for the first 100 miles she drove, plus a fee of \$0.30 for each additional mile over 100 miles. When Liz received the bill for her rental car, she was charged \$57.50 for the miles she drove. How many miles did Liz drive on her business trip?

   F. 175
   G. 225
   H. 325
   J. 430
   K. 515

11. If b is a positive integer greater than 1, what is the smallest integer value of a for which there exists a value of b such that $\sqrt{a} - b^2 > 0$?

   A. 5
   B. 16
   C. 25
   D. 36
   E. 49

15. When the lines $4x - y = 4$ and $x + 4y = 18$ are graphed in the standard (x,y) coordinate plane, which of the following (x,y) pairs represents the point of intersection?

   A. $(-2, 5\ )$
   B. $(\ 0, 4.5)$
   C. $(\ 2, 4\ )$
   D. $(\ 4, 3.5)$
   E. $(\ 6, 3\ )$

18. Amethyst's route to work is 48 miles long. Along the way, she stops for coffee and notices that the ratio of the number of miles she's driven so far to the number of miles left to go is 3:1. How many miles does she have left to drive?

   F. 6
   G. 12
   H. 24
   J. 30
   K. 36

Medium

21. In a dog park on a Sunday morning, all dogs belonged to exactly 1 of 3 groups: hounds, terriers, or mixed breed dogs. There were 27 dogs in the park. There were 6 fewer hounds than terriers and 9 fewer terriers than mixed breed dogs. How many mixed breed dogs were in the park that morning?

   A. 8
   B. 9
   C. 10
   D. 17
   E. 19

23. If $\dfrac{w-1}{2} = z$ and $\dfrac{w+z}{2} = 11$, then which of the following is equivalent to z ?

   A. 5
   B. 7
   C. 11
   D. 13
   E. 15

28. Tim draws a parallelogram whose height is 2 times its base. If the area of the parallelogram is 18 square inches, how long is the base, in inches?

(Note: The area of a parallelogram is given by the equation $A = Bh$, where B is the base and h is the height.)

   F. 3
   G. 4
   H. 6
   J. 9
   K. 10

30. If $|2n + 6| = |3n + 4|$, then what are the possible values of n ?

   F. 0 and 2
   G. 0 and –2
   H. –2 and 2
   J. 2 only
   K. –2 only

33. If $\sqrt[3]{343} - \sqrt[3]{a} = \sqrt[3]{27}$, what is the value of a ?

   A. 4
   B. 7
   C. 16
   D. 49
   E. 64

Hard

45. Which of the following gives the solution set for $\sqrt[3]{(n^2 - 6n)} = 3$?

   A. {3}
   B. $\{2 \pm \sqrt{3}\}$
   C. {–3, 9}
   D. {3, –9}
   E. {27}

49. If n is a real number, then what is the solution to the equation $27^{2n} = 81^{(n+1)}$?

   A. $n = 0$
   B. $n = 1$
   C. $n = 2$
   D. $n = 3$
   E. $n = 4$

52. Real numbers $x = a$ and $x = b$ satisfy $h(x) = 2$. If $h(x) = 2^{x^2 + 2x - 2}$, what are the values of a and b ?

   F. {–3, 0}
   G. {–3, 1}
   H. {–3, 3}
   J. {–1, 1}
   K. { 0, 1}

55. Which of the following is an irrational value of n that is a solution to the equation $|n^2 - 30| - 6 = 0$?

   A. $\sqrt{6}$
   B. 6
   C. $2\sqrt{6}$
   D. $3\sqrt{6}$
   E. $4\sqrt{6}$

PLUGGING IN THE ANSWERS DRILL ANSWER KEY

Easy		Medium		Hard	
2.	K	21.	D	45.	C
6.	G	23.	B	49.	C
11.	C	28.	F	52.	G
15.	C	30.	H	55.	C
18.	G	33.	E		

PLUGGING IN THE ANSWERS DRILL EXPLANATIONS

Easy

2. **K** The question asks for the value of n. Since the question asks for a specific value and the answers contain numbers in increasing order, plug in the answers. Begin by labeling the answers as n and start with (H), $\frac{7}{3}$. The equation becomes $\frac{3 \times \frac{7}{3}}{4} - 7 = 2$ or $\frac{7}{4} - 7 = 2$. This is not true, so eliminate (H). Since $\frac{7}{4} - 7$ would result in a negative value, the correct answer must be greater than (H), $\frac{7}{3}$, in order to result in 2. Eliminate (F) and (G) and try (J), 9. The equation becomes $\frac{3 \times 9}{4} - 7 = 2$ or $\frac{27}{4} - 7 = 2$. This can be rewritten as $\frac{27}{4} - \frac{28}{4} = 2$ or $-\frac{1}{4} = 2$. This is also not true, so eliminate (J). Only (K) remains, but check $n = 12$ just to make sure. The equation becomes $\frac{3 \times 12}{4} - 7 = 2$ or $\frac{36}{4} - 7 = 2$. This simplifies to $9 - 7 = 2$, which is true. The correct answer is (K).

6. **G** The question asks for the number of miles Liz drove. Since the question asks for a specific value and the answers contain numbers in increasing order, plug in the answers. Begin by labeling the answers as "miles driven" and start with (H), 325 miles. The question specifies that Liz is charged $20.00 for the first 100 miles driven and $0.30 for each additional mile driven. Calculate Liz's cost for 325 miles by adding $20, for the first 100 miles, to $0.30(325 − 100) or $0.30(225) for the remaining 225 miles. This becomes $20 + $0.30(225) = $20 + $67.50 = $87.50. This does not match the charge of $57.50 as the question states, so (H) is not the correct answer. Since this answer choice yielded a cost that was too high, try a lesser value such as (G), 225 miles. Calculate Liz's cost for 225 miles by adding $20, for the first 100 miles, to $0.30(225 − 100) or $0.30(125) for the remaining 125 miles. Since $20 + $0.30(125) = $20 + $37.50 = $57.50, stop here. The correct answer is (G).

11. **C** The question asks for the smallest value of a that satisfies the conditions in the question. Since the question asks for a specific value and the answers contain numbers in increasing order, plug in the answers. Begin by labeling the answers as "a" and, because the question asks for the *smallest* value of a, start with the *smallest* answer choice: (A). Choice (A) becomes $\sqrt{5} - b^2 > 0$, then $2.24 > b^2$ or $1.5 > b$. Because b must be an *integer greater than 1*, meaning it must be equal to or greater than 2, eliminate (A). Try (B), 16. Choice (B) becomes $\sqrt{16} - b^2 > 0$, then $4 > b^2$ or $2 > b$. Because b must be an integer *greater than 1*, meaning it must be equal to or greater than 2, eliminate (B). Try (C), 25. Choice (C) becomes $\sqrt{25} - b^2 > 0$, then $5 > b^2$ or $\sqrt{5} > b^2$. Since b could equal 2, a positive integer greater than 1, stop here. The correct answer is (C).

15. **C**   The question asks for the point of intersection between the two lines with given equations $4x - y = 4$ and $x + 4y = 18$. The point of intersection must satisfy both equations. There are specific points in the answers, so plug in the answers. Test the ordered pairs in both equations from the question and look for a pair that makes both equations true. Start by plugging the x- and y-values from (C) into the first equation to get $4(2) - 4 = 8 - 4 = 4$, which is true. Test the second equation with the same ordered pair. It becomes $2 + 4(4) = 2 + 16 = 18$, which is also true. There is no need to plug in any other answer choices. The correct answer is (C).

18. **G**   The question asks for the number of miles Amethyst has left to drive. Since the question asks for a specific value and the answers contain numbers in increasing order, plug in the answers. Begin by labeling the answers as "miles left to drive" and start with (H), 24 miles. If she has 24 miles left to drive, she has so far driven $48 - 24 = 24$ miles. This makes the ratio of miles driven to miles left 24:24, which is not equal to the 3:1 ratio given in the question. Eliminate (H). Because the number of miles driven so far is the 3 in the 3:1 ratio desired, the number of miles driven so far must be greater and the number of miles left to drive must be less. Try (G), which is 12. If she has 12 miles left to drive, she has so far driven $48 - 12 = 36$ miles. Now the ratio is 36:12, which is equal to a 3:1 ratio of miles driven so far to miles left to drive, so stop here. The correct answer is (G).

Medium

21. **D**   The question asks for the number of mixed breed dogs in the park. Since the question asks for a specific value and the answers contain numbers in increasing order, plug in the answers. Begin by labeling the answers as "mixed breed" and start with (C), 10. Since there are 9 fewer terriers than mixed breed dogs, the number of terriers is $10 - 9 = 1$. Since there are 6 fewer hounds than terriers, the number of hounds would be negative, which is impossible. Eliminate (C). Since (C) resulted in too few dogs, eliminate (A) and (B), as well, and try (D), 17. The number of terriers is now $17 - 9 = 8$. If there are 8 terriers, then the number of hounds is $8 - 6 = 2$. With 17 mixed breed dogs, 8 terriers and 2 hounds, the total number of dogs becomes $17 + 8 + 2 = 27$. This matches the total number of dogs given in the question, so stop here. The correct answer is (D).

23. **B**   The question asks for the value of z. Since the question asks for a specific value and the answers contain numbers in increasing order, plug in the answers. Begin by labeling the answers as "z" and start with (C), 11. Plug 11 in for z in the first equation to find a value for w. In the first equation, $\frac{w-1}{2} = 11$. This simplifies to $w - 1 = 22$, so $w = 23$. Now plug the values for z and w into the second equation: $\frac{23+11}{2} = 11$. This simplifies to $\frac{34}{2} = 11$ or $17 = 11$, which is not true. Eliminate (C). If it's not immediately apparent whether a greater number or a smaller number is needed, simply pick a direction and try that answer. Try (B), 7. In the first equation, $\frac{w-1}{2} = 7$. This simplifies to $w - 1 = 14$, so $w = 15$. In the second equation, this becomes $\frac{15+7}{2} = 11$. This simplifies to $\frac{22}{2} = 11$ or $11 = 11$. This is true, so stop here. The correct answer is (B).

28. **F**   The question asks for the length of the base of Tim's parallelogram. Since the question asks for a specific value and the answers contain numbers in increasing order, plug in the answers. Begin by labeling the answers as "base" and start with (H), 6. Since the height of the parallelogram is given as *two times its base*, the height is equal to $6 \times 2 = 12$. Calculate the area by multiplying base by height, as given. The area is therefore $(6)(12) = 72$. Since 72 is greater than the area of 18 given in the question, eliminate (H) and try a smaller answer, such as (G), 4. When the base is 4, the height is equal to $4 \times 2 = 8$. The area is therefore $(4)(8) = 32$. Since 32 is greater than the area of 18 given in the question, eliminate (G). Choice (F) is likely to be correct, but to check, plug in 3 for the base. This makes the height equal to $3 \times 2 = 6$. The area is therefore $(3)(6) = 18$, which matches the value given in the question. The correct answer is (F).

30. **H**   The question asks for the possible values of n. Since the question asks for a specific value and the answers contain numbers, plug in the answers. Begin by labeling the answers as n. Try $n = 0$. The expression becomes $|2(0) + 6| = |3(0) + 4|$, which simplifies to $|6| = |4|$ or $6 = 4$. This is not true, so 0 is not part of the solution set. Eliminate (F) and (G). Try $n = -2$. The expression becomes $|2(-2) + 6| = |3(-2) + 4|$, which simplifies to $|-4 + 6| = |-6 + 4|$ or $|2| = |-2|$. This is $2 = 2$, so -2 is part of the solution set. Eliminate (J). Try $n = 2$. The expression becomes $|2(2) + 6| = |3(2) + 4|$, which simplifies to $|4 + 6| = |6 + 4|$ or $|10| = |10|$. This is true, so 2 is also part of the solution set. Eliminate (K). The correct answer is (H).

33. **E**   The question asks for the value of a. Since the question asks for a specific value and the answers contain numbers in increasing order, plug in the answers. Begin by labeling the answers as "a," and start with (C), 16. The equation becomes $\sqrt[3]{343} - \sqrt[3]{16} = \sqrt[3]{27}$. Use a calculator as needed to find that $\sqrt[3]{343}$ is 7, $\sqrt[3]{16}$ as about 2.52, and $\sqrt[3]{27}$ is 3. The equation becomes $7 - 2.52 = 3$ or $4.48 = 3$, which is not true, so eliminate (C). A larger value is needed for a to make the value of the left side of the equation smaller, so eliminate (A) and (B). Try (E). The equation becomes $\sqrt[3]{343} - \sqrt[3]{64} = \sqrt[3]{27}$ or $7 - 4 = 3$. This is true, so stop here. The correct answer is (E).

Hard

45. **C**   The question asks for the solution set of a given equation. Since the question asks for a specific value and the answers contain numbers, plug in the answers. Begin by labeling the answers as "n." Try $n = 3$ from (A). The given expression becomes $\sqrt[3]{3^2 - (6)(3)} = 3$ or $\sqrt[3]{-9} = 3$. This is not true, so 3 is not part of the solution set. Eliminate (A) and (D). Rather than trying the complicated numbers in (B), try $n = -3$ from (C) next. The given expression becomes $\sqrt[3]{(-3)^2 - (6)(-3)} = 3$ or $\sqrt[3]{9 + 18} = 3$. This simplifies to $\sqrt[3]{27} = 3$. This is true, so -3 is part of the solution set. Because only (C) includes -3 as part of the solution set, stop here. The correct answer is (C).

49. **C** The question asks for the solution, the value of n, to a given equation. Since the question asks for a specific value and the answers contain numbers in increasing order, plug in the answers. Begin by labeling the answers as "n" and start in the middle with (C), 2. The expression becomes $27^{2(2)} = 81^{(2+1)}$ or $27^4 = 81^3$. Either use a calculator to compare the two values or notice that both 27 and 81 can be converted to the same base of 3:27 is the same as 3^3 and 81 is the same as 3^4. Replace 27 with 3^3 and replace 81 with 3^4 in the given expression. The expression becomes $(3^3)^4 = (3^4)^3$. When dealing with questions about exponents, remember the MADSPM rules. The PM part of the acronym indicates that raising a base with an exponent to another Power means to Multiply the exponents. The equation becomes $3^{12} = 3^{12}$. Since this is a true statement, stop here. The correct answer is (C).

52. **G** This question asks for the values of a and b that satisfy the given function. Since the question asks for specific values and the answers contain numbers, plug in the answers. Since both a and b are equal to x, begin by labeling the answers as "x" and start with an easy number from the answers. Try $x = 0$. In function notation, the number inside the parentheses is the x-value that goes into the function, and the value that comes out of the function is the y-value. If $x = 0$, then $h(0) = 2^{(0^2 + 2(0) - 2)} = 2^{(0 + 0 - 2)} = 2^{-2} = \dfrac{1}{2^2} = \dfrac{1}{4}$. This does not match the information in the question that $h(x) = 2$. Eliminate any answer containing 0: eliminate (F) and (K). Next, plug in another choice from the remaining answers. Try $x = 1$. If $x = 1$, then $h(1) = 2^{(1^2 + 2(1) - 2)} = 2^{(1 + 2 - 2)} = 2^1 = 2$. This matches the information in the question that $h(x) = 2$. Eliminate any remaining answers that do not contain 1. Eliminate (H). Try one of the remaining answers. Try $x = -1$. If $x = -1$, then $h(-1) = 2^{((-1)^2 + 2(-1) - 2)} = 2^{(1 - 2 - 2)} = 2^{-3} = \dfrac{1}{2^3} = \dfrac{1}{8}$. This does not match the information in the question that $h(x) = 2$. Eliminate any answer containing -1. Eliminate (J). This leaves only (G) remaining. The correct answer is (G).

55. **C** The question asks for an irrational solution to the given equation. Since the question asks for a specific value and the answers contain numbers in increasing order, plug in the answers. Begin by labeling the answers as "n." First, eliminate (B) because it is a rational number; it can be expressed as a fraction using integers. The remaining choices are all irrational numbers, so start in the middle with (C), $2\sqrt{6}$. The expression becomes $\left| \left(2\sqrt{6} \right)^2 - 30 \right| - 6 = 0$ or $|4(6) - 30| - 6 = 0$. This becomes $|24 - 30| - 6 = 0$, or $|-6| - 6 = 0$. Finally, this becomes $6 - 6 = 0$. Since this is a true statement, stop here. The correct answer is (C).

Chapter 6
Plane Geometry

You've seen in the Plugging In chapters that a smart test-taking strategy, in and of itself, can improve your Math score. That is no less true for Geometry questions, but for these you typically have to bring a bit more to the table. ACT doesn't give you the formulas like SAT does, so you need to have them stored in your brain (or your calculator) when test day rolls around. Remember, counting Trigonometry, Geometry makes up about half of any given ACT Math test.

THE BASIC APPROACH
Let's try a straightforward Geometry question.

22. In right triangle $\triangle STU$ shown below, V is the midpoint of $\overline{TU}$. In inches, what is the length of $\overline{UV}$?

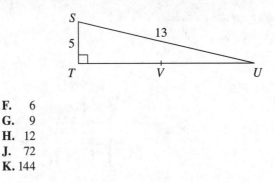

F. 6
G. 9
H. 12
J. 72
K. 144

STEP 1

Step 1: Ballpark
First, ACT has actually done you a big favor on this question. While they claim that "illustrative figures are NOT necessarily drawn to scale," it's usually safe to assume that they are at least close. Remember what you're looking for here: the length of $\overline{UV}$. Look closely at this figure: you can tell just by looking at it that the longest side is $\overline{SU}$, which has a length of 13, so it's not likely that any smaller part of the triangle will have a longer length, eliminating (J) and (K). You can probably eliminate (H) as well because $\overline{SU}$ is so much longer than $\overline{UV}$. This way, if you were running short on time and had to guess, you have improved your chances of guessing from 20% to 50%. Not bad for no work, huh?

STEP 2

Step 2: Draw the Figure
If the ACT hasn't given you a figure, draw your own. If you're taking the ACT on the computer, you'll need to copy down or draw the figure on your whiteboard. Don't worry about being perfectly accurate but do get all the necessary details in a figure so you can do the next step. In this case, ACT has given you a figure, so you'll only need to draw triangle STU yourself if you're taking the test on a computer.

STEP 3

Step 3: Write on the Figure
Now, dig in to get your final answer. Rather than trying to keep everything in your mind, make sure you are writing all over your figure. The question says that V is the midpoint of $\overline{TU}$, so make sure you mark that on your figure. It's probably worth emphasizing the portion, $\overline{UV}$, that you are looking for as well.

Step 4: Write Down Formulas

As for the formulas, get those down before you begin working the question as well. For this question, you are dealing with the sides of a right triangle, so it is likely that you will need the Pythagorean Theorem: $a^2 + b^2 = c^2$, where c is the longest side. Plug in the information you have, and write anything new that you find on the figure:

$$a^2 + b^2 = c^2$$

$$(5)^2 + \left(\overline{TU}\right)^2 = (13)^2$$

$$\left(\overline{TU}\right)^2 = (13)^2 - (5)^2$$

$$\left(\overline{TU}\right)^2 = 169 - 25$$

$$\left(\overline{TU}\right)^2 = 144$$

$$\overline{TU} = 12$$

Don't make your brain work any harder than it needs to! Make sure you're writing everything down. Hopefully by now your scratch paper looks something like this:

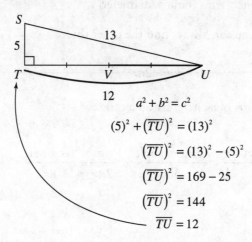

Now, once you have got all the information on the figure, it's probably very clear that the answer is (F) because $\overline{TU}$ is 12, and $\overline{UV}$ is one-half of this value. If you know your Pythagorean triples, you may have found $\overline{TU}$ even more quickly, but make sure you're reading the question carefully. If you don't read all the way, you might fall into the trap and pick (H).

Know Your Pythagorean Triples

Pythagorean triples are easy-to-remember, commonly tested ratios for the sides of a right triangle. Memorizing them can save you a lot of time by enabling you to bypass the Pythagorean Theorem. The most common Pythagorean triples are 3:4:5, 6:8:10, and 5:12:13, each listed from the shortest to the longest side. Which one does question 22 use?

So let's review the Basic Approach for Geometry questions.

The Basic Approach for Geometry

1. Use Ballparking to eliminate wrong answers on questions in which a figure is given.

2. If the question doesn't provide a figure, draw your own.

3. Write any information given by the question on the provided figure.

4. Write down any formulas you need and plug in any information you have.

THE FORMULAS

Here are some of the formulas you may find useful on Geometry questions.

Circles

Think CArd! (Circumference, Area, radius, diameter)

If you have one of these, you can always find the other three.

$$d = 2r \qquad C = \pi d = 2\pi r \qquad A = \pi r^2$$

When dealing with the parts of a circle, set up a ratio.

$$\frac{\text{part}}{\text{whole}} = \frac{\text{central angle}}{360°} = \frac{\text{arc}}{2\pi r} = \frac{\text{sector area}}{\pi r^2}$$

Triangles

$$\text{Area} = A = \frac{1}{2}bh$$

Perimeter: P = sum of the sides

Sum of all angles: 180°

Similar triangles have congruent angles and proportional sides.

Right Triangles

The Triangle rules listed above apply, but there are also some special rules for right triangles.

Pythagorean Theorem, where a, b, and c are the sides of the triangle, and c is the hypotenuse:

$$a^2 + b^2 = c^2$$

SOHCAHTOA (ratios between sides and angles of right triangles)

$$\sin \theta = \frac{opposite}{hypotenuse} \qquad \cos \theta = \frac{adjacent}{hypotenuse} \qquad \tan \theta = \frac{opposite}{adjacent}$$

Special Right Triangles

When you've determined the angles of your right triangle, you may be able to use the following ratios to bypass the Pythagorean Theorem:

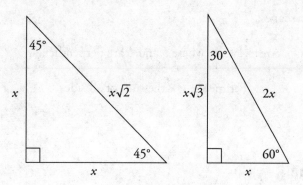

If a triangle question contains a $\sqrt{2}$ or a $\sqrt{3}$, you can most likely use one of these special triangles.

If you don't know the angles, you can often bypass the Pythagorean Theorem with the Pythagorean triples:

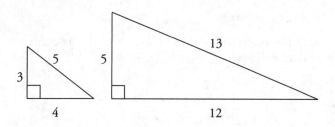

These Pythagorean triples are basic ratios, so they can be multiplied to be used with larger numbers.

Although 6:8:10 is commonly cited as a Pythagorean triple, it is just the 3:4:5 triple multiplied by 2.

Four-Sided Figures (Quadrilaterals)

Parallelogram:	Opposite sides parallel, opposite sides and angles equal
Rhombus:	Opposite sides parallel, ALL sides equal, opposite angles equal A rhombus is a *parallelogram* in which all four sides are equal.
Rectangle:	Opposite sides parallel, opposite sides equal, ALL angles 90° A rectangle is a *parallelogram* with four right angles.
Square:	Opposite sides parallel, ALL sides equal, ALL angles 90° A square is a type of *parallelogram*, *rhombus*, and *rectangle*.

For any of these four shapes:

Area: $A = bh$, where b and h are perpendicular

Perimeter: $P =$ the sum of all sides

THE QUESTIONS

Plane Geometry

Let's use these formulas and the Basic Approach to solve some questions.

31. If the perimeter of a square is 36 inches, what is the length of one side of the square, in inches?

    A. 72
    B. 36
    C. 12
    D. 9
    E. 6

Here's How to Crack It

The question asks for the length of one side of a square with a perimeter of 36 inches. Is a figure provided for you? No, so draw one! Label it with the information from the question.

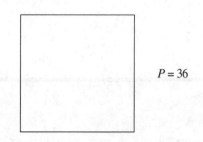

$P = 36$

The perimeter of a square is the sum of the lengths of all the sides. In a square, every side is the same length, which means you can divide 36 by 4 to get the length of each side. This becomes $36 \div 4 = 9$, so the correct answer is (D). Be sure to read the question carefully—if you mistake 36 for the area of the square instead of the perimeter, you'll get 6 as the length of one side. More complex questions will then ask you to determine something else about the square, such as the area.

Now apply the Basic Approach to a question about circles.

44. A circle has a diameter of 8 inches. What is the area of the circle, to the nearest 0.1 square inch?

    F. 12.6
    G. 25.1
    H. 50.3
    J. 64.0
    K. 201.1

Here's How to Crack It

The question asks for the area of a circle with a diameter of 8 inches. Remember the Basic Approach. There's no figure, so draw your own. Once you've done that, mark it up with information from the question, and get all your formulas down. Think CArd!

Your paper should look something like this:

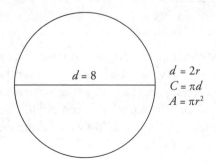

$d = 8$

$d = 2r$
$C = \pi d$
$A = \pi r^2$

> **Write It Down!**
> If there's no figure given to you, draw your own. This will allow you to better grasp what the question is asking and make sense of the provided information. See the figure to the left for an example.

Now work the formulas to get the answer. You know that the diameter of this circle is 8, which means its radius is 4. Use the radius in the Area formula, and use your calculator to find this Area:

$$A = \pi r^2$$
$$A = \pi (4)^2$$
$$A = 16\pi$$
$$A \approx 50.3$$

This matches up nicely with (H). If you don't have a calculator, or you're not especially handy with it, no question. Use Ballparking. You know that π is roughly equivalent to 3, so your answer will need to be close to 16 × 3, or 48. Only (H) is close enough.

Let's look at another one.

5. The length and width of a rectangle are 20 feet and 48 feet, respectively. What is the length, in feet, of the diagonal of the rectangle?

    A. 30
    B. 34
    C. $\sqrt{1,904}$
    D. 52
    E. 68

Here's How to Crack It

The question asks for the length of the diagonal of a rectangle with a given length and width. First, draw the figure and transfer all the information from the question to the figure. You should get something that looks like this:

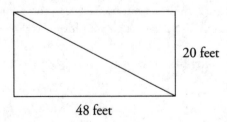

While this may seem like a rectangle question, the diagonal is really the hypotenuse of the two triangles that make up the rectangle. To solve for the hypotenuse, use the Pythagorean Theorem, $a^2 + b^2 = c^2$. Opposite sides of a rectangle are equal, so the vertical side on the left is also 20 feet. Therefore, a and b are 48 and 20. The equation becomes $(48^2) + (20^2) = c^2$. Solve the equation to get $2,304 + 400 = c^2$, which simplifies to $2,704 = c^2$. Taking the square root of both sides results in $c = 52$. The correct answer is (D).

Now let's look at another triangle concept the ACT likes to test.

23. In the figure below, $\triangle ABC$ is similar to $\triangle DEF$. The measures given are in inches. The corresponding side lengths of the 2 triangles are in a ratio of 2:5. What is the perimeter, in inches, of the larger triangle, $\triangle DEF$?

A. 70

B. 35

C. 28

D. 14

E. $5\dfrac{3}{5}$

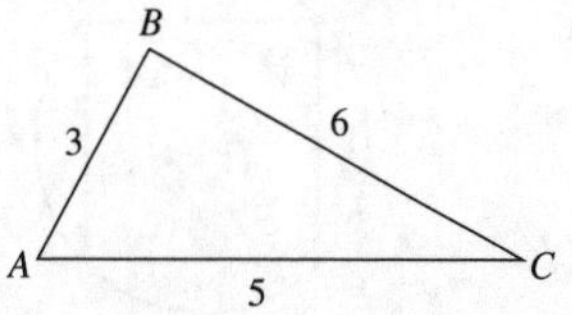

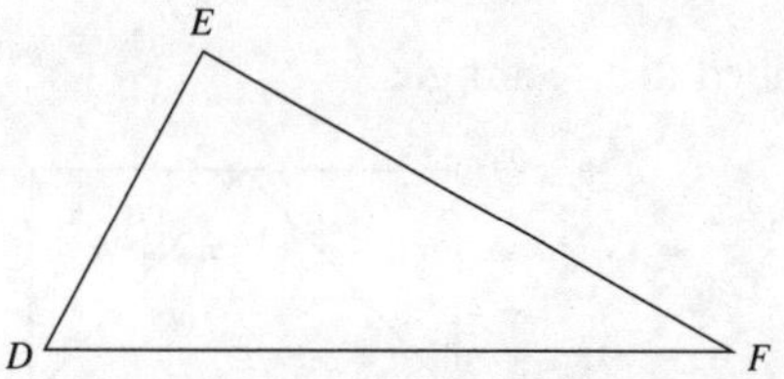

Here's How to Crack It

The question asks for the perimeter of the larger of two similar triangles. When triangles are "similar," it means that all the angles are the same and all the sides are proportional. The question asks for the perimeter of the larger triangle, so try to find that rather than each individual side. If the ratio of the sides is 2:5, then the ratio of the perimeters is also 2:5. The smaller triangle has a perimeter of 3 + 5 + 6 = 14. Ratios can also be written as fractions, so the perimeter of the smaller triangle is $\dfrac{2}{5}$ of the perimeter of the larger triangle. To get the perimeter of the larger triangle, set up the following equation: $\dfrac{2}{5}P = 14$. Multiply both sides by 5 to get $2P = 70$, then divide both sides by 2 to get $P = 35$. The correct answer is (B).

Shapes Within Shapes: What's the Link?

ACT's favorite way to ask hard Geometry questions is to put shapes within shapes. You know the drill: some shape inscribed in some other shape, or two shapes share a common side. They've got all kinds of ways to ask these questions. But when you see a shape drawn within another shape, there's usually one question that will blow the question wide open: *What's the link between the two shapes?* Let's try a few.

1. A square inscribed in a circle

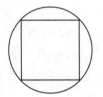

2. A triangle inscribed in a rectangle

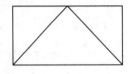

3. A square overlapping with a circle

So, what's the link?

1. What's the link? The diagonal of the square is the diameter of the circle.

2. What's the link? The base of the triangle is the long side of the rectangle, and the height of the triangle is the short side of the rectangle.

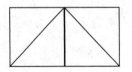

3. What's the link? The side of the square is equivalent to the radius of the circle.

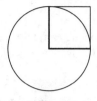

Let's try a couple of questions that deal with these concepts.

25. In the figure below, Q is a point on side $\overline{MN}$ of parallelogram $MNOP$. The measures given are in centimeters. What is the area of $\triangle NOP$, in square centimeters?

A. 8
B. 9
C. 24
D. 33
E. 66

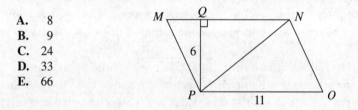

Here's How to Crack It

The question asks for the area of a triangle that is part of a parallelogram. Use the Basic Approach and write out the necessary formula. The formula for the area of a triangle is $A = \frac{1}{2}bh$. For $\triangle NOP$, 11 is the base, but it may be tricky to see the height. Since $MNOP$ is a parallelogram, any line perpendicular to MN and OP will have the same measurement. Therefore, the length of QP will equal the length of a height dropped down from point N to meet the base of $\triangle NOP$ at a right angle. This means that the height is 6, so $A = \frac{1}{2}(11)(6) = 33$ square centimeters. Note, you can also solve this question by finding the area of the parallelogram, $A = bh = 66$, and dividing that by 2. Either way, the correct answer is (D).

Now let's look at a more difficult one.

37. In the square shown below, points E and F are the midpoints of sides $\overline{AB}$ and $\overline{CD}$, respectively. Two semicircles are drawn with centers E and F. What is the perimeter, in feet, of the shaded region?

A. $12 + 12\pi$
B. $24 + 12\pi$
C. $24 + 24\pi$
D. $48 + 12\pi$
E. $48 + 24\pi$

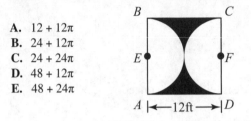

Here's How to Crack It

The question asks for the perimeter of the shaded region on the figure. Make sure you write everything you need on the figure, including the relevant square and circle formulas. Since you are dealing with shapes within shapes, now is also a good time to figure out what the link is, what these two (or three, in this case) shapes have in common. Don't worry about digging up a formula for the perimeter of that hourglass-shaped thing. Stick with the shapes you know.

For this question, the links occur on the right and left sides of the figure: the left and right sides of the square are the same as the diameters of each of the semicircles. You can therefore say that if all sides of a square are equal, each of these sides is 12. Since the diameter of each semicircle is equivalent to a side of the square, then the diameters of both semicircles must also be 12.

Let's use this information to find the perimeters of each of these semicircles. Remember, when you're dealing with circles, the perimeter is called the *circumference*, which can be found with the formula $C = \pi d$. Since you're dealing with a semicircle here, you'll need to divide its circumference in half. Let's find the circumference of the semicircle with center E.

$$\frac{C_E}{2} = \frac{\pi d}{2}$$
$$= \frac{\pi(12)}{2}$$
$$= 6\pi$$

The semicircle with center F will have the same circumference because it has the same diameter. Now all you need to do is add up the perimeters to find your answer. You know the sides of the square will each be 12 and the circumference of each semicircle will be 6π, so the total perimeter of the shaded region will be $12 + 12 + 6\pi + 6\pi = 24 + 12\pi$, as in (B).

Basic Trigonometry

There's a common misconception about the ACT regarding Trigonometry. Many believe that if you don't have a solid foundation in Trigonometry, you can't get a good score on the ACT Math test. However, rest assured that there are only a handful of these questions on the test—usually only four!

What's more, two of these questions will deal with basic SOHCAHTOA, which you clearly don't need a whole semester or year of trig to learn. The other two questions may deal with radians, or the unit circle, or some of the trig identities, but you shouldn't worry about these until you've solidified a math score of at least 28.

So let's have a look at one of these basic SOHCAHTOA questions.

42. According to the measurements given in the figure below, which of the following expressions gives the distance, in meters, from the house to the garage?

F.   40 tan 38°

G.   40 cos 38°

H.   40 sin 38°

J. $\dfrac{40}{\cos 38°}$

K. $\dfrac{40}{\sin 38°}$

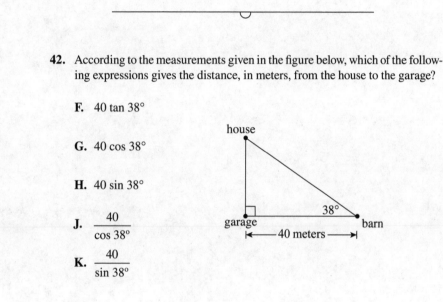

Here's How to Crack It

The question asks for the trigonometric expression that gives the distance from the house to the garage. They've already written most of the information you'll need on the figure, but it can be worth noting the side that you are looking for: the side that shows the distance from the house to the garage.

Let the answer choices help. These choices tell you a lot more than you may think. First of all, they offer the main indication that this will be a SOHCAHTOA question by showing that you will need to choose sine, cosine, or tangent. Next, they tell you that you'll be dealing with only one angle, the 38° one. Finally, they tell you that you won't need to do any weird rounding with decimals because they want just the sine, cosine, or tangent expression.

Have a close look at the sides you're dealing with. Where are they relative to the 38° angle? The base of the triangle is touching the 38° angle, so it's *adjacent*, and the side you're looking for is *opposite* the 38° angle. It looks like you won't be dealing with the *hypotenuse* at all. So which trig function deals with the *opposite* and *adjacent* sides? Remember SOHCAH**TOA**. The function you'll need is tangent. And don't do more work than you need to. Only (F) offers an expression featuring the tangent function, so it must be the correct answer.

Now go ahead and give some of these concepts a try in the following drills.

PLANE GEOMETRY DRILL

8. In the figure below, $\overline{AB} \parallel \overline{CD}$. What is the value of y ?

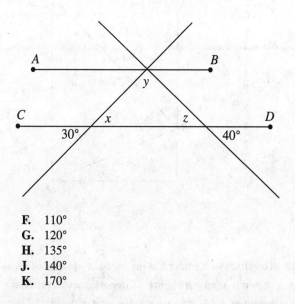

   F. 110°
   G. 120°
   H. 135°
   J. 140°
   K. 170°

9. In the figure below, $\angle BAC$ measures 50°, $\angle BDC$ measures 80°, and $\angle BCD$ measures 55°. What is the measure of $\angle ACB$?

   A. 30°
   B. 45°
   C. 75°
   D. 85°
   E. 100°

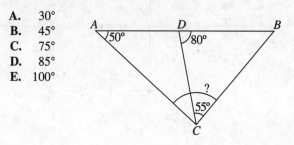

14. The 8-sided figure below is divided into 6 congruent squares. The total area of the 6 squares is 96 square centimeters. What is the perimeter, in centimeters, of the figure?

   F. 16
   G. 28
   H. 48
   J. 56
   K. 96

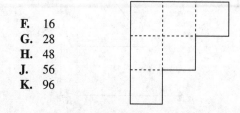

22. The base of triangle M is four times the base of triangle N, while the height of triangle N is half the height of triangle M. The area of triangle M is how many times that of triangle N ?

   F. 2
   G. 4
   H. 8
   J. 10
   K. 16

26. A rectangular horse corral is built along one side of a square barn whose area is 5,776 square feet. The length of the corral is the same as the length of the side of the barn, while the width of the corral is one-fourth the length of the side of the barn. What is the area of the horse corral, in square feet?

   F.   76
   G. 1,016
   H. 1,284
   J. 1,444
   K. 5,776

27. In right triangle $\triangle FHK$ below, $\overline{GJ}$ is parallel to $\overline{FK}$, and $\overline{GJ}$ is perpendicular to $\overline{HK}$ at J. The length of $\overline{HK}$ is 12 inches, the length of $\overline{GJ}$ is 6 inches, and the length of $\overline{GH}$ is 10 inches. What is the length, in inches, of $\overline{FK}$?

A. 7
B. 8
C. 9
D. 10
E. 11

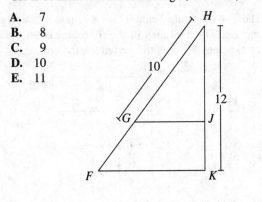

30. The diameter of circle A is twice that of circle B. If the area of circle A is 36π, then what is the circumference of circle B ?

F. π
G. 3π
H. 6π
J. 9π
K. 18π

32. A rectangular whiteboard is 12 centimeters wide and 16 centimeters long. Which of the following is closest to the length, in centimeters, of the diagonal of this whiteboard?

F. 4
G. $\sqrt{112}$
H. 14
J. 20
K. 28

36. In the figure below, the distance from A to B is $\dfrac{1}{3}$ the distance from B to C. The area of $\triangle BDE$ is what fraction of the area of rectangle $ACDE$?

F. $\dfrac{1}{6}$
G. $\dfrac{1}{3}$
H. $\dfrac{1}{2}$
J. $\dfrac{3}{5}$
K. $\dfrac{2}{3}$

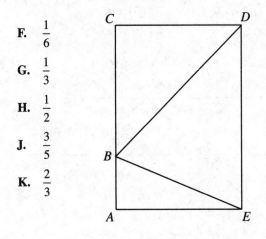

39. The circle with center E is inscribed in square $ABCD$, as shown in the figure below. If line $\overline{AC}$ (not shown) has a length of $8\sqrt{2}$, then what is the area of the circle?

A. π
B. 4π
C. 8π
D. 12π
E. 16π

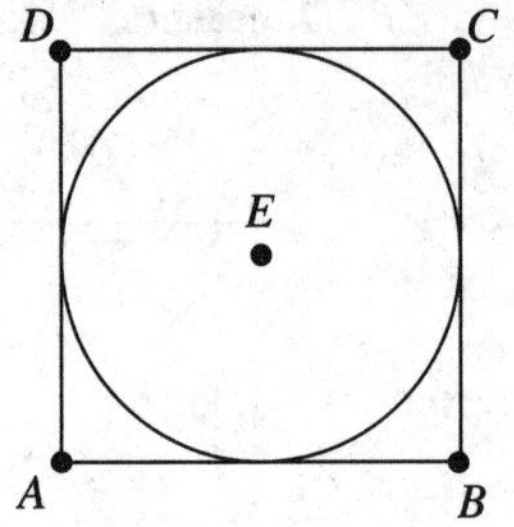

41. For isosceles trapezoid *PQRS* shown below, *QR* = 5 inches, *PS* = 5 inches, *SR* = 16 inches, and the height of the trapezoid is 4 inches. What is the area, in square inches, of *PQRS* ?

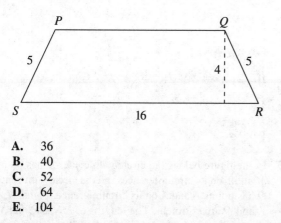

- **A.** 36
- **B.** 40
- **C.** 52
- **D.** 64
- **E.** 104

43. In △*ABC*, $\overline{AB} \cong \overline{BC}$ and the measure of ∠*B* is 38°. What is the measure of ∠*A* ?

- **A.** 142°
- **B.** 76°
- **C.** 71°
- **D.** 38°
- **E.** 19°

44. What is the volume, in cubic inches, of a cube if the perimeter of 1 square face is 60 inches?

- **F.** 45
- **G.** 900
- **H.** 3,375
- **J.** 27,000
- **K.** 216,000

48. In the figure below, the circle with center *X* has a radius of 8 centimeters, and the measure of ∠*SRX* is 70°. What is the measure of $\overparen{RS}$?

- **F.** 20°
- **G.** 40°
- **H.** 50°
- **J.** 55°
- **K.** 70°

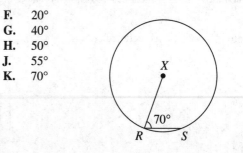

49. Each angle of a quadrilateral is 90°. Which of the following must also describe this quadrilateral?

  I. Square (sides of equal length and 90° angles)
  II. Rhombus (sides of equal length)
  III. Rectangle (90° angles)
  IV. Parallelogram (opposite sides parallel)

- **A.** I and III only
- **B.** I and IV only
- **C.** II and III only
- **D.** II and IV only
- **E.** III and IV only

51. When a ball strikes the side of a pool table at an angle, it will rebound off the side at the same angle. On the pool table below, what is the measure of the indicated angle?

(Note: A pool table is rectangular.)

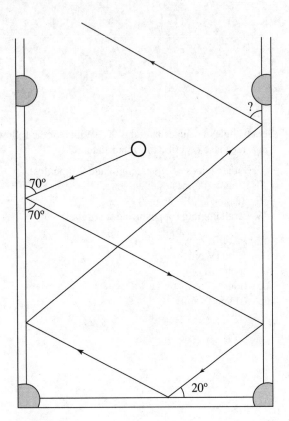

A. 50°
B. 60°
C. 70°
D. 75°
E. 80°

54. The side of an equilateral triangle is *s* inches longer than the side of a second equilateral triangle. How many inches longer is the altitude of the first triangle than the altitude of the second triangle?

F. $\dfrac{\sqrt{3}}{2}s$

G. $\sqrt{2}s$

H. $2s$

J. $3s$

K. s^3

55. In the figure below, the circle with center *N* has points *M* and *Y* on its circumference, and the circle with center *O* has points *P* and *X* on its circumference. Points *N*, *X*, *Y*, and *O* are collinear. The lengths of $\overline{MN}$, $\overline{OP}$, and $\overline{XY}$ are 10, 8, and 3 inches, respectively. What is the length, in inches, of $\overline{NO}$?

A. 10
B. 11
C. 12
D. 15
E. 18

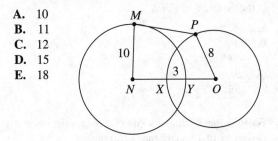

57. The five semicircles in the figure below touch only at their corners. If the distance from A to F along the diameters of the semicircles is 60 inches, what is the distance, in inches, from F to A along the arcs of these semicircles?

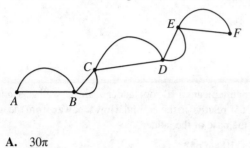

    A. 30π
    B. 40π
    C. 60π
    D. 72π
    E. 90π

60. In the figure below, both solids consist of 5 cubes, each 2 inches on a side. In the solid on the right, 4 of the cubes form a rectangular box that is 4 inches long, 2 inches wide, and 4 inches high. The solid on the left is the result of moving Cube 1 from its position to the right of Cube 2 to above it so that Cubes 1, 2, and 3 form a rectangular box 2 inches long, 2 inches wide, and 6 inches high. To the nearest percent, the total surface area of the solid on the left is what percent greater than the total surface area of the solid on the right?

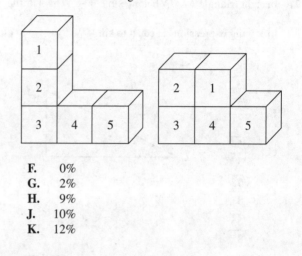

    F.   0%
    G.   2%
    H.   9%
    J.   10%
    K.   12%

TRIGONOMETRY

Basic Trigonometry Drill

21. In right triangle $\triangle LMN$ below, $\sin L = \dfrac{3}{8}$. Which of the following expressions is equal to $\sin M$?

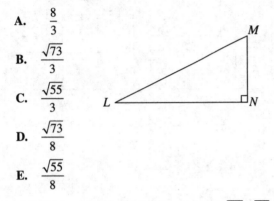

    A. $\dfrac{8}{3}$

    B. $\dfrac{\sqrt{73}}{3}$

    C. $\dfrac{\sqrt{55}}{3}$

    D. $\dfrac{\sqrt{73}}{8}$

    E. $\dfrac{\sqrt{55}}{8}$

23. In isosceles right triangle ABC (not shown), $\overline{AB} = \overline{AC} = 3$. Which of the following represents the value of $\cos \angle ABC$?

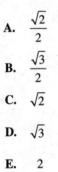

    A. $\dfrac{\sqrt{2}}{2}$

    B. $\dfrac{\sqrt{3}}{2}$

    C. $\sqrt{2}$

    D. $\sqrt{3}$

    E. 2

25. A painter leans a 10-foot ladder against a wall at an angle of 65° relative to the ground. How far away from the wall is the base of the ladder?

    A. $10 \tan 65°$

    B. $10 \sin 65°$

    C. $10 \cos 65°$

    D. $\dfrac{10}{\sin 65°}$

    E. $\dfrac{10}{\cos 65°}$

29. For the polygon below, which of the following represents the length, in inches, of $\overline{FK}$?

    A. 10

    B. 30

    C. $\dfrac{10}{\sin 70°}$

    D. $\dfrac{30}{\sin 70°}$

    E. $\sin 70°$

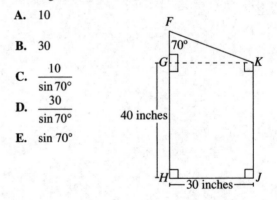

37. A straight ladder is leaned against a house so that the top of the ladder is 12 feet above level ground, as shown in the figure below. Which of the following gives the length, in feet, of the ladder?

A. $x = 12\cos 65°$

B. $x = 12\sin 65°$

C. $x = \dfrac{12}{\cos 65°}$

D. $x = \dfrac{12}{\sin 65°}$

E. $x = \dfrac{12}{\tan 65°}$

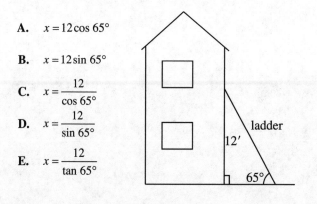

PLANE GEOMETRY DRILL ANSWER KEY

8. F
9. D
14. H
22. H
26. J
27. C
30. H
32. J
36. H
39. E
41. C
43. C
44. H
48. G
49. E
51. C
54. F
55. D
57. A
60. J

BASIC TRIGONMETRY DRILL ANSWER KEY

21. E
23. A
25. C
29. D
37. D

PLANE GEOMETRY DRILL EXPLANATIONS

8. **F**   The question asks for the value of y in the given geometric figure. Use the Geometry Basic Approach and start by labeling the provided figure. Mark line segments $\overline{AB}$ and $\overline{CD}$ as parallel. Notice that x, y, and z are the angles within a triangle. The angle labeled x is across from the angle that is 30°, and opposite angles are equal, so $x = 30°$. The same applies to the angle labeled z and the angle that is 40°, so $z = 40°$. Since y is the final angle in the triangle and the interior angles of a triangle equal 180°, y can be determined by the equation $y = 180° - 30° - 40° = 110°$. The correct answer is (F).

9. **D**   The question asks for the measure of $\angle ACB$ on the figure. The information from the question is already provided on the figure, so look for a way to start determining the measures of the remaining angles. The measure of $\angle ACB$ is 55° plus the measure of $\angle ACD$. As a result, it must be greater than 55°, so eliminate (A) and (B). There are 180° in a triangle such as ABC, so finding the measure of $\angle ABC$ will lead to finding the measure of $\angle ACB$. Start with the measures of $\triangle BCD$ to find $\angle DBC = 180° - \angle BDC - \angle BCD = 180° - 80° - 55° = 45°$. Label this on the figure. This is also the measure of $\angle ABC$. Now find the measure of $\angle ACB$ the same way: $\angle ACB = 180° - \angle BAC - \angle ABC = 180° - 50° - 45° = 85°$. The correct answer is (D).

14. **H**   The question asks for the perimeter, in centimeters, of the given figure. Use the Geometry Basic Approach and start by labeling the provided figure. The question states that there are 6 congruent squares, so mark all sides of the squares as congruent. The question provides the area and asks for the perimeter, so write down the formulas for both: $A = s^2$ and $P =$ sum of the sides. To calculate the area of each individual square, divide the total area, 96, by the number of squares, 6: $96 \div 6 = 16$. Determine the side length of the squares: $A = s^2 = 16$, so $\sqrt{s^2} = \sqrt{16}$, and $s = 4$. The question asks for perimeter, so label each side of a square that is also the side of the large figure as 4. Now count the labeled sides. There are 12, so $P = 4(12) = 48$. The correct answer is (H).

22. **H**   The question asks for a comparison of *the area of triangle M* to *that of triangle N*. Use the Geometry Basic Approach. The question does not have a figure, so draw two triangles labeled M and N. The question asks about area, so write the formula for the area of a triangle: $A = \frac{1}{2}bh$. The question provides a relationship between the triangles, so plug in numbers for the triangles' measurements. According to the question, *the base of triangle M is four times the base of triangle N*, so plug in 2 for the base of triangle N and 8 for the base of triangle M. The question also states that *the height of triangle N is half the height of triangle M*, so plug in 6 for the height of triangle M, and 3 for the height of triangle N. Now find the areas of both triangles: $A_M = \frac{1}{2}(8)(6) = 24$, and $A_N = \frac{1}{2}(2)(3) = 3$. To find how many times larger M is than N, divide 24 by 3 to get 8. The correct answer is (H).

26. **J** The question asks for *the area of the horse corral, in square feet.* Use the Geometry Basic Approach. The question does not have a figure, so draw a square to represent the barn and a rectangle to represent the corral that shares a side with the barn. Write down the formula for the area of a square and the area of a rectangle: $A = s^2$ and $A = lw$, respectively. The question states that *the length of the corral is the same as the length of the side of the* barn; begin by finding the side of the barn using the given area of 5,776 square feet. This becomes $A = s^2 = 5{,}776$, so $s = \sqrt{5{,}776} = 76$. The question also states that *the width of the corral is one-fourth the length of the side of the barn*, so the length can be calculated as $76\left(\dfrac{1}{4}\right) = 19$. Now that the length and width of the rectangular corral are known, solve for the area A as $lw = (76)(19) = 1{,}444$. The correct answer is (J).

27. **C** The question asks for *the length, in inches, of* $\overline{FK}$. Use the Geometry Basic Approach and start by labeling the provided figure with the information from the question. $\overline{GJ}$ is parallel to $\overline{FK}$ and they are both perpendicular to $\overline{HK}$, so label $\angle FKH$ and $\angle GJH$ as right angles; finally, label $\overline{GJ}$ as 6. Notice that there are two triangles that have two sets of congruent angles: $\angle FKH$ and $\angle GJH$ are both right angles, and $\angle FHK \cong \angle GHJ$ because the same angle is part of both triangles. Therefore, this question is testing similar triangles. Similar triangles have corresponding sides that are in a ratio. The question asks for the measure of $\overline{FK}$, which corresponds to $\overline{GJ}$. To solve the ratio, another pair of corresponding sides is needed, but the question did not provide a pair. Use the Pythagorean Triple 6:8:10 or the Pythagorean Theorem to find the measure of side $\overline{HJ}$: $6^2 + (HJ)^2 = 10^2$, which simplifies to $36 + (HJ)^2 = 100$. Subtract 36 from both sides to get $(HJ)^2 = 64$; then take the square root of both sides to get $HJ = 8$. Now set up the proportion and solve for the length of $\overline{FK}$: $\dfrac{FK}{GJ} = \dfrac{HK}{HJ}$. Plug in the known information to get $\dfrac{FK}{6} = \dfrac{12}{8}$; then cross-multiply to get $(FK)(8) = (6)(12)$. Divide both sides by 8 to get $FK = \dfrac{(6)(12)}{8} = \dfrac{72}{8} = 9$. The correct answer is (C).

30. **H** The question asks for *the circumference of circle B.* Use the Geometry Basic Approach. Start by drawing two circles and labeling them A and B. The question gives an area and asks for a circumference, so write down both of those formulas: $A = \pi r^2$ and $C = \pi d$. The question also states that the area of circle A is 36π. Use the area formula to determine the radius of circle A: $A = \pi r^2 = 36\pi$, so divide both sides by π to get $r^2 = 36$; then take the square root of each side to get $r = 6$. The diameter of circle A is $2r = 2(6) = 12$. According to the question, *the diameter of circle A is twice that of circle B*, so the diameter of circle B is half of 12, or 6. Use the formula for circumference to find that the circumference of circle B is $\pi d = 6\pi$. The correct answer is (H).

32. **J** The question asks for the length of a diagonal of a rectangular whiteboard. Use the Geometry Basic Approach. Start by drawing a rectangle and labeling it as 12 cm wide and 16 cm long. Draw the diagonal as well, which divides the rectangle into two right triangles. Either notice that this is a 3:4:5 Pythagorean triple with each side multiplied by 4 or use Pythagorean Theorem, $a^2 + b^2 = c^2$, to solve for the hypotenuse, which is also the diagonal. This becomes $12^2 + 16^2 = c^2$, which simplifies to $144 + 256 = c^2$ or $400 = c^2$. Take the square root of both sides to get $c = 20$. The correct answer is (J).

36. **H** The question asks *what fraction of the area* of the given rectangle is the area of $\square BDE$. Use the Geometry Basic Approach. The figure is provided, so write down the formulas for the areas of a rectangle and a triangle: $A = lw$ and $A = \frac{1}{2}bh$, respectively. Since no lengths are given in the question, plug in numbers that fit the rules given in the question. The question says that *the distance from A to B is* $\frac{1}{3}$ *the distance from B to C*. Label $AB = 2$ and $BC = 6$. The sum $AB + BC$ is equal to the side of the rectangle, so the length of the side $\overline{AC}$ is $2 + 6 = 8$. To find the area of the rectangle, plug in a number for the width that will make solving for the area easy, such as 4, and label side $AE = 4$. Now calculate the area of the rectangle: $A = lw = (8)(4) = 32$. Solve for the area of $\triangle BDE$. The base is side $\overline{DE}$, which has length equal to $AC = 8$, and the height is equal to $AE = 4$. The area of $\triangle BDE$ becomes $A = \frac{1}{2}bh = \frac{1}{2}(8)(4) = 16$. Finally, divide the area of $\triangle BDE$ by the area of the rectangle to find the ratio: $\frac{16}{32} = \frac{1}{2}$. The correct answer is (H).

39. **E** The question asks for *the area of the circle*. Use the Geometry Basic Approach and start by labeling the given figure by drawing the diagonal, line $\overline{AC}$, and labeling it $8\sqrt{2}$. The diagonal of a square cuts the square into two 45°-45°-90° triangles, which have sides with a length of s and a hypotenuse with a length of $s\sqrt{2}$. Set $8\sqrt{2} = s\sqrt{2}$ and solve for s to find that the side of the square is 8 units long. The side of the square is equal to the diameter of the inscribed circle, so the diameter of the circle is also 8 and the radius is 4. Write down the formula for the area of a circle, $A = \pi r^2$, and plug in the radius to get $A = \pi r^2 = \pi(4^2) = 16\pi$. The correct answer is (E).

41. **C** The question asks for the area of the trapezoid. There is a formula for this, but it may be easier to divide the shape into a rectangle and two triangles than to recall it. Use the Geometry Basic Approach and start by labeling the given figure. Most of the sides are already labeled, but drop a line down from P to create a triangle on the left like the one on the right.

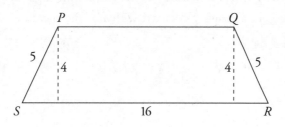

Next, take the area of each of the pieces and add them together. The area of a triangle is $A = \frac{1}{2}bh$. The base of the triangle is not given, but this is a 3:4:5 Pythagorean triple, so the base is 3. Therefore, the area of each triangle is $A = \frac{1}{2}(3)(4) = 6$. Next, calculate the area of the rectangle using the formula $A = bh$. The height is 4, so determine the base. Each of the triangles takes up 3 units of the base, meaning the base of the rectangle is $16 - 2(3) = 16 - 6 = 10$. Therefore, the area of the rectangle is $A = (10)(4) = 40$. The sum of the areas is $40 + 6 + 6 = 52$. The correct answer is (C).

43. **C** The question asks for the measure of $\angle A$ in a triangle. Use the Geometry Basic Approach and start by drawing a triangle with equal sides AB and BC and label $\angle B$ as 38°. The figure will look like this:

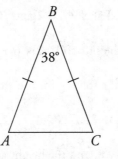

The interior angles of a triangle add up to 180°. Angle B is 38°, so the remaining degrees are $180° - 38° = 142°$. Since AB and BC are the same length, the angles of A and C are equal. Divide 142° by 2 to find that each angle is 71°. The correct answer is (C).

44. **H** The question asks for the volume of a cube if the perimeter of a face is 60 inches. Use the Geometry Basic Approach and start by drawing a cube, which is a 3-dimensional figure with equal square sides. Perimeter is defined as the sum of all the sides of a figure. If the perimeter of one of the faces is 60 inches, each side of the face is $60 \div 4 = 15$ inches. The volume of a rectangular solid is $V = lwh$, but on a cube all those dimensions are the same. The volume becomes $(15)(15)(15) = 3,375$ cubic inches. The correct answer is (H).

48. **G** The question asks for *the measure of* $\overset{\frown}{RS}$. Use the Geometry Basic Approach and start by labeling $\overline{XR}$ in the given figure as 8 cm because it is a radius. Also draw line segment $\overline{XS}$ because the length of the arc is equal to the size of the central angle and creating a triangle will make it possible to solve for the central angle, $\angle RXS$. $\overline{XS}$ is also a radius, so label it as 8 cm. An isosceles triangle has been created. The measure of $\angle RXS$ is also 70°, as angles opposite equal sides in an isosceles triangle are also equal. There are 180° in a triangle, so the measure of the remaining angle, $\angle RXS$ is $180° - 70° - 70° = 40°$. Because $\angle RXS$ is the central angle associated with $\overset{\frown}{RS}$, the measure of $\overset{\frown}{RS}$ is also 40°. The correct answer is (G).

49. **E** The question asks for a description of a quadrilateral with angles of 90°. Use the Geometry Basic Approach and draw a quadrilateral. It could look like this:

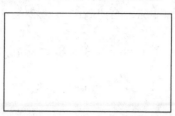

Now evaluate each of the descriptions given. Statement (I) says that this figure must also be a square. Based on this drawing, it does not *have* to be a square, so eliminate any answer choice that has (I) in it. Eliminate (A) and (B). Statement (II) says that it must also be a rhombus. Based on this drawing, it does not *have* to be a rhombus. Eliminate (C) and (D). No matter how the figure is drawn, it will be a rectangle and the opposite sides will be parallel. The correct answer is (E).

51. **C** The question asks for the measure of the indicated angle. Following the path of the ball, the first bounce off the left side is given as 70°. The second bounce will be off the right side of the table, which is parallel to the left side. The path of the ball crosses these two parallel lines, so it creates the same 70° angle. Mark the angles on either side of the bounce on the right of the table (not the one in the middle) as 70°. The third bounce is given as 20°, which will also be the angle at which it bounces off the wall. Label the angle of this bounce as 20°. The path of the ball and the corner of the table create a right triangle, and the interior angles of a triangle add up to 180°. Thus, the fourth bounce back on the right side of the table will be 180° − 90° − 20° = 70°. The last and final bounce will come off the left side and hit on the right side, so it will also be 70°, same angle as the fourth bounce. The correct answer is (C).

54. **F** The question asks for *how many inches longer the altitude of the first triangle is than the altitude of the second triangle.* Use the Geometry Basic Approach. Because no figures are provided, draw the two equilateral triangles. There are variables in the answer choices, and the question is about a relationship between figures, so plug in numbers. Label the sides of the second triangle 2 and assign a value to s, such as 4. Then label the sides of the first triangle 2 + 4 = 6, since the side of the first *equilateral triangle is s inches longer that the side of the second triangle.* To find the altitude of each equilateral triangle, draw a line from the top vertex to the base. This splits the equilateral triangle into two 30°-60°-90° triangles. Use the rules of special right triangles: the shortest leg measures x, the longer leg measures $x\sqrt{3}$, and the hypotenuse measures $2x$. In the second triangle, the hypotenuse measures 6 and $x = 3$. The altitude is the longer leg of the triangle and measures $x\sqrt{3} = 3\sqrt{3}$. Completing the same steps for the first triangle gives hypotenuse of 2 and altitude of $1\sqrt{3}$ or $\sqrt{3}$. The question asks for the difference in the altitudes, so subtract: $3\sqrt{3} - \sqrt{3} = 2\sqrt{3}$. This is the target value; circle it. Now plug $s = 4$ into the answer choices

to see which matches the target value. Choice (F) becomes $\frac{\sqrt{3}}{2}(4) = 2\sqrt{3}$. Keep (F) but check the remaining answers just in case. Choice (G) becomes $\sqrt{2}(4) = 4\sqrt{2}$. This does not match the target value, so eliminate (G). Choice (H) becomes $2(4) = 8$, so eliminate (H). Choice (J) becomes $(3)(4) = 12$; eliminate (J). Choice (K) becomes $4^3 = 64$; eliminate (K). The correct answer is (F).

55. **D**   The question asks for the length of $\overline{NO}$. The figure is already labeled with the information from the question, so look at $\overline{NO}$. The question states that N and O are the centers of their respective circles, point Y lies on circle N, and point X lies on circle O. This means that $\overline{NY}$ is a radius of circle N, and $\overline{OX}$ is a radius of circle O. Since $\overline{MN}$ is also a radius of circle N, $NY = MN = 10$. The same is true for circle O: $OX = PO = 8$. Since $XY = 3$ and is part of $\overline{NY}$, then $NX = NY - XY = 10 - 3 = 7$, and $OY = OX - XY = 8 - 3 = 5$. The length of $NO = NX + XY + OY = 7 + 3 + 5 = 15$. The correct answer is (D).

57. **A**   The question asks for *the distance, in inches, from F to A along the arcs of* the semicircles. Since the question gives no information on the relative lengths of the different diameters, plug in numbers that sum to 60 for the lengths of the diameters. The easiest approach is to make them all equal. Divide 60 by 5 and assign each diameter a value of 12. Calculate the distance of the length along the semicircle using the circumference formula $C = \pi d$. Since a semicircle is exactly half a circle, modify the circumference formula to calculate half the circumference: $C_{semicircle} = \frac{1}{2}\pi d$. Now plug in $d = 12$ and solve to get the circumference of one semicircle $C_{semicircle} = \frac{1}{2}\pi(12) = 6\pi$. There are 5 semicircles, so to get the total distance from F to A along the curves, multiply the circumference of one semicircle by 5: $(5)(6\pi) = 30\pi$. The correct answer is (A).

60. **J**   The question asks for the percent difference between the surface areas of the two shapes. Surface area is the sum of the areas of all faces of the figures. In the figure on the left, there are 22 faces on the outside of the figure: 5 in front, 5 in back, 3 on top, 3 on the bottom, 3 on the right, and 3 on the left. In the figure on the right, there are 20 faces: 5 in front, 5 in back, 3 on top, 3 on the bottom, 2 on the right, and 2 on the left. The faces are all congruent squares, as the figures are made up of congruent cubes. Rather than calculate the actual surface area, just find the percent change of the number of congruent faces. Percent change is calculated as $\frac{difference}{original} \times 100$. In this case, that is $\frac{22 - 20}{20} \times 100 = \frac{2}{20} \times 100 = 10$. The correct answer is (J).

Basic Trigonometry Drill

21. **E**   The question asks which expression *is equal to sin M* given that $sin\ L = \dfrac{3}{8}$. Use the Geometry Basic

Approach. Write out SOHCAHTOA to remember the trig functions and use it to label the figure.

The SOH part defines sine as $\dfrac{opposite}{hypotenuse}$, so *opposite* = MN = 3 and *hypotenuse* = LM = 8. Label those

side lengths on the figure. To find sin *M*, use the sine definition again. In relation to angle *M, opposite*

is $\overline{LN}$, and $\overline{LM}$ is still the hypotenuse. Therefore, $sin\ M = \dfrac{LM}{8}$. Eliminate (A), (B), and (C), as those

are not over 8. Next, determine the measure of $\overline{LN}$. Use Pythagorean Theorem: $3^2 + (LN)^2 = 8^2$,

which becomes $9 + (LN)^2 = 64$. Subtract 9 from both sides to get $(LN)^2 = 55$, so $LN = \sqrt{55}$. Thus,

$sin\ M = \dfrac{\sqrt{55}}{8}$. The correct answer is (E).

23. **A**   The question asks for *the value of cos* $\angle ABC$ given an *isosceles right triangle ABC* where *AB = AC = 3*.

Use the Geometry Basic Approach and draw and label triangle *ABC*. The right angle is *A*, and the

length of each leg of the triangle, $\overline{AB}$ and $\overline{AC}$, is 3. The two non-right angles will be 45°, since the

triangle is isosceles. It will look like this:

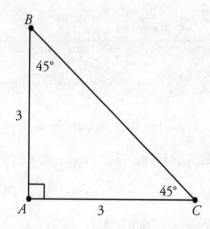

Write out SOHCAHTOA to remember the trig functions and use it to label the figure. The CAH

part defines cosine as $\dfrac{adjacent}{hypotenuse}$. The length of the adjacent side $\overline{AB}$ is 3. Use the rules for a

45°-45°-90° special right triangle, or the Pythagorean Theorem, to find the length of the

hypotenuse is $3\sqrt{2}$. Therefore, $cos\ \angle ABC = \dfrac{3}{3\sqrt{2}} = \dfrac{1}{\sqrt{2}}$. However, $\dfrac{1}{\sqrt{2}}$ is not an available answer,

so rationalize the denominator by multiplying the numerator and the denominator by $\sqrt{2}$ to get

$\left(\dfrac{1}{\sqrt{2}}\right)\left(\dfrac{\sqrt{2}}{\sqrt{2}}\right) = \dfrac{\sqrt{2}}{\left(\sqrt{2}\right)\left(\sqrt{2}\right)} = \dfrac{\sqrt{2}}{2}$. The correct answer is (A).

25. **C** The question asks *how far away from the wall is the base of the ladder.* Use the Geometry Basic Approach and draw a triangle. The ladder creates the hypotenuse of a triangle with the vertical side represented by the wall and the horizontal side representing the distance the ladder is from the wall. Label the hypotenuse as 10 and the angle that the hypotenuse makes with the horizontal side as 65°. Label the horizontal side x since this is the value for which the question asks. It will look like this:

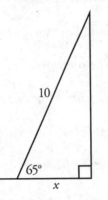

Write out SOHCAHTOA to remember the trig functions. In relation to the angle that is 65°, the side labeled x is the adjacent side, and the side labeled 10 is the hypotenuse. The CAH part of SOHCAHTOA defines sine as $\dfrac{adjacent}{hypotenuse}$, so cosine is the function that is needed. Eliminate (A), (B), and (D) since these use other trig functions. Plug in the values from the triangle to get $\cos 65° = \dfrac{x}{10}$. Multiply both sides by 10 to get $x = 10 \cos 65°$. The correct answer is (C).

29. **D** The question asks for the length of $\overline{FK}$. Use the Geometry Basic Approach and start by labeling the figure. Note that *GHJK* has 4 right angles and is therefore a rectangle. Opposite sides of a rectangle are equal, so $GK = 30$ and $JK = 40$. Label these measurements on the figure. There are trigonometric expressions in some of the answer choices, so write out SOHCAHTOA to remember the trig functions. In relation to the angle that is 70°, $\overline{GK}$ is the opposite side, and $\overline{FK}$ is the hypotenuse. The SOH part of SOHCAHTOA defines sine as $\dfrac{opposite}{hypotenuse}$, so $\sin 70° = \dfrac{30}{FK}$. Multiply both sides of the equation by *FK* to get $FK \sin 70° = 30$; then divide both sides by sin 70° to get $FK = \dfrac{30}{\sin 70°}$. The correct answer is (D).

37. **D** The question asks for *the length, in feet, of the ladder leaned against the house*. Use the Geometry Basic

Approach. Label the ladder as x. There are trigonometric expressions in the answer choices, so write

out SOHCAHTOA to remember the trig functions. In relation to the angle that is 65°, the side labeled

12 is the opposite side, and the side labeled x is the hypotenuse. The SOH part of SOHCAHTOA

defines sine as $\dfrac{opposite}{hypotenuse}$. Eliminate (A), (C) and (E) because they do not use sine. Now set up the

equation to solve for the length of the ladder, x. Plug in the values from the triangle to get $\sin 65° = \dfrac{12}{x}$.

Multiply both sides by x to get $x \sin 65° = 12$. Divide both sides by $\sin 65°$ to get $x = \dfrac{12}{\sin 65°}$. The

correct answer is (D).

Chapter 7
Coordinate
Geometry

ACT likes to make a big deal about the distinction between Plane and Coordinate Geometry, but your approach toward the two question types won't really differ that much. When a figure of the coordinate plane is not given, draw your own. Mark the figure with all the information given in the question, to avoid having to keep track of it in your head. Write out any formulas you'll need to answer the question before filling in the given information.

THE FORMULAS

All points are written (x, y), where x gives the x-coordinate and y gives the y-coordinate.

Two lines *intersect* when they meet at a single point

$$\text{Slope}: \frac{\text{rise}}{\text{run}} = \frac{y_2 - y_1}{x_2 - x_1}$$

where (x_1, y_1) and (x_2, y_2) are two points on a line.

Equations of a line will appear in two forms on the ACT.

- Slope-intercept form of a line: $y = mx + b$

  o In this form, (x, y) is a point on the line, m is the slope, and b is the y-intercept, or the point at which the line crosses the y-axis.

You can use the slope-intercept form to find the slope of a line. Then the slope of a line perpendicular to it will be the negative reciprocal, or $-\dfrac{1}{m}$. That is, if the slope of a line is 2, the slope of a *perpendicular* to that line will be $-\dfrac{1}{2}$. *Parallel* lines have equal slopes.

- Standard form of a line: $Ax + By = C$

  o In this form, (x, y) is a point on the line, the slope is $-\dfrac{A}{B}$, and the y-intercept is $\dfrac{C}{B}$.

Occasionally, a Coordinate Geometry question will deal with a circle in the coordinate plane. Here is the equation:

- Standard form of a circle: $(x - h)^2 + (y - k)^2 = r^2$

  o In this form, (x, y) is a point on the circle, (h, k) is the center of the circle, and r is the radius.

THE QUESTIONS

Let's try a few Coordinate Geometry questions now. We'll start with a question about slope.

---

18. What is the slope of the line parallel to the line represented by the equation $16x + 4y = 8$?

    F. −2
    G. −4
    H. −16
    J. −24
    K. 16

Here's How to Crack It

The question asks for the slope of a line *parallel* to the one given. Parallel lines have the same slope, so to solve this question, determine the slope of the given line. You may be in a rush to put the line into slope-intercept form, $y = mx + b$, where m represents slope. However, if you recognize that the equation is already in the standard form $Ax + By = C$, you can avoid that work. For an equation in standard form, slope is $-\dfrac{A}{B}$. For this equation, $A = 16$ and $B = 4$, so the slope is $-\dfrac{16}{4} = -4$. The correct answer is (G).

Of course, using slope-intercept form would have worked as well, but why take up precious time or risk making a careless mistake in manipulating the equation?

> Parallel lines have the same slope.
>
> Perpendicular lines have slopes that are negative reciprocals.

Now let's look at a question that specifically asks for slope-intercept form.

50. The points (2,−1) and (−1,8) lie on a straight line. What is the slope-intercept equation of the line?

   F. $y = 5x$
   G. $y = 2x − 1$
   H. $y = x − 2$
   J. $y = −2x + 5$
   K. $y = −3x + 5$

Here's How to Crack It

The question asks for the slope-intercept equation of a line given two points on the line. The first step to answering this question is determining the slope of the line. Slope is defined as $\dfrac{y_2 − y_1}{x_2 − x_1}$ for any two points on the line. For the points given, this becomes $\dfrac{−1−8}{2−(−1)} = \dfrac{−9}{3} = −3$. Rather than continuing to find the full equation, as your math teacher would want you to do, stop and see if you can eliminate any answers. Each of the equations in the answers is given in slope intercept form, $y = mx + b$, where m stands for slope. Only (K) has the correct slope, so the correct answer is (K).

Let's look at a Coordinate Geometry question about a circle in the *xy*-plane.

30. In the standard (x,y) coordinate plane, $O(−6,9)$ is the center of circle O. If AB is a diameter of circle O, and A has coordinates (2,3), what are the coordinates of B ?

   F.   (−2, −15)
   G.   (−2, −3)
   H.   (−2, 6)
   J.   (−14, 12)
   K.   (−14, 15)

Here's How to Crack It

The question asks for the coordinates of B, which is one endpoint of the diameter of a circle. Start by drawing the circle and given points in the *xy*-plane:

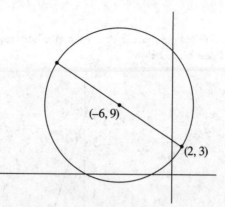

Our sketch does not need to be exactly to scale as long as it is close enough to show you what is going on. This question seems like it is about a circle, but really, it is all about the midpoint of a line. The center of the circle (–6, 9) is the midpoint of the diameter, line $\overline{AB}$. The midpoint of a line is given by the average of the coordinates of the endpoints. Since the coordinates of B are unknown, label them x and y. The x-value of the midpoint is then the average of the x-coordinates of A and B: $\frac{2+x}{2} = -6$. Multiply both sides of the equation by 2 to get $2 + x = -12$; then add 2 to both sides to get $x = -14$. The x-coordinate of B must be –14. Eliminate (F), (G), and (H), which have different x-coordinates. The average of the two y-coordinates is $\frac{3+y}{2} = 9$. Solve for y to get $3 + y = 18$, and $y = 15$. Eliminate (J). The correct answer is (K).

Midpoint is defined as $\left(\frac{x_1 + x_2}{2}, \frac{y_1 + y_2}{2} \right)$ for points (x_1, y_1) and (x_2, y_2).

Of course, Coordinate Geometry isn't just about equations and points. It all takes place in the *xy*-plane, so many of the questions will also involve graphing. Here's an example.

---

17. Which of the following equations represents the line graphed in the standard (x,y) coordinate plane below?

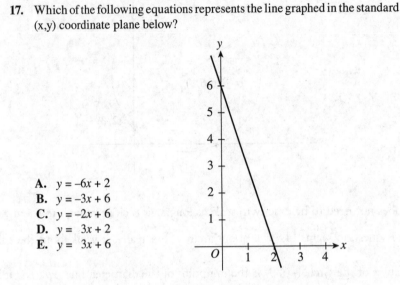

A. $y = -6x + 2$
B. $y = -3x + 6$
C. $y = -2x + 6$
D. $y = 3x + 2$
E. $y = 3x + 6$

Here's How to Crack It

The question asks for the equation of the line graphed above. The answer choices are already in $y = mx + b$ form, where m is the slope and b is the *y*-intercept. Start by eliminating answers that do not have the correct slope or *y*-intercept. The slope of the line is negative because the line descends as it moves in the positive *x*-direction, so eliminate (D) and (E). The *y*-intercept is the point at which the line crosses the *y*-axis, and this line crosses at $y = 6$. Eliminate (A), which has a value of 2 for *b*. The difference between (B) and (C) is the slope, so find the slope using the points (2, 0) and (0, 6). The *rise* is –6 and the *run* is 2, so the slope is $\frac{-6}{2} = -3$. Another option is to plug in the point (2, 0) to see which equation is true. Choice (B) becomes $0 = -3(2) + 6$ or $0 = -6 + 6$. This is true, so that is the equation of the line. Either way, the correct answer is (B).

Some ACT Math questions will combine graphing with word problems. The graphs of real-world situations can still be handled in much the same way as graphs of algebraic equations—with POE and plugging in points. Try one now.

20. The graph below shows the distance, *m* miles, Rachel is from school *t* minutes after the start of a drive. Which of the following statements accurately describes Rachel's drive?

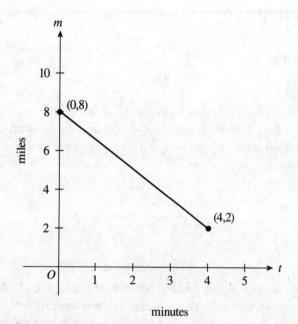

F. Rachel starts 8 miles from school, and after 4 minutes is 2 miles from school.

G. Rachel starts 8 miles from school, and after 2 minutes is 4 miles from school.

H. Rachel starts 4 miles from school, and after 8 minutes is 2 miles from school.

J. Rachel starts 2 miles from school, and after 4 minutes is 8 miles from school.

K. Rachel starts at school, and after 8 minutes is 4 miles from school.

Here's How to Crack It

Even some of the tried-and-true math class methods can be avoided using simpler methods. Let's look at a question about distance in the coordinate plane.

The question asks for a true statement based on the graph. This question is asking you to describe what you see. For this graph, $t = 0$ is the starting point. The *m*-value at $t = 0$ is 8, meaning that Rachel is 8 miles from school when she starts. This eliminates (H), (J), and (K). At 4 minutes into the drive, when $t = 4$, the *y*-value is 2. This means that Rachel travels 4 minutes and ends up 2 miles from school, eliminating (G). The correct answer is (F).

Even some of the tried-and-true math class methods can be avoided using simpler methods. Let's look at a question about distance in the coordinate plane.

23. In the standard (x,y) coordinate plane, point G lies at $(-3,-4)$, and point H lies at $(2,5)$. What is the length of $\overline{GH}$ in coordinate units?

A. $\sqrt{14}$

B. 4

C. $\sqrt{45}$

D. 7

E. $\sqrt{106}$

Here's How to Crack It

The question asks for the length of a line segment, which is the distance between the two endpoints of the segment. Your first impulse here will probably be to whip out the distance formula and complete this question in lightning-fast time. The only problem is that the distance formula looks like this:

$$d = \sqrt{(x_2 - x_1)^2 + (y_2 - y_1)^2}$$

Yikes. If you've got this formula stored somewhere in your head, great. Unfortunately, for most of us, this is a really easy formula to forget, or worse, to remember incorrectly. What you'll find about ACT Geometry is that for 90% of the questions, you're best off just dealing with the basics. For weird shapes in Plane Geometry, this will mean carving things up into recognizable shapes and working from there. On Coordinate Geometry, you will find that simple formulas and the Basic Approach can get you plenty of points.

Let's use the Basic Approach. First and foremost, this is a Geometry question, and they haven't given you a figure. Draw your own. It should look something like this:

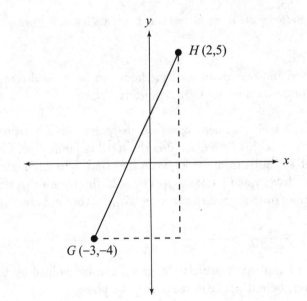

Now, look carefully at the line you've drawn for $\overline{GH}$. Remind you of anything? How about the hypotenuse of a right triangle? Remember, you want to work with the basics, and you know your triangles, so let's turn this thing into a right triangle.

Draw in the sides and find the lengths of those sides. To find the base of the triangle, figure out how much you're moving from one x-coordinate to the other. The points are (–3, –4) and (2, 5), so the x-coordinate will go from –3 to 2, or 5 units. The y-coordinate will go from –4 to 5, or 9 units. After you've drawn all this in and marked up your figure, you should have something like this:

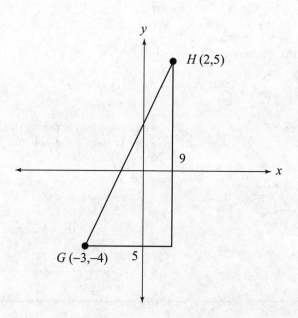

And now this is just a plain old ("plane" old?) Plane Geometry question. You know two sides of a right triangle and need the third. Sounds like a job for the Pythagorean Theorem.

$$a^2 + b^2 = c^2$$
$$(5)^2 + (9)^2 = \left(\overline{GH}\right)^2$$
$$\left(\overline{GH}\right)^2 = 25 + 81$$
$$\left(\overline{GH}\right)^2 = 106$$
$$\overline{GH} = \sqrt{106}$$

The answer is (E). No distance formula required.

COORDINATE GEOMETRY DRILL

3. A point at (5,–4) in the standard (*x*,*y*) coordinate plane is shifted left 3 units and up 6 units. What are the new coordinates of the point?

   A. (11, 7)
   B. (8, 2)
   C. (8,10)
   D. (2, 2)
   E. (2,10)

13. The points $A(-6,8)$ and $B(10,2)$ lie in the standard (*x*,*y*) coordinate plane. What is the midpoint of $\overline{AB}$?

   A. (–3, 4)
   B. (2, 5)
   C. (4,10)
   D. (5, 1)
   E. (8,–3)

19. What is the *x*-intercept of the line $y = 5x + 2$?

   A. $\left(0, -\dfrac{2}{5}\right)$

   B. $\left(0, \dfrac{2}{5}\right)$

   C. $(2, 0)$

   D. $\left(\dfrac{2}{5}, 0\right)$

   E. $\left(-\dfrac{2}{5}, 0\right)$

24. Points $O(5,3)$ and $P(-3,8)$ lie in the standard (*x*,*y*) coordinate plane. What is the slope of a line that is perpendicular to line $\overline{OP}$?

   F. $-\dfrac{8}{5}$

   G. $-\dfrac{5}{8}$

   H. $\dfrac{5}{8}$

   J. 1

   K. $\dfrac{8}{5}$

26. Points $L(-3,2)$ and $M(4,7)$ lie in the standard (*x*,*y*) coordinate plane. What is the slope of LM ?

   F. 9

   G. $-\dfrac{5}{7}$

   H. $\dfrac{5}{7}$

   J. $-\dfrac{1}{9}$

   K. $\dfrac{1}{9}$

33. Which quadrants of the standard (*x*, *y*) coordinate plane below contain points on the graph of the equation $8x + 4y = 12$?

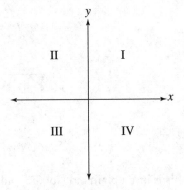

Quadrants of the standard
(*x*,*y*) coordinate plane

   A. II and IV only
   B. I, II, and III only
   C. I, II, and IV only
   D. I, III, and IV only
   E. II, III, and IV only

35. Triangle XYZ has vertices in the standard (*x*,*y*) coordinate plane at $X(-3,-5)$, $Y(4,-1)$, and $Z(-2,6)$. A translation of triangle XYZ is a second triangle, $X'Y'Z'$, with vertices X' $(6,-10)$, Y' $(13,-6)$, and Z' (a,b). What are the coordinates of Z' ?

   A. (2, 6)
   B. (7, 1)
   C. (7,–5)
   D. (7,–6)
   E. (–11, 1)

39. On a map in the standard (x,y) coordinate plane, the cities of Everton and Springfield are represented by the points $(-3,-5)$ and $(-6,-8)$, respectively. Each unit on the map represents an actual distance of 20 kilometers. Which of the following is closest to the distance, in kilometers, between these 2 cities?

A. 316
B. 120
C. 85
D. 60
E. 49

41. The figure below shows the graph in the standard (x,y) coordinate plane of one of the following functions. Which function is shown?

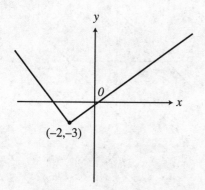

(−2,−3)

A. $y = |x + 2| + 3$

B. $y = |x - 2| - 3$

C. $y = |x + 2| - 3$

D. $y = |x + 3| - 2$

E. $y = |x - 3| + 2$

42. A circle in the standard (x,y) coordinate plane has a radius of 8 coordinate units and a center at $(-4,3)$. Which of the following is an equation of the circle?

F. $(x - 4)^2 - (y + 3)^2 = 8$
G. $(x - 4)^2 - (y + 3)^2 = 64$
H. $(x - 4)^2 + (y + 3)^2 = 64$
J. $(x + 4)^2 + (y - 3)^2 = 8$
K. $(x + 4)^2 + (y - 3)^2 = 64$

47. The figure below shows the graph of line ℓ in the standard (x,y) coordinate plane. Which of the following could be the equation of line ℓ ?

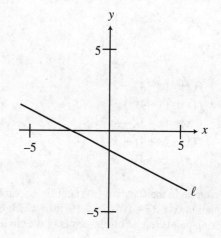

A. $y = -\dfrac{5}{2}x - 1$

B. $y = \dfrac{5}{2}x + 1$

C. $y = -\dfrac{2}{5}x - 1$

D. $y = -\dfrac{2}{5}x + 1$

E. $y = \dfrac{2}{5}x - 1$

48. The graph of $f(x) = x^3$ is shown in the standard (x,y) coordinate plane below. For which of the following equations is the graph of the cubic function shifted 4 units to the left and 3 units up?

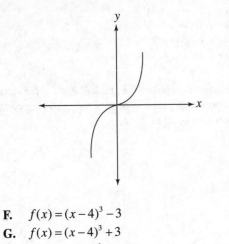

    F. $f(x) = (x-4)^3 - 3$
    G. $f(x) = (x-4)^3 + 3$
    H. $f(x) = (x+3)^3 - 4$
    J. $f(x) = (x+4)^3 + 3$
    K. $f(x) = (x+4)^3 - 3$

50. If a circle in the standard (x,y) coordinate plane has the equation $(x + 3)^2 + (y - 5)^2 = 16$, then which of the following points represents the center of the circle?

    F. $(-5,\ 3)$
    G. $(-3,-5)$
    H. $(\ 3,\ 5)$
    J. $(-5,-3)$
    K. $(-3,\ 5)$

54. Which of the following graphs in the standard (x,y) coordinate plane represents the solution set of the inequality $|x - y| \leq 2$?

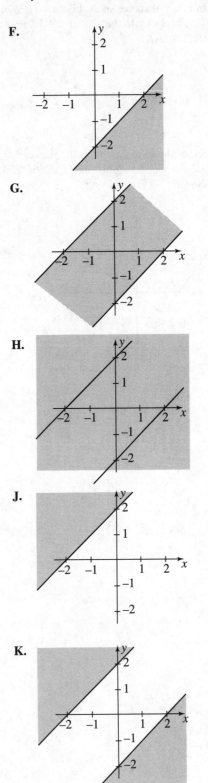

56. The graph below shows the distance a hot-air balloon is from the ground for a period of 10 minutes. A certain order of 3 of the following 5 actions describes the balloon's movement in relation to the position of the ground. Which order is it?

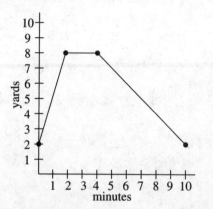

- I. Remains stationary for 2 minutes
- II. Moves away at 3 yards per minute
- III. Moves toward at 3 yards per minute
- IV. Moves away at 1 yard per minute
- V. Moves toward at 1 yard per minute

F. I, II, II
G. II, I, V
H. III, I, IV
J. IV, I, III
K. V, I, II

57. Trapezoid *WXYZ* is shown below in the standard (x,y) coordinate plane. The line $y = mx + 10$ connects the midpoint of side *XY* to the point *W*. What is the value of *m* ?

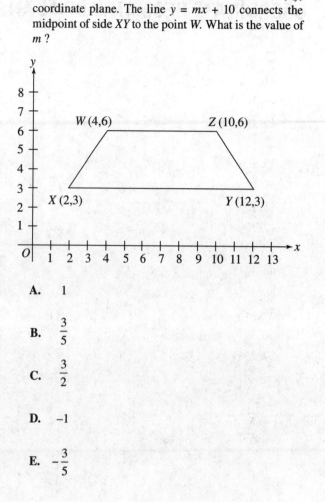

A. 1

B. $\dfrac{3}{5}$

C. $\dfrac{3}{2}$

D. -1

E. $-\dfrac{3}{5}$

COORDINATE GEOMETRY DRILL ANSWER KEY

3. D
13. B
19. E
24. K
26. H
33. C
35. B
39. C
41. C
42. K
47. C
48. J
50. K
54. G
56. G
57. D

COORDINATE GEOMETRY DRILL EXPLANATIONS

3. D   The question asks for the *new coordinates of the point* (5, –4) after it has been shifted. Drawing the coordinate plane and graphing the point can be helpful, so use the Geometry Basic Approach to draw the figure if needed. The question states that point (5, –4) is *shifted left 3 units*; left-right shifts happen along the *x*-axis. Shifting to the left decreases the *x*-coordinate, so subtract: 5 – 3 = 2. The new *x*-coordinate will be 2. Eliminate (A), (B), and (C) because they do not contain an *x*-coordinate of 2. The question also states that the point is shifted *up 6 units*. Up-down shifts happen along the *y*-axis. Shifting up increases the *y*-coordinate, so add: –4 + 6 = 2. The new *y*-coordinate is 2. The new point is (2, 2). The correct answer is (D).

13. B   The question asks for *the midpoint of $\overline{AB}$*. Use the Geometry Basic Approach and write the formula for the midpoint: $\left(\dfrac{x_2 + x_2}{2}, \dfrac{y_2 + y_2}{2} \right)$. Substitute the given points (–6, 8) and (10, 2) into the equation: $\left(\dfrac{-6 + 10}{2}, \dfrac{8 + 2}{2} \right) = \left(\dfrac{4}{2}, \dfrac{10}{2} \right) = (2, 5)$. The correct answer is (B).

19. E   The question asks for *the x-intercept of the line y = 5x + 2*. Make sure to read the question carefully; this formula is in the slope-intercept form $y = mx + b$, where b is the *y*-intercept, but the question asks for the *x*-intercept. The *x*-intercept is where the line crosses the *x*-axis; the value of *y* on the *x*-axis is always zero, so the *y*-coordinate of the *x*-intercept should be 0. Eliminate (A) and (B) because they do not have a *y*-value of 0. Now substitute *y* = 0 into the equation and solve for *x* to find the *x*-coordinate of the *x*-intercept. This becomes 0 = 5x + 2, so subtract 2 from each side to get –2 = 5x; then divide both sides by 5 to get $-\dfrac{2}{5} = x$. The coordinates of the *x*-intercept are $\left(-\dfrac{2}{5}, 0 \right)$. The correct answer is (E).

24. K   The question asks for *the slope of the line that is perpendicular to line $\overline{OP}$*. The question provides two points, so use the Geometry Basic Approach and write the formula for the slope of a line given two points: *slope* = $\dfrac{y_2 - y_1}{x_2 - x_1}$. Use points *O* (5, 3) and *P* (–3, 8) to solve for the slope of line $\overline{OP}$: $\dfrac{8 - 3}{-3 - 5} = -\dfrac{5}{8}$. The question asks for the slope of the line perpendicular to $\overline{OP}$, and perpendicular slopes are negative reciprocals. The negative reciprocal of $-\dfrac{5}{8}$ is $\dfrac{8}{5}$. The correct answer is (K).

26. **H**   The question asks for the slope of a line given two points. Use the Geometry Basic Approach and write the formula for the slope of a line given two points: $slope = \dfrac{y_2 - y_1}{x_2 - x_1}$. For the points (–3, 2) and (4, 7), the slope is $\dfrac{7-2}{4-(-3)} = \dfrac{5}{4+3} = \dfrac{5}{7}$. The correct answer is (H).

33. **C**   The question asks for the quadrants through which the line $8x + 4y = 12$ passes. First, manipulate the equation into the slope-intercept form $y = mx + b$ by isolating y. Subtract $8x$ from both sides of the equation to get $4y = -8x + 12$; then divide both sides by 4 to get $y = -2x + 3$. If a graphing calculator is available, graph this equation and observe the quadrants through which the line passes. If a calculator is not available, draw tick marks on the provided coordinate plane. The y-intercept of the equation is 3, so plot the point (0, 3). The slope of the line is –2, so move down two and move one to the right from point (0, 3). Plot point (1, 1). Connect these points and extend the line to see that it passes through Quadrants I, II, and IV. The correct answer is (C).

35. **B**   The question asks for the coordinates of a point after a triangle is moved in the coordinate plane. Check the changes to the coordinates of the other points to determine how the triangle moved. For each of the x-coordinates, the value increased by 9. The translated x-coordinate of Z will be –2 + 9 = 7, so eliminate (A) and (E), since they do not have this x-coordinate. For each of the y-coordinates, the value decreased by 5, so the new y-coordinate will be 6 – 5 = 1. Eliminate (C) and (D). The correct answer is (B).

39. **C**   The question asks for *the closest to the distance, in kilometers,* between the cities of Everton and Springfield. Use the Word Problem Basic Approach and break the question into bite-sized pieces. The question provides points on the coordinate plane and asks for the distance between those points, so use the Geometry Basic Approach and sketch the given two points: Everton (–3, –5) and Springfield (–6, –8). Draw a line connecting these points, and then draw a line from Everton directly to the left until just above Springfield. Finally, draw a line straight down to Springfield. This creates a right triangle. Since both legs have length 3, the triangle is an isosceles right triangle: a right triangle with side lengths of s and a hypotenuse of $s\sqrt{2}$. The hypotenuse, and the distance between the cities, is $s\sqrt{2} = 3\sqrt{2}$ in the coordinate plane. The question also states that *each unit on the map represents an actual distance of 20 kilometers,* so multiply the distance on the graph, $2\sqrt{3}$, by 20 to get 84.85, which is approximately 85 km. The correct answer is (C).

41. **C**   The question asks *which function is shown* on the graph. Since the answers contain variables and the point (–2, –3) is given on the graph, plug the given point into the answers to see which one works. Choice (A) becomes $-3 = |-2 + 2| + 3$ or $-3 = 3$. This is not true, so eliminate (A). Choice (B) becomes $-3 = |-2 - 2| + 3$ or $-3 = 7$. This is not true, so eliminate (B). Choice (C) becomes $-3 = |-2 + 2| - 3$ or $-3 = -3$. This is true, so keep (C), but check the remaining answers just in case. Choice (D) becomes $-3 = |-2 + 3| - 2$ or $-3 = 1$; eliminate (D). Choice (E) becomes $-3 = |-2 - 3| + 2$ or $-3 = 7$; eliminate (E). Another option is to graph the equations in the answer choices on a graphing calculator to see which one matches the given graph. Either way, the correct answer is (C).

42. **K** The question asks for the equation of a circle in the coordinate plane. The formula for the equation of a circle is $(x - h)^2 + (y - k)^2 = r^2$, where (h, k) is the center of the circle and r is the radius. The equation must have addition between the x and y terms, so eliminate (F) and (G), which have subtraction there. The question states that the radius is 8, so the right side of the equation should be 8^2 or 64. Eliminate (J) because the right side is not 64. The center is $(-4, 3)$, so the equation becomes $[x - (-4)]^2 + (y - 3)^2 = 64$, which simplifies to $(x + 4)^2 + (y - 3)^2 = 64$. The correct answer is (K).

47. **C** The question asks for the answer that *could be the equation of line l*. Since there are no points available to determine the equation of the line, look to the answers for help. The answers are in slope-intercept form: $y = mx + b$, where m is the slope and b is the y-intercept. Look first at the y-intercept. It is below the origin, so the y-intercept is negative. Eliminate (B) and (D) because they do not have a negative value for b. The slope of the line is negative, so eliminate (E). The slope of a line is the representation of the rise (change in y) over the run (change in x). If a graphing calculator is available, graph the equations in (A) and (D) to observe which has a slope most like the provided figure. If no calculator is available, note that (A) has a slope of $-\frac{5}{2}$, which means the line will fall 5 units for every 2 units it moves to the right. This produces a slope steeper than that of the line represented on the graph, so eliminate (A). The correct answer is (C).

48. **J** The question asks which of the answers shows the equation of *the graph of the cubic function shifted 4 units to the left and up 3 units*. Note that the answer choices contain variables and that one point on the graph of the cubic equation is at the origin. If the point at the origin is shifted *4 units to the left and up 3 units*, the new point would be $(-4, 3)$; plug this point into the answers and eliminate any that aren't true. Choice (F) becomes $3 = (-4 - 4)^3 - 3$, which simplifies to $3 = -8^3 - 3$ and then $3 = -512 - 3$ or $3 = -515$. This is not true; eliminate (F). Choice (G) becomes $3 = (-4 - 4)^3 + 3$ and simplifies to $3 = -8^3 + 3$ then $3 = -512 + 3$ and finally $3 = -509$. This is not true; eliminate (G). Choice (H) becomes $3 = (-4 + 3)^3 - 4$, which simplifies to $3 = -1 - 4$ or $3 = -5$. This is not true; eliminate (H). Choice (J) becomes $3 = (-4 + 4)^3 + 3$, which simplifies to $3 = 3$. This is true, so keep (J), but check the remaining answer just in case. Choice (K) becomes $3 = (-4 + 4)^3 - 3$, which simplifies to $3 = -3$. Eliminate (K). Another option is to graph the answer equations on a graphing calculator to see which one matches the given graph. Either way, the correct answer is (J).

50. **K** The question asks which answer represents *the center of the circle* with equation $(x + 3)^2 + (y - 5)^2 = 16$. Use the Geometry Basic Approach and write down the equation of a circle in standard form: $(x - h)^2 + (y - k)^2 = r^2$, where (h, k) is the center of the circle and r is the radius. Rewrite the equation of the given circle as $[x - (-3)]^2 + (y - 5)^2 = 16$, so $h = -3$ and $k = 5$. The center of the circle is $(-3, 5)$. The correct answer is (K).

54. **G** The question asks for the graph that represents the inequality. Enter points from the graphs in the answer choices into the equation to determine which graph matches. First, try (0, 0). Putting this into the inequality results in $|0 - 0| \leq 2$ or $0 \leq 2$, which is true. Therefore, the point (0, 0) should either be on the line or in a shaded region of the graph. Eliminate (F), (J), and (K), since these do not include (0, 0). Next, test a point that is in (H) but is not in (J), such as (2, –2). In the inequality, this becomes $|2 - (-2)| \leq 2$. This simplifies to $|4| \leq 2$, which is not true. Therefore, the point (2, –2) should not be shaded or on a line of the graph. Eliminate (H). The correct answer is (G).

56. **G** The question asks for *the order* of the actions performed by the *hot-air balloon* as it moves during a 10-minute period. Complete this question in bite-sized pieces. First, note that the graph shows that the balloon rises from 2 yards to 8 yards in minutes 0 to 2, for a total distance of 6 yards. This means the balloon is moving away from the ground at $\frac{6}{2} = 3$ yards per minute, which matches statement (II). Eliminate (F), (H), (J), and (K) because they do not start with (II). The correct answer is (G).

57. **D** The question asks for the value of m, which is the slope of the line connecting the midpoint of $\overline{XY}$ to point W. First, ballpark the slope, which will connect the upper left corner of the trapezoid to the middle of the base of the trapezoid. This slope will be negative, so eliminate (A), (B), and (C), which are positive. Now determine the midpoint of $\overline{XY}$. The midpoint is determined by finding the averages of the x- and y-values. Given that the y-values are the same, find the average of the x-values: $\frac{2+12}{2} = \frac{14}{2} = 7$. Therefore, the midpoint of $\overline{XY}$ is (7, 3). Now use this and the coordinates of W in the slope formula, $\frac{y_2 - y_1}{x_2 - x_1}$, to determine m: $\frac{6-3}{4-7} = \frac{3}{-3} = -1$. The correct answer is (D).

Part III
Practice Tests

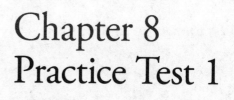

Chapter 8
Practice Test 1

ACT MATHEMATICS TEST
60 Minutes—60 Questions

DIRECTIONS: Solve each problem, choose the correct answer, and then darken the corresponding oval on your answer document.

Do not linger over problems that take too much time. Solve as many as you can; then return to the others in the time you have left for this test.

You are permitted to use a calculator on this test. You may use your calculator for any problems you choose, but some of the problems may best be done without using a calculator.

Note: Unless otherwise stated, all of the following should be assumed:

1. Illustrative figures are NOT necessarily drawn to scale.

2. Geometric figures lie in a plane.

3. The word *line* indicates a straight line.

4. The word *average* indicates arithmetic mean.

---

1. A tree that had a diameter of 5 inches when it was first planted grows at a constant rate such that its diameter increases by 2 inches per year. From the time that the tree is planted, which of the following functions best represents the diameter of the tree, D, in inches y years after planting?

   A. $D(y) = 5 + 2y$

   B. $D(y) = 5y + 2$

   C. $D(y) = 5y + 2y^2$

   D. $D(y) = 7 + y$

   E. $D(y) = 5\left(\dfrac{1}{2}\right)^y$

DO YOUR FIGURING HERE.

2. For all real values of a, b, and c, which of the following expressions is equivalent to $\dfrac{a^{12}b^{10}c^{21}}{a^3b^5c^7}$?

   F. $a^3b^2c^{14}$
   G. $a^4b^2c^3$
   H. $a^4b^5c^3$
   J. $a^9b^2c^3$
   K. $a^9b^5c^{14}$

3. What is the value of y in the equation $-2y + 14 = 4y - 10$?

   A. -4

   B. $-\dfrac{2}{3}$

   C. $\dfrac{2}{3}$

   D. 4

   E. 12

GO ON TO THE NEXT PAGE.

DO YOUR FIGURING HERE.

4. Jin has a credit card that earns 2 bonus points for each dollar up to $1,000 that he charges to the card in one month. For each dollar over $1,000 that he charges that month, Jin receives $2\frac{1}{2}$ times the bonus points that he receives for each dollar up to $1,000. How many points does Jin earn if he charges $1,250 in a given month?

F. 2,500
G. 3,250
H. 3,500
J. 4,750
K. 6,250

5. A fourth grade class is having an end-of-the-year party. The teachers ordered 8 pizzas to feed the class. The girls in the class ate $1\frac{2}{3}$ pizzas, and the boys in the class ate $2\frac{1}{6}$ pizzas. How many pizzas were left for the teachers?

A. $2\frac{1}{3}$

B. $3\frac{5}{6}$

C. $4\frac{1}{6}$

D. $5\frac{5}{6}$

E. $6\frac{1}{3}$

6. The height of a certain rectangle is 50 centimeters, and the length of the diagonal of the rectangle is 130 centimeters. What is the width, in centimeters, of the rectangle?

F. 80
G. 90
H. 120
J. 140
K. 180

GO ON TO THE NEXT PAGE.

7. In the geometric sequence below, the 1st term is –1,296. What is the 5th term in the sequence, if it can be determined?

$$-1{,}296, \ 432, \ -144, \ 48, \ \ldots$$

A. –16
B. –12
C. 12
D. 16
E. Cannot be determined from the given information

DO YOUR FIGURING HERE.

8. How many *seconds* would it take a snail moving at a constant speed of 75 centimeters per minute to travel 240 centimeters?

(Note: There are 60 seconds in 1 minute.)

F. 19
G. 31
H. 165
J. 192
K. 300

9. What is the value of $\dfrac{y^2}{x} + \dfrac{7}{z}$ for $x = 2$, $y = 4$, and $z = 9$?

A. $\dfrac{23}{11}$

B. $\dfrac{15}{9}$

C. $\dfrac{16}{9}$

D. $\dfrac{43}{9}$

E. $\dfrac{79}{9}$

10. What is the least common denominator of the fractions below?

$$\frac{3}{10}, \frac{5}{18}, \frac{2}{27}$$

F. 90
G. 135
H. 270
J. 1,620
K. 4,860

GO ON TO THE NEXT PAGE.

11. The storeroom of a furniture retailer contains 300 chairs, 15% of which are recliners. Of the chairs that are NOT recliners, 52 are chairs that can swivel. How many of the chairs in the storeroom that are NOT recliners are non-swiveling chairs?

A. 203
B. 230
C. 233
D. 248
E. 255

12. A grocery store employee is creating a pyramid display of boxes at the end of an aisle. The display will have 9 tiers of boxes, and the top tier will contain 1 box. Each tier below the top tier will have 1 more box than the previous tier. How many boxes will the employee need to create the pyramid display?

F. 55
G. 45
H. 44
J. 18
K. 9

13. In the standard (x,y) coordinate plane, point F is located at $(-2,5)$. If point G is the reflection of point F across the x-axis, what are the coordinates of G ?

A. $(-2, -5)$
B. $(2, -5)$
C. $(2, 5)$
D. $(-5, -2)$
E. $(5, -2)$

14. For the equation $a^2 - 5a - 66 = 0$, what is the product of the solutions?

F. -66
G. -6
H. 0
J. 5
K. 11

15. The relationship between the measurement of temperature in number of degrees Fahrenheit, F, and the temperature in number of degrees Celsius, C, can be determined by the equation $C = \frac{5}{9}(F - 32)$. On a certain day, the temperature measures 10° Celsius. What is this temperature measurement in degrees Fahrenheit?

A. 18
B. 34
C. 42
D. 50
E. 82

DO YOUR FIGURING HERE.

GO ON TO THE NEXT PAGE.

16. In the figure shown below, triangle *OPQ* has a height of 4 cen-

timeters and a base of 8 centimeters, and $\overline{LO} \cong \overline{MP} \cong \overline{NQ}$.

The area of triangle *OPQ* is one-fourth the area of triangle *LMN*.

What is the length, in centimeters, of $\overline{MP}$?

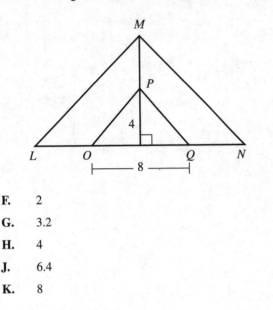

F.   2

G.   3.2

H.   4

J.   6.4

K.   8

17. If $x = 6.2 \times 10^4$, what is 16% of *x* ?

A.   3,875

B.   9,920

C.   38,750

D.   99,200

E.   992,000

18. In the figure below, the side lengths of the triangle are given in inches. Which of the following expressions can be used to represent *h* ?

F.   12 sin 40°

G.   cos 40°

H.   tan 40°

J. $\frac{1}{12}$ cos 40°

K. $\frac{1}{12}$ tan 40°

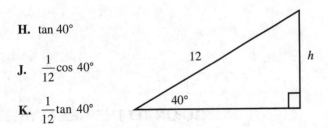

GO ON TO THE NEXT PAGE.

19. If the perimeter of a given square is 48 feet, what is the area of the square, in square feet?

    A. 12
    B. 24
    C. 36
    D. 144
    E. 192

DO YOUR FIGURING HERE.

20. $\dfrac{d}{1} \times \dfrac{4}{2} \times \dfrac{5}{3} \times \dfrac{6}{4} \times \dfrac{7}{5} \times \dfrac{8}{6} \times \dfrac{9}{7} \times \dfrac{10}{8} =$

    F. $\dfrac{19d}{6}$

    G. $\dfrac{10d}{3}$

    H. 15

    J. d

    K. 15d

21. A business analyst predicted the costs of a certain project and then plotted the actual data related to the costs in a scatterplot in the standard (x,y) coordinate plane. His initial prediction for the line of best fit was $y = 0.19x + 1.5$. The line for the predicted equation and the scatterplot of the actual costs are shown below.

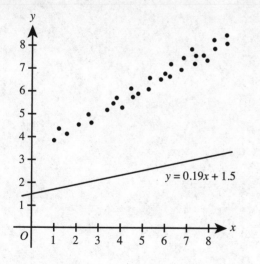

The analyst wants to alter the equation to better fit the actual data for the project. To change the given best fit line equation to better match the actual data, he *must*:

    A. decrease the y-intercept and decrease the slope.
    B. decrease the y-intercept and increase the slope.
    C. not change the y-intercept but increase the slope.
    D. increase the y-intercept and decrease the slope.
    E. increase the y-intercept and increase the slope.

GO ON TO THE NEXT PAGE.

DO YOUR FIGURING HERE.

22. There is a probability of 0.3 that Occurrence X will happen, and there is a probability of 0.5 that Occurrence Y will happen. What is the probability that both Occurrence X *and* Occurrence Y will happen?

    F. 0.15
    G. 0.2
    H. 0.5
    J. 0.6
    K. 0.8

23. A band director is using stickers as a reward for her students. She has 42 students this year and has enough stickers so that all the students can receive the same number of stickers with none left over. If there are 198 stickers on each sheet, which of the following integers could NOT be the number of sheets of stickers the band director has?

    A. 7
    B. 21
    C. 42
    D. 57
    E. 63

24. The circle below contains points W, X, Y, and Z on its circumference. Minor arc $\overset{\frown}{WY}$ measures 86°, and minor arc $\overset{\frown}{XZ}$ measures 54°. Chords $\overline{WX}$ and $\overline{YZ}$ meet at point V such that $\overline{VW} \cong \overline{VY}$ and $\overline{VX} \cong \overline{VZ}$. What is the measure of minor arc $\overset{\frown}{WZ}$?

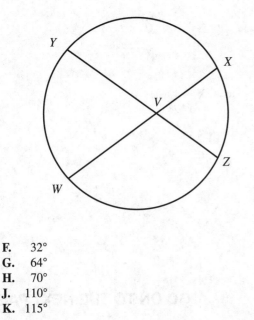

    F. 32°
    G. 64°
    H. 70°
    J. 110°
    K. 115°

GO ON TO THE NEXT PAGE.

DO YOUR FIGURING HERE.

Use the following information to answer questions 25–28.

The National Basketball Association (NBA) is a men's professional basketball association in North America founded in 1946. The table below gives some information about the 14 NBA players with the highest scores in a single game.

Player	Date of Highest Score	Points Scored
Joe Fulks	2-10-1949	63
Elgin Baylor	11-15-1960	71
Jerry West	1-17-1962	63
Wilt Chamberlain	3-2-1962	100
Rick Barry	3-26-1974	64
Pete Maravich	2-25-1977	68
David Thompson	4-9-1978	73
George Gervin	4-9-1978	
Michael Jordan	3-28-1990	69
David Robinson	4-24-1994	
Tracy McGrady	3-10-2004	62
Kobe Bryant	1-22-2006	81
Carmelo Anthony	1-24-2014	62
Devin Booker	3-24-2017	70

25. A sports statistician will select one of the players on the list at random to write an analysis of his high scoring game. What is the probability that the player she chooses has a last name that starts with the letter B, given that the player earned his highest score after 1970 ?

   A. $\dfrac{3}{4}$

   B. $\dfrac{3}{10}$

   C. $\dfrac{4}{10}$

   D. $\dfrac{4}{14}$

   E. $\dfrac{10}{14}$

26. For Devin Booker's high scoring game in 2017, he scored 60% of his total points for the game in the first three of four quarters. Which of the following is the number of points he scored in the fourth quarter?

   F. 10
   G. 14
   H. 28
   J. 35
   K. 42

GO ON TO THE NEXT PAGE.

27. David Robinson's high score was 8 points higher than George Gervin's. The sum of George Gervin's high score and two times David Robinson's high score is 2 points less than three times Michael Jordan's high score. What is the sum of the high scores earned by David Robinson and George Gervin?

   A. 117
   B. 129
   C. 134
   D. 181
   E. 205

28. What is the median number of points scored by the 12 players whose high scores are included in the table?

   F. 68
   G. 68.5
   H. 69
   J. 70
   K. 70.5

---

29. For angle θ with measure $0 < \theta < \dfrac{\pi}{2}$, the value of $\tan \theta$ is $\dfrac{24}{7}$. What is the value of $\sin \theta$?

   A. $-\dfrac{24}{25}$

   B. $-\dfrac{7}{24}$

   C. $\dfrac{7}{24}$

   D. $\dfrac{25}{24}$

   E. $\dfrac{24}{25}$

30. Given that the equation $\dfrac{2}{5} = \dfrac{a+3b}{4a+b}$ is true, what is the value of $\dfrac{b}{a}$?

   F. $\dfrac{3}{13}$

   G. $\dfrac{5}{13}$

   H. $\dfrac{2}{5}$

   J. $\dfrac{3}{7}$

   K. $\dfrac{3}{2}$

DO YOUR FIGURING HERE.

GO ON TO THE NEXT PAGE.

31. The vectors **a**, **b**, and **c** are represented in the standard (x, y) coordinate plane below.

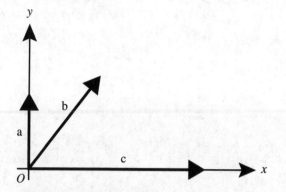

In what general direction will the vector **a** + **b** – **c** point?

A. To the left but neither up nor down
B. Down and to the right
C. Down and to the left
D. Up and to the right
E. Up and to the left

32. For matrices X and Y, given below, which of the following matrices is $X + Y$?

$$X = \begin{bmatrix} -2 & 3 \\ -1 & 8 \end{bmatrix} \qquad Y = \begin{bmatrix} -5 & -2 \\ 7 & -3 \end{bmatrix}$$

F. $\begin{bmatrix} -7 & 6 \\ 1 & 5 \end{bmatrix}$

G. $\begin{bmatrix} -7 & 1 \\ 6 & 5 \end{bmatrix}$

H. $\begin{bmatrix} -3 & -1 \\ -6 & -5 \end{bmatrix}$

J. $\begin{bmatrix} -3 & 5 \\ 8 & 11 \end{bmatrix}$

K. $\begin{bmatrix} 3 & -8 \\ 5 & 11 \end{bmatrix}$

33. Each year, approximately 742,650 liters of blood are needed for medical patients in the United States and Canada. If the average blood donation is 500 milliliters and a person can donate no more than 6 times per year, what is the minimum number of donors needed each year to meet this demand?

A. 24,755
B. 123,775
C. 247,550
D. 371,325
E. 371,325,000

GO ON TO THE NEXT PAGE.

34. Which of the following numbers has the least value?

F. 0.727

G. 0.$\overline{722}$

H. 0.7$\overline{27}$

J. $\dfrac{72}{99}$

K. $\dfrac{720}{1,001}$

DO YOUR FIGURING HERE.

35. A botanist affects the growth of a tree in a lab by decreasing the temperature, creating periods of dormancy. She maintains dormancy conditions for a whole number of months each time. The graph below shows the relationship between time, in months, since the experiment began and growth, in inches, of the tree above its initial height. Which of the following is the average growth of the tree, in inches per month, during the parts of the experiment that the tree was growing?

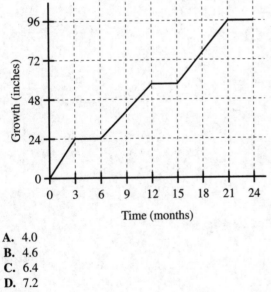

A. 4.0
B. 4.6
C. 6.4
D. 7.2
E. 10.7

GO ON TO THE NEXT PAGE.

36. As shown below, a movie with a runtime of 3 hours and 48 minutes will be paused halfway through for an intermission. What is the length, to the nearest minute, of each half of the movie?

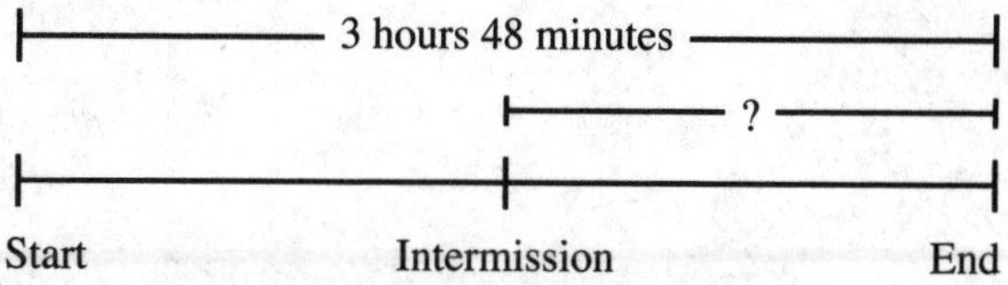

```
|——————— 3 hours 48 minutes ———————|
                    |——————— ? ———————|
|———————————————————|———————————————|
Start          Intermission         End
```

- **F.** 1 hour and 30 minutes
- **G.** 1 hour and 36 minutes
- **H.** 1 hour and 42 minutes
- **J.** 1 hour and 54 minutes
- **K.** 2 hours and 12 minutes

37. For the general quadratic expression in x shown below, which of the following are the linear factors?

$afx^2 - (ag + bf)x + bg$

- **A.** $(af + g)$ and $(fx - b)$
- **B.** $(ax + b)$ and $(fx - g)$
- **C.** $(ax + b)$ and $(fx + g)$
- **D.** $(ax - b)$ and $(fx + g)$
- **E.** $(ax - b)$ and $(fx - g)$

38. Given the function below, what is $g(8)$?

$$g(x) = \begin{cases} \frac{3}{4}x + 5; \ x \le 8 \\ -x - 2; \ x > 8 \end{cases}$$

- **F.** -10
- **G.** $-\dfrac{3}{4}$
- **H.** 1
- **J.** 11
- **K.** 21

GO ON TO THE NEXT PAGE.

39. Trapezoid *WXYZ* shown below is formed from a rectangle and a triangle, with the lengths of sides $\overline{XY}$ and $\overline{WZ}$ marked in inches. If *P* is on $\overline{WZ}$, what is the ratio of the area of $\triangle PYZ$ to the area of *WXYZ* ?

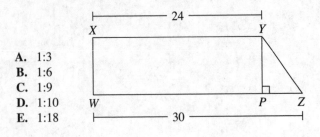

A. 1:3
B. 1:6
C. 1:9
D. 1:10
E. 1:18

40. For $h(x) = \dfrac{x^2}{2}$ and $j(x) = 2x + 4$, which of the following expressions gives $h(j(x))$ for all values of *x* ?

F. $x^2 + 4$
G. $x^3 + 2x^2$
H. $2x^2 + 4x + 8$
J. $2x^2 + 8x + 8$
K. $2x^3 + 2$

41. In rectangle *FGHJ* below, *K* is on $\overline{FG}$, $\overline{JK}$ bisects $\angle FJG$, and the measure of $\angle FGJ$ is 28°. What is the measure of $\angle FKJ$?

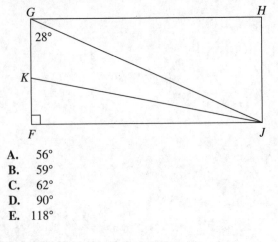

A. 56°
B. 59°
C. 62°
D. 90°
E. 118°

GO ON TO THE NEXT PAGE.

DO YOUR FIGURING HERE.

42. Which of the following expressions is NOT equivalent to

    $\cos \theta$ for all real values of x such that $0 < \theta < \dfrac{\pi}{2}$?

    F. $(\sin \theta)(\cot \theta)$

    G. $\dfrac{1}{\sec \theta}$

    H. $\dfrac{\sin \theta}{\tan \theta}$

    J. $\dfrac{\cot \theta}{\csc \theta}$

    K. $\dfrac{\csc \theta}{\tan \theta}$

43. While playing a video game, Everett has 97.5 points, which is 25% more than the number of points James has. How many more points than James does Everett have?

    A.   0.78
    B.   3.9
    C.   19.5
    D.   24.375
    E.   72.5

44. What real value of a satisfies the equation $3a = \log_2(8^3)$?

    F.   2
    G.   3
    H.   9
    J.   16
    K.   27

45. In the figure below, point P is on semicircles MPN and LPO inside square $LMNO$. Semicircle MPN has its diameter on side MN, and semicircle LPO has its diameter on side LO. Both semicircles have a radius of 1 inch. What is the area, in square inches, of the shaded region?

    A. $4 - \dfrac{\pi}{2}$

    B. $4 - \pi$

    C. $4 - 2\pi$

    D. $8 - \pi$

    E. $8 - 2\pi$

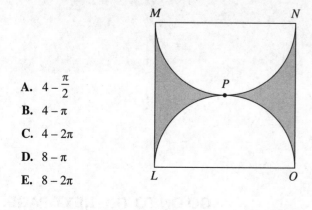

GO ON TO THE NEXT PAGE.

DO YOUR FIGURING HERE.

46. Tanja is a volunteer for a music booster club. A raffle will be held to award prizes to 3 of the 30 volunteers who helped with a recent event. The names of each volunteer who helped will be written on a ticket, and the tickets will be placed in a bowl. At a concert, the club president will randomly pull 3 tickets from the bowl without replacing any of the tickets. What is the probability that Tanja will NOT win a prize?

F. $\dfrac{1}{10}$

G. $\dfrac{9}{10}$

H. $\dfrac{13}{15}$

J. $\dfrac{1}{30}$

K. $\dfrac{29}{30}$

47. The table below shows the number of students in a class that have a given number of first cousins.

Number of first cousins	Number of students
0	3
1	1
2	6
3	4
4	5
5	2
6	3
7	0
8 or more	1

If only one student is chosen and each student has the same probability of being chosen, which of the following is the probability that the chosen student has exactly 2 first cousins?

A. 0.08
B. 0.12
C. 0.15
D. 0.20
E. 0.24

GO ON TO THE NEXT PAGE.

48. The paddle steamer shown below has a paddle with a diameter of 22 feet, and the midline of the paddle is level with the water surface of the river.

DO YOUR FIGURING HERE.

The paddle moves at a constant rate of one full revolution every 3.15 seconds. The variable x can be defined as the number of seconds since the paddle began moving from its starting position, which is shown above. The variable y can be defined as the distance that the point marked on the rim at the bottom of the wheel is below or above the surface of the water. Which of the following graphs in the standard (x,y) coordinate plane shows the distance, y, as a function of time, x ?

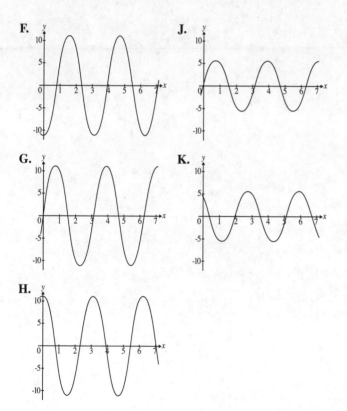

Use the following information to answer questions 49–50.

A toy manufacturer produces a series of geometric blocks. The most popular one is in the shape of a *hexagonal pyramid*. A hexagonal pyramid is a solid that has a base that is a regular hexagon and 6 congruent faces, each of which is an isosceles triangle, for a total of 7 faces. Each edge is shared by two faces, and each vertex of the hexagonal base is shared by 2 triangular faces. The vertex shown at top in the image below shares all 6 triangular faces, 3 of which are visible in the image.

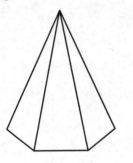

49. How many *edges* does the geometric block have?

A. 7
B. 12
C. 14
D. 21
E. 24

50. For each triangular face of the geometric block, the short edge is 1.4 inches and the long edges are each 2.5 inches. What is the area, in square inches, of 1 triangular face of the block?

F. 0.84
G. 1.4
H. 1.68
J. 2.4
K. 3.36

51. In a reality show competition, there are 16 contestants. For a certain challenge, 4 distinct contestants will be chosen to receive the same advantage over the remaining contestants. Which of the following expressions gives the maximum number of possible groupings for the contestants with the advantage?

A. 16^4

B. $16(4)$

C. $16(15)(14)(13)$

D. $16(15)(14)(13)(4)(3)(2)(1)$

E. $\dfrac{16(15)(14)(13)}{4(3)(2)(1)}$

GO ON TO THE NEXT PAGE.

52. Amy and Rachel began their current jobs as project managers at the same time some years ago. Amy has now spent $\frac{2}{3}$ of her professional career in her current job, and Rachel has spent $\frac{5}{7}$ of her professional career in her current job. Which of the following represents the length of Amy's professional career in terms of R, the length of Rachel's professional career?

F. $\frac{10}{21}R$

G. $\frac{5}{7}R$

H. $\frac{14}{15}R$

J. $\frac{15}{14}R$

K. $\frac{7}{5}R$

53. A 5K event included both runners and walkers in heats throughout the day. The 64 participants who ran in the first heat had an average time of 31 minutes. The 48 participants who walked in the first heat had an average time of 59 minutes. What was the average time, in minutes, for all the participants in the first heat?

A. 31
B. 38
C. 43
D. 45
E. 59

54. Bob keeps track of some data regarding his score in the first 3 bowling games of the league season, as shown in the table below.

Data	Score
Mean	207
Minimum	178
Median	218

What is the maximum score Bob has received in his first 3 bowling games, if it can be determined?

F. 198
G. 207
H. 215
J. 225
K. Cannot be determined from the given information

DO YOUR FIGURING HERE.

GO ON TO THE NEXT PAGE.

DO YOUR FIGURING HERE.

55. A carnival game consists of 48 rubber ducks in a row on a narrow shelf and a water blaster to spray the ducks. Alex chooses an integer, *n*. Counting from the first duck on the left, Alex goes down the row and sprays every *n*th duck, knocking it over. She continues until she reaches the end of the row, then continues counting with the first duck in the row, counting each duck whether it has been knocked over or not. She goes down the line spraying the ducks over and over, until she has knocked over every duck on the shelf. Which of the following could be Alex's value for the integer *n* ?

A. 2
B. 3
C. 4
D. 5
E. 6

56. What is the digit in the ones place when 18^{55} is multiplied out?

F. 0
G. 2
H. 4
J. 6
K. 8

57. An ellipse is inscribed in rectangle *FGHJ* as shown below.

When the figure is drawn in the standard (*x,y*) coordinate plane,

the ellipse can be described by the equation $\dfrac{(x+2)^2}{25}+\dfrac{y^2}{4}=1$.

Points *W*, *X*, *Y*, and *Z* are the midpoints of the sides of *FGHJ*,

the line connecting points *X* and *Z* is the minor axis, and the

line connecting points *W* and *Y* is the major axis. What will

be the coordinates of points *F* and *J* ?

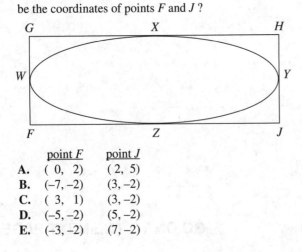

	point *F*	point *J*
A.	(0, 2)	(2, 5)
B.	(−7, −2)	(3, −2)
C.	(3, 1)	(3, −2)
D.	(−5, −2)	(5, −2)
E.	(−3, −2)	(7, −2)

GO ON TO THE NEXT PAGE.

58. For all positive values of a and b, which of the following radical forms is equivalent to $a^{\frac{7}{5}}b^{\frac{1}{2}}$?

F. $a\sqrt[10]{a^4 b^5}$

G. $ab\sqrt[10]{a^7 b^7}$

H. $\sqrt[10]{ab^7}$

J. $\sqrt[10]{a^5 b^2}$

K. $\sqrt[10]{a^7 b^7}$

59. A salesclerk in a shoe store must stack 48 shoe boxes on a shelf. Each box is 13.5 centimeters tall, and each stack cannot have a combined height of more than 72 centimeters. No box will be in more than one stack, and the clerk will place the maximum number of shoeboxes into a stack before starting a new stack. What is the combined height, in centimeters, of the boxes that are in the short stack?

A. 3.0
B. 9.0
C. 28.2
D. 40.5
E. 67.5

60. Which of the following expressions is equivalent to

$$\frac{5}{x^2 + 9x + 20} - \frac{2}{x^2 + 6x + 8} \ ?$$

F. $\dfrac{3}{3x + 12}$

G. $\dfrac{3}{(x+2)(x+4)(x+5)}$

H. $\dfrac{x}{(x+1)(x+2)(x+3)}$

J. $\dfrac{3x}{(x+2)(x+4)(x+5)}$

K. $\dfrac{3x + 20}{(x+2)^2 (x+5)}$

END OF TEST.
STOP! DO NOT TURN THE PAGE UNTIL TOLD TO DO SO.

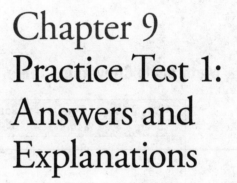

Chapter 9
Practice Test 1:
Answers and
Explanations

SCORE YOUR PRACTICE TEST

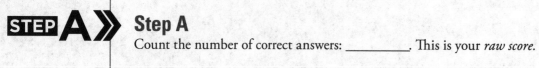

Step A

Count the number of correct answers: _____. This is your *raw score*.

Step B

Use the score conversion table below to look up your raw score. The number to the left is your *scale score*: _____.

Math Scale Conversion Table

Scaled Score	Raw Score	Scaled Score	Raw Score	Scaled Score	Raw Score
36	58–60	27	41–43	18	24–25
35	56–57	26	39–40	17	21–23
34	54–55	25	37–38	16	17–20
33	53	24	35–36	15	13–16
32	51–52	23	33–34	14	10–12
31	49–50	22	31–32	13	8–9
30	48	21	30	12	6–7
29	46–47	20	28–29	11	5
28	44–45	19	26–27	10	4

MATH PRACTICE TEST 1 ANSWER KEY

1.	A	31.	E
2.	K	32.	G
3.	D	33.	C
4.	G	34.	K
5.	C	35.	C
6.	H	36.	J
7.	A	37.	E
8.	J	38.	J
9.	E	39.	C
10.	H	40.	J
11.	A	41.	B
12.	G	42.	K
13.	A	43.	C
14.	F	44.	G
15.	D	45.	B
16.	H	46.	G
17.	B	47.	E
18.	F	48.	F
19.	D	49.	B
20.	K	50.	H
21.	E	51.	E
22.	F	52.	J
23.	D	53.	C
24.	J	54.	J
25.	B	55.	D
26.	H	56.	G
27.	C	57.	B
28.	G	58.	F
29.	E	59.	D
30.	F	60.	J

MATH PRACTICE TEST 1 EXPLANATIONS

1. **A** The question asks for an equation that represents a situation. Translate the English into math in Bite-Sized Pieces and use Process of Elimination. The tree's diameter increases by two inches per year, and y represents years. This can be represented by $2y$. Eliminate any answer choice that does not include this expression, which gets rid of everything except (A). There are variables in the answer choices, so Plugging In is also an option. Make $y = 2$. If the tree starts with a diameter of 5 inches and grows 2 inches per year for 2 years, it will have a diameter of $5 + 2(2) = 5 + 4 = 9$. This is the target value; circle it. Now plug $y = 2$ into the answer choices to see which one matches the target value. Choice (A) becomes $D(2) = 5 + 2(2) = 5 + 4 = 9$. This matches the target, so keep (A) but check the remaining answers just in case. Choice (B) becomes $D(2) = 5(2) + 2 = 10 + 2 = 12$. Eliminate (B). Choice (C) becomes $D(2) = 5(2) + 2(2)^2 = 10 + 2(4) = 10 + 8 = 18$. Eliminate (C). Choice (D) becomes $7 + 2 = 9$. Keep (D) but check (E) as well. Choice (E) becomes $D(2) = 5\left(\frac{1}{2}\right)^2 = 5\left(\frac{1}{4}\right) = \frac{5}{4}$. Eliminate (E). Now plug in $y = 3$. With an extra year, the tree will grow 2 more inches for a new target of $9 + 2 = 11$. Choice (A) becomes $D(3) = 5 + 2(3) = 5 + 6 = 11$ and (D) becomes $D(3) = 7 + 3 = 10$. Only (A) matches the new target. Either way, the correct answer is (A).

2. **K** The question asks for an equivalent expression. Although there are variables in the answer choices, Plugging In on this question would be difficult, given three variables and large exponents. Instead, use Bite-Sized Pieces and Process of Elimination to tackle this question. When dealing with questions about exponents, remember the MADSPM rules. The DS part of the acronym indicates that Dividing matching bases means to Subtract the exponents. Start with the a terms. The result of subtracting the exponents of the a terms is $a^{12-3} = a^9$. Eliminate (F), (G), and (H), which do not contain this term. Next work with the b terms. The result of subtracting the exponents of the b terms is $b^{10-5} = b^5$. Eliminate (J). The correct answer is (K).

3. **D** The question asks for the value of y in the equation. Since the question asks for a specific value and the answers contain numbers in increasing order, Plugging In the Answers is an option. However, the equation is not too complicated and there are fractions and negatives in the answer choices, so it may be faster to solve for y. Begin by subtracting $4y$ from both sides of the equation to get $-6y + 14 = -10$, then subtract 14 from both sides to get $-6y = -24$. Divide both sides by -6 to get $y = 4$. The correct answer is (D).

4. **G** The question asks for the number of points Jin earns in a month. Read carefully and use Bite-Sized Pieces to tackle this question. The question states that Jin *earns 2 bonus points for each dollar up to*

$1,000 that he charges. For the first $1,000, Jin will earn (2)(1,000) = 2,000 points. Jin earns a different amount of points for dollars over $1,000, so figure out how many dollars over $1,000 he charged. The difference is $1,250 − $1,000 = $250. For these $250, Jin earns $2\frac{1}{2}$ *times the bonus points he receives for each dollar up to $1,000.* Therefore, for each of these dollars, he earns $\left(2\frac{1}{2}\right)(2) = 5$ points. For $250 additional dollars, Jin earns (5)(250) = 1,250 points. Add this to the 2,000 points he already earned to get a total of 2,000 + 1,250 = 3,250 points. The correct answer is (G).

5. **C**   The question asks for the number of pizzas left after some are eaten. Use Ballparking and Bite-Sized Pieces to tackle this question. The class started with 8 pizzas and ate about 4 of them, so there would be about 4 left. Eliminate (A), which is too small, and (D) and (E), which are too big. To find out exactly how much pizza was left, subtract the amount that was eaten from the original amount. Either use a calculator to find the decimal equivalents or find a common denominator. A common denominator for 3rds and 6ths is 6. The portion eaten by the girls becomes $1\frac{4}{6}$ or $\frac{10}{6}$, and the total eaten by the boys is $2\frac{1}{6}$ or $\frac{13}{6}$. The original 8 pizzas can be expressed as $\frac{48}{6}$. Now subtract to find out how much pizza was left: $\frac{48}{6} - \frac{10}{6} - \frac{13}{6} = \frac{25}{6}$. Turn the improper fraction back into a mixed number, which is $4\frac{1}{6}$. The correct answer is (C).

6. **H**   The question asks for the width of a rectangle. Use the Geometry Basic Approach. Start by drawing a figure and labeling it with the given information. It will look like this:

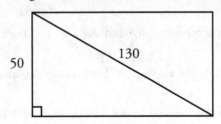

Since the question asks for a specific value and the answers contain numbers in increasing order, plug in the answers. Begin by labeling the answers as "width" and start with (H), 120. Label the third side of the triangle as 120. Notice that this is a 5:12:13 Pythagorean triple with each side multiplied by 10, or use the Pythagorean ($a^2 + b^2 = c^2$) to check the dimensions. The Pythagorean Theorem becomes $50^2 + 120^2 = 130^2$, or 2,500 + 14,400 = 16,900. This is true and matches the information given in the question, so stop here. The correct answer is (H).

7. **A**   The question asks for the 5th term in a geometric sequence. Use Process of Elimination first. The 1st and 3rd terms are negative, and the 2nd and 4th terms are positive. Therefore, the 5th term will follow the pattern and be negative. Eliminate (C) and (D), which are positive. In a geometric sequence, the ratio of adjacent terms is always the same. To find the ratio between terms, take adjacent terms such as -144 and 48, and divide them. The ratio is $\frac{3rd}{4th} = \frac{-144}{48} = -3$, and this will also be the ratio of the 4th term to the 5th term. If x represents the 5th term, this becomes $\frac{4th}{5th} = \frac{48}{x} = -3$. Multiply both sides of the equation by x to get $48 = -3x$, then divide both sides by -3 to get $x = -16$. The correct answer is (A).

8. **J**   The question asks for the time something will take and gives conflicting units. Begin by reading the question to find information on the snail's pace. The question states that the snail moves at a pace of *75 centimeters per minute* and that there are *60 seconds in 1 minute*. This means that the pace is 75 centimeters per 60 seconds. Set up a proportion, being sure to match up the units, to determine how far the snail will go in 240 seconds: $\frac{75 \text{ centimeters}}{60 \text{ seconds}} = \frac{240 \text{ centimeters}}{x \text{ seconds}}$. Cross-multiply to get $75x = 14,400$. Divide both sides of the equation by 75 to get $x = 192$. The correct answer is (J).

9. **E**   The question asks for the value of an expression for given values. Plug $x = 2$, $y = 4$, and $z = 9$ into the expression to get $\frac{4^2}{2} + \frac{7}{9}$. This simplifies to $\frac{16}{2} + \frac{7}{9} = 8 + \frac{7}{9}$. Either ballpark that the result is between 8 and 9 or rewrite 8 as a fraction with a denominator of 9 to get $\frac{72}{9} + \frac{7}{9} = \frac{79}{9}$. Either way, the correct answer is (E).

10. **H**   The question asks for the least common denominator of the given fractions. The least common denominator will be the smallest number that is divisible by the denominators of all three fractions. Since the question asks for a specific value and the answers contain numbers in increasing order, test the answers. Begin by labeling the answers as "least common denominator" and start with the smallest value, (F), 90. To be a common denominator, the number divided by each denominator must result in an integer. For (F), $\frac{90}{10} = 9$, which is an integer, and $\frac{90}{18} = 5$, which is also an integer. However, $\frac{90}{27} = 3.\overline{3}$, which is not an integer, so eliminate (F). For (G), $\frac{135}{10} = 13.5$, which is not an integer, so eliminate (G). For (H), $\frac{270}{10} = 27$; $\frac{270}{18} = 15$; and $\frac{270}{27} = 10$. All of these are integers, so 270 is a

common denominator. Because the question asked for the *least* common denominator, stop here. The correct answer is (H).

11. **A** The question asks for the number of chairs that are NOT recliners and are non-swiveling. Read the question carefully and use Bite-Sized Pieces. One piece of information is that there are 300 chairs and 15% are recliners. *Percent* means divide by 100, so the number of recliners is $\frac{15}{100} \times 300 = 45$. Another piece of information refers to the number of chairs that are NOT recliners, so subtract the number of recliners from the total to get $300 - 45 = 255$ non-recliners. Of those, 52 can swivel, and the question asks for the number of non-swiveling chairs. Subtract the number of swiveling chairs from the number of non-recliners to get $255 - 52 = 203$ non-swiveling chairs that are not recliners. The correct answer is (A).

12. **G** The question asks for the number of boxes in the display. The top tier will have 1 box and each of the remaining 8 tiers will have one more box than the previous tier. The number of boxes in the display will be the sum of the number of boxes in each tier. Rather than trying to remember a formula for this, write out the number of boxes in each tier and add them up. The top tier will have 1, the next will have 2, and so on until the 9th tier. The total will be $1 + 2 + 3 + 4 + 5 + 6 + 7 + 8 + 9 = 45$ boxes. The correct answer is (G).

13. **A** The question asks for the coordinates of a reflected point in the coordinate plane. Use the Geometry Basic Approach. Start by sketching the original point, *F*, in the coordinate plane. Next, determine where to draw point *G*. A point that is *reflected* over the *x*-axis is flipped over that axis as if that axis were a mirror. It will look like this:

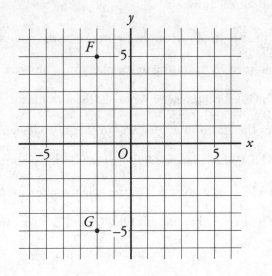

The new point has the same *x*-coordinate of –2, but its *y*-coordinate is –5. The correct answer is (A).

14. **F** The question asks for the product of the solutions to a quadratic equation. For a quadratic in the standard form $ax^2 + bx + c$, the product of the solutions is $\dfrac{c}{a}$. For this quadratic, $c = -66$ and $a = 1$, so the product of the solutions is $\dfrac{-66}{1} = -66$. It is also possible to answer this question by factoring the quadratic. Look for two numbers that multiply to -66 and add to -5. These numbers are -11 and 6, so this quadratic factors into $(a - 11)(a + 6) = 0$. Set each binomial equal to 0 to find that $a = 11$ or $a = -6$. The product of these is $(11)(-6) = -66$. Either way, the correct answer is (F).

15. **D** The question asks for the temperature in degrees Fahrenheit for a corresponding measurement in Celsius. Since the question asks for a specific value and the answers contain numbers in increasing order, Plugging In the Answers is an option. Begin by labeling the answers as "temperature in Fahrenheit" and start with (C), 42. Plug 42 into the equation in place of F to get $C = \dfrac{5}{9}(42 - 32) = \dfrac{5}{9}(10) = \dfrac{50}{9} = 5.\overline{5}$. This does not match the information in the question, so eliminate (C). The resulting value for C was too small, so try a larger value like (D), 50. Plug 50 into the equation to get $C = \dfrac{5}{9}(50 - 32) = \dfrac{5}{9}(18) = \dfrac{90}{9} = 10$. This matches the value for C given in the question, so stop here. Solving the equation algebraically is also an option. Plug in the value for C as $10°$ and solve for F. The equation becomes $10 = \dfrac{5}{9}(F - 32)$. Isolate the F by multiplying both sides of the equation by 9 to get $90 = 5(F - 32)$; then divide both sides by 5 to get $18 = F - 32$. Add 32 to both sides to get $50 = F$. The correct answer is (D).

16. **H** The question asks for the length of $\overline{MP}$ on the figure. Since the question asks for a specific value and the answers contain numbers in increasing order, plug in the answers. Begin by labeling the answers as "$\overline{MP}$" and start with (H), 4 centimeters. Write out the formula for the area of a triangle: $A = \dfrac{1}{2}bh$. The question compares the area of triangle OPQ to that of triangle LMN, so find the area of both triangles. The base and height of triangle OPQ are given in the question, so the area of triangle OPQ becomes $A = \dfrac{1}{2}(8)(4) = 16$. For triangle LMN, the height is the sum of $\overline{MP}$ and 4, so if $\overline{MP} = 4$, the height is $4 + 4 = 8$. The base is the sum of $\overline{LO}$, $\overline{OQ}$, and $\overline{QN}$. Because $\overline{LO} \cong \overline{MP} \cong \overline{NQ}$, the base becomes $4 + 8 + 4 = 16$. For triangle LMN, the area becomes $A = \dfrac{1}{2}(16)(8) = 64$. The question states that the area of triangle OPQ is one-fourth of the area of LMN. One-fourth of 64 is 16. This matches the information given in the question, so stop here. The correct answer is (H).

17. **B** The question asks for a percent of a number. Translate the English to math in Bite-Sized Pieces. *Percent* means to divide by 100, and *of* means to multiply. Thus, the value of 16% of x is calculated as $\frac{16}{100}\left(6.2\times10^4\right)$. This can be rewritten as $(0.16)(6.2)(10{,}000)$. Multiply these with a calculator to get 9,920. The correct answer is (B).

18. **F** The question asks for the expression that represents h on the figure. There are trigonometric expressions in the answer choices, so write out SOHCAHTOA to remember the trig functions. In relation to the 40° angle, the side labeled h is the opposite side, and the side labeled 12 is the hypotenuse. The SOH part defines the sine as $\frac{opposite}{hypotenuse}$, so $\sin40°=\frac{h}{12}$. Multiply both sides of the equation by 12 to get $12\sin40°=h$. The correct answer is (F).

19. **D** The question asks for the area of a square with a perimeter of 48 feet. Use the Geometry Basic Approach. Start by drawing a figure of a square. The only information given is that the perimeter is 48. The perimeter is the sum of all the sides, and on a square all sides are equal. Therefore, $P=4s$, so $48=4s$. Divide both sides of the equation by 4 to get $12=s$. Label each side of the square as 12. Write out the formula for the area of a square, $A=s^2$. Plug in the length of the side to get $A=12^2=144$. The correct answer is (D).

20. **K** The question asks for the product of a series of fractions. Rather than multiplying out all the numerators and all the denominators, cancel out as many factors as possible. Any number that appears in one of the numerators and one of the denominators can be crossed out. This applies to the 4s, 5s, 6s, 7s, and 8s. The expression becomes $\frac{d}{1}\times\frac{4}{2}\times\frac{5}{3}\times\frac{6}{4}\times\frac{7}{5}\times\frac{8}{6}\times\frac{9}{7}\times\frac{10}{8}$. Multiplying the remaining values in the numerators and the denominators leaves $\frac{d\times9\times10}{1\times2\times3}$. Multiply across to get $\frac{90d}{6}=15d$. The correct answer is (K).

21. **E** The question asks for the change that will make the line of best fit better match the data represented on a graph. Use Bite-Sized Pieces and Process of Elimination to tackle this question. Compare features of the existing line to the data represented in the scatterplot. The dots approximate a line that starts near a y-value of about 3.8. The current line of best fit has a y-intercept of 1.5. Increasing the y-intercept to something closer to 3.8 will better match the data. Eliminate (A), (B), and (C) as they do not indicate an increase in the y-intercept. The y-values of the dots increase faster as the x-values increase. The slope must be increased to make the line of best fit steeper. Eliminate (D), which indicates a decrease in the slope. The correct answer is (E).

22. **F**   The question asks for the probability that two events will both occur. The probability of each event is given. When finding the probability of two or more events occurring together, multiply the probabilities of each event occurring on its own. This becomes $(0.3)(0.5) = 0.15$. The correct answer is (F).

23. **D**   The question asks for the number that could NOT be the number of sheets of stickers the band director has. Since the question asks for a specific value and the answers contain numbers in increasing order, plug in the answers. Begin by labeling the answers as "sheets" and start with (C), 42. There are 198 stickers on each sheet, so with 42 sheets the band director will have $198(42) = 8{,}316$ stickers. There are 42 students, so each student would get $8{,}316 \div 42 = 198$ stickers. This matches the information in the question that there are *none left over*, so 42 could be the number of sheets. Eliminate (C). Since the question asks for the value that could not work, there is no way to tell if a smaller or greater number is needed. Just pick a direction and go. Try (D) next. If there are 57 sheets, the band director will have $198(57) = 11{,}286$ stickers. Each student would get $11{,}286 \div 42 = 268.71$ stickers. Since students can't receive fractional stickers, then there will be some stickers left over. Therefore, 57 is NOT a number of sheets the band director could have. The correct answer is (D).

24. **J**   The question asks for the measure of a minor arc on the figure. Use the Geometry Basic Approach. Start by labeling the figure with the given information. Mark arcs $\overset{\frown}{WY}$ and $\overset{\frown}{XZ}$ with the given measurements. The measure of arc $\overset{\frown}{WZ}$ is greater than either of these labeled arcs, so ballpark and eliminate (F), (G), and (H) as these values are too small. Also label the figure to indicate that $\overline{VW} \cong \overline{VY}$ and $\overline{VX} \cong \overline{VZ}$. Because of these segment congruencies, sector XVY and sector WVZ are congruent and will have the same arc measures. There are $360°$ in a circle, and the labeled arcs take up $86° + 54° = 140°$. This leaves $360° - 140° = 220°$ for arcs $\overset{\frown}{WZ}$ and $\overset{\frown}{XY}$. The arcs are congruent, so divide this by 2 to find that the measure of arc $\overset{\frown}{WZ}$ is $\dfrac{220°}{2} = 110°$. The correct answer is (J).

25. **B**   The question asks for a probability, which is defined as $\dfrac{want}{total}$. Read the table carefully to find the numbers to make the probability. On the table, there are 10 players who earned their highest score *after 1970*, from Rick Barry to the bottom of the table, so 10 is the *total*. Of these players, 3 have last names that start with B (Barry, Bryant, and Booker), so 3 is the *want*. Therefore, the probability is $\dfrac{3}{10}$. The correct answer is (B).

26. **H** The question asks for the number of points Devin Booker scored in the fourth quarter. Since the question asks for a specific value and the answers contain numbers in increasing order, plug in the answers. Begin by labeling the answers as "fourth quarter" and start with (H), 28. The question states that Booker scored *60% of his total* points in the first three quarters, and the table indicates that his score was 70 points. If he scored 28 points in the fourth quarter, he scored $70 - 28 = 42$ points in the other three quarters. Check whether 42 is 60% of 70 by multiplying 70 by $\frac{60}{100}$ to get $\frac{60}{100} \times 70 = 42$. Thus, he scored a total of $42 + 28 = 70$ points. This matches the information in the question, so stop here. The correct answer is (H).

27. **C** The question asks for the sum of the high scores earned by Robinson and Gervin, neither of which is listed in the table. Translate the English to math in Bite-Sized Pieces to create equations that can be solved for these values. Let Robinson's score be represented as R and Gervin's score as G. The question states that Robinson's score was *8 points higher* than Gervin's. This can be written as $R = G + 8$. The sum in the second sentence is compared to Michael Jordan's score, so look on the table to find that Jordan's score was 69. This is related to the *sum* of Gervin's score and *two times* Robinson's score, which can be written as $G + 2R$. The sum is *two points less than three times Michael Jordan's score*. The equation becomes $G + 2R = 3(69) - 2$, which simplifies to $G + 2R = 207 - 2$ or $G + 2R = 205$. Use the two equations to solve for G and R. In the first equation, subtract G from both sides to get $-G + R = 8$. Stack the equations and add them together to eliminate the Gs.

$$
\begin{array}{r}
-G + R = 8 \\
+ \; G + 2R = 205 \\
\hline
3R = 213
\end{array}
$$

Divide both sides of the equation by 3 to get $R = 71$. Plug this into the first equation to get $71 = G + 8$. Subtract 8 from both sides to get $G = 63$. Now find the sum by adding to get $R + G = 71 + 63 = 134$. The correct answer is (C).

28. **G** The question asks for the median of the list of scores on the table. The median of a list of numbers is the middle number when all values are arranged in order. In lists with an even number of items, the median is the average of the middle two numbers. List all 12 numbers in order to get {62, 62, 63, 63, 64, 68, 69, 70, 71, 73, 81, 100}. On this list, the middle values are 68 and 69. The average of these values is $\frac{68 + 69}{2} = \frac{137}{2} = 68.5$. The correct answer is (G).

29. **E** The question asks for the value of the sine of an angle in the coordinate plane. Use the Geometry Basic Approach. Start by drawing a figure and labeling it with the given information. The angle is between 0 and $\frac{\pi}{2}$, so it is in Quadrant I. In this quadrant, sine is positive, so eliminate (A) and (B). Write out SOHCAHTOA to remember the trig functions. The TOA part defines the tangent as $\frac{opposite}{adjacent}$, so label the side opposite θ as 24 and the side adjacent θ as 7. It will look like this:

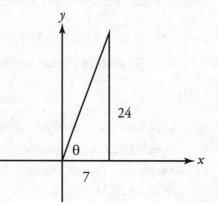

The question asks for sin θ, and the SOH part of SOHCAHTOA defines the sine as $\frac{opposite}{hypotenuse}$. The hypotenuse isn't known yet, but the *opposite* is still 24. Therefore, sin θ must have 24 in the numerator. Eliminate (C) and (D). Only one answer remains, so there is no need to calculate the hypotenuse, which must be 25. The correct answer is (E).

30. **F** The question asks for the value of $\frac{b}{a}$ given the equation. There is not enough information to solve for a and b separately, so manipulate the equation to get it into the desired form. When two rational expressions are set equal, solve by cross-multiplying. The equation becomes $2(4a + b) = 5(a + 3b)$. Distribute on both sides to get $8a + 2b = 5a + 15b$. Combine all the a terms on one side and all the b terms on the other. Subtract $5a$ from both sides to get $3a + 2b = 15b$; then subtract $2b$ from both sides to get $3a = 13b$. Isolate b by dividing both sides by 13 to get $\frac{3a}{13} = b$; then divide both sides by a to get $\frac{3}{13} = \frac{b}{a}$. The correct answer is (F).

31. **E** The question asks for the general direction in which the vector **a** + **b** − **c** will point. Vectors are added "head-to-tail," which means that the arrow of one connects to the tail of the next. Start with the vector **a** + **b** by redrawing **b** with its current orientation but moved up, so its tail starts at the tip of the arrow of vector **a**. To subtract vectors, first reverse the direction of the one being subtracted, which is **c** in this case. Then add **c** head-to-tail with **b.** It will look like this:

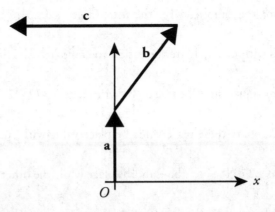

Finally, connect the starting point of the tail of **a** at the origin to the ending point of the tip of **c** to get the vector **a** + **b** − **c**. It will point up and to the left in the coordinate plane. The correct answer is (E).

32. **G** The question asks for the sum of two matrices. To add matrices, add the values in each position. Use Bite-Sized Pieces to add one pair of numbers at a time and eliminate after each calculation. Adding the numbers in the upper left position of the matrices results in (−2) + (−5) = −7. Eliminate (H), (J), and (K) because these do not have that value in the upper left position. Compare the remaining choices. There are different values in the upper right position of (F) and (G), so calculate that next. The result is 3 + (−2) = 1. Eliminate (F) because it does not have that value in the upper right position. The correct answer is (G).

33. **C** The question asks for the minimum number of blood donors needed to meet the demand. Since the question asks for a specific value and the answers contain numbers in increasing order, plug in the answers. Begin by labeling the answers as "donors" and start with the least value in (A). Read the question carefully and use Bite-Sized Pieces. The question says that each donor *can donate no more than 6 times per year*. To minimize the number of donors, assume that each one donates the maximum number of times. If there are 24,755 donors giving blood 6 times per year, the result is (24,755)(6) = 148,530 donations. Each donation averages 500 milliliters of blood, but the demand is given in liters. Set up a proportion, being sure to match the units. There are 1,000 milliliters in 1 liter, so the proportion is $\frac{1,000 \text{ mL}}{1 \text{ L}} = \frac{500 \text{ mL}}{x}$. Cross-multiply and then divide both sides by 1,000 to find that each donation is 0.5 liters. Multiply this by the number of donations to find that the volume of blood donated is (148,530)(0.5) = 74,265 liters. The demand is 742,650 liters, so this is not nearly enough. Eliminate (A). The result using (A) was exactly one-tenth of the needed supply, so try a number of donors that is 10 times the number in (A). This is found in (C). If there are 247,550 donors giving blood 6 times per year, the number of donations is (247,550)(6) = 1,485,300. The volume donated is (1,485,300)(0.5) = 742,650. This matches the value given in the question, so stop here. The correct answer is (C).

34. **K**   The question asks for the number with the *least* value. Compare the choices and use Process of Elimination. Choices with decimals are the easiest to compare. The line over the numbers in (G) and (H) indicate repeating digits, so (G) can also be written as 0.722722722… and (H) can be rewritten as 0.727727727…. Compare these place value by place value with the number in (F). All three start with 0.72, but (G) has a 2 in the one-thousandths place while the other two have a 7 there. This means that the value of (G) is less than that of (F) and (J), so eliminate (F) and (J). To compare (G) to the fractions in (J) and (K), use a calculator. The value of $\frac{72}{99}$ as a decimal is 0.72727272…, making it greater than (G). Eliminate (J). The value of $\frac{720}{1,001}$ is 0.71928, which is less than 0.72222. Eliminate (G). The correct answer is (K).

35. **C**   The question asks for the average growth of a tree during the times that the tree was growing. Use the formula $T = AN$, in which T is the total, A is the average, and N is the number of things. The graph represents the time, in months, on the *x*-axis and the growth, in inches, on the *y*-axis. First determine the *total* growth of the tree. The lowest point on the *y*-axis is 0 and the highest point is 96, meaning the total growth was 96 – 0 = 96 inches. Next determine the *number of things*, which is the number of months that the tree was growing. This is represented by segments of the graph with a positive slope, as the flat horizontal lines indicate no change in growth. The tree was growing from months 0 to 3, months 6 to 12, and months 15 to 21. This represents a total of 3 + 6 + 6 = 15 months of growth. Now use the formula to calculate the *average*: 96 = A(15). Isolate A by dividing both sides by 15, and the result is $\frac{96}{15}$ = 6.4 inches per month. The correct answer is (C).

36. **J**   The question asks for the length of each half of a movie. Start by ballparking. The movie was almost but not quite 4 hours, so each half would be slightly less than 2 hours. Eliminate (F), which is too small, and (K) which is too big. Now divide the time by two. It can be tricky to divide mixed measurements like hours and minutes, so either convert the time to minutes or take half of the hours and half of the minutes separately and add the results together. The second approach may be easier. Take half of 3 hours to get 1.5 hours or 1 hour 30 minutes. Take half of 48 minutes to get 24 minutes. Add these together to get 1 hour 30 minutes + 24 minutes = 1 hour 54 minutes. The correct answer is (J).

37. **E**   The question asks for the factors of a quadratic expression. There are variables in the answer choices, so Plugging In is an option. However, with this many terms and negative signs, it may be easier to use Bite-Sized Pieces and Process of Elimination to tackle this question. Multiply out the factors in the answer choices using FOIL to see if the result matches the original expression. Start with the

first terms (the F in FOIL). The first terms in (A) become $(af)(fx) = af^2x$. This does not match the first term of the original expression, so eliminate (A). Multiplying the first terms in the other answer choices results in $(ax)(fx) = afx^2$, which does match the original expression. Try multiplying the last two terms in each remaining answer (the L in FOIL). Choice (B) becomes $(b)(-g) = -bg$. This does not match the last term in the original expression, so eliminate (B). Choice (C) becomes $(b)(g) = bg$. This does match, so keep (C). Choice (D) becomes $(-b)(g) = -bg$. Eliminate (D). Choice (E) becomes $(-b)(-g) = bg$. This matches, so keep (E). Finally, try the middle terms (the O and I in FOIL) for the two remaining answers. Choice (C) becomes $(ax)(g) + (b)(fx) = axg + bfx$. Factor out the x to get $x(ag + bf)$. The middle term of the original expression is negative, not positive. Eliminate (C). Choice (E) is all that's left, but to check it multiply the middle terms: $(ax)(-g) + (-b)(fx) = -axg + (-bfx)$. Factor out $-x$ to get $-x(ag + bf)$. This matches the middle term of the original expression. The correct answer is (E).

38. **J**   The question asks for the value of a function. In function notation, the number inside the parentheses is the x-value that goes into the function, and the value that comes out of the function is the y-value. This function is a piecewise function, or one that has a sequence of intervals. The value of x is 8, so plug $x = 8$ into the top segment of the function as that is the part defined for $x \leq 8$. The function becomes $g(8) = \frac{3}{4}(8) + 5 = \frac{24}{4} + 5 = 6 + 5 = 11$. The correct answer is (J).

39. **C**   The question asks for the ratio of the area of a triangle to the area of a trapezoid on a figure. Use the Geometry Basic Approach. There is a figure provided and it is labeled, so think of the formulas for area. There is a formula for the area of a trapezoid, but this trapezoid is already divided into a rectangle and a triangle, so use those formulas. The area of a rectangle is $A = lw$, and the area of a triangle is $A = \frac{1}{2}bh$. The area of the trapezoid will be the area of the rectangle plus the area of the triangle, and both the rectangle and the triangle have the same height. That height is not given, so plug in a value such as $h = 2$. Plug the information into the rectangle area formula to get $A = (24)(2) = 48$. The base of the triangle is the difference between the measures of the top and bottom of the trapezoid, so the base of the triangle is $30 - 24 = 6$. Plug the information into the triangle area formula to get $A = \frac{1}{2}(6)(2) = 6$. The area of the trapezoid is then $48 + 6 = 54$. The ratio of the area of the triangle to the area of the trapezoid is 6:54, which reduces to 1:9. The correct answer is (C).

40. **J**   The question asks for the expression that gives $h(j(x))$. In function notation, the number inside the parentheses is the x-value that goes into the function, and the value that comes out of the function is the y-value. This is a compound function, which is solved from the inside out. There are variables in the answer choices, so plug in. Make $x = 2$. The expression becomes $h(j(2))$. Plugging 2 into the j function results in $j(2) = 2(2) + 4 = 4 + 4 = 8$. Substitute 8 for $j(2)$ in the h function, which results in $h(8) = \frac{8^2}{2} = \frac{64}{2} = 32$. This is the target value; circle it. Now plug $x = 2$ into the answer choices to see

which one matches the target value. Choice (F) becomes $2^2 + 4 = 4 + 4 = 8$. This does not match the target, so eliminate (F). Choice (G) becomes $2^3 + 2(2^2) = 8 + 2(4) = 8 + 8 = 16$. Eliminate (G). Choice (H) becomes $2(2^2) + 4(2) + 8 = 2(4) + 8 + 8 = 8 + 16 = 24$. Eliminate (H). Choice (J) becomes $2(2^2) + 8(2) + 8 = 2(4) + 16 + 8 = 8 + 24 = 32$. Keep (J) but check (K) just in case. Choice (K) becomes $2(2^3) + 2 = 2(8) + 2 = 16 + 2 = 18$. Eliminate (K). The correct answer is (J).

41. **B**   The question asks for the measure of an angle on a figure. Start by ballparking. The question asks for the measure of $\angle FKJ$, which is part of triangle FJK in the figure. The measure of $\angle KFJ$ is marked as 90°, so the measure of $\angle FKJ$ must be less than 90°. Eliminate (D) and (E). Now use the Geometry Basic Approach and label the figure with the given information. The question states that $\overline{JK}$ bisects $\angle FJG$, which means that it divides $\angle FJG$ into two equal angles. Mark $\angle FJK$ and $\angle GJK$ as congruent. Use the information about the measures of the angles in triangle FGJ to determine the measures of the angles in triangle FJK. The measure of $\angle FGJ$ is 28°, and the angle at F is 90°. There are 180° in a triangle, so the measure of $\angle FJG = 180° - 28° - 90° = 62°$. Divide this in half to find that $\angle FJK = 31°$. There are also 180° in triangle FJK, so the measure of $\angle FKJ = 180° - 31° - 90° = 59°$. The correct answer is (B).

42. **K**   The question asks for the trigonometric function that is NOT equivalent to the given function. There is an unknown quantity θ in the answer choices, so plug in. Make $\theta = \dfrac{\pi}{3}$ to meet the restriction that $0 < \theta < \dfrac{\pi}{2}$. With a calculator in radians, find the value of $\cos\dfrac{\pi}{3}$, which is 0.5. The question asks for the expression NOT equal to this, so plug $\theta = \dfrac{\pi}{3}$ into the answer choices to see which one does NOT match this value. Choice (F) becomes $\left(\sin\dfrac{\pi}{3}\right)\left(\cot\dfrac{\pi}{3}\right)$. The cotangent function is the reciprocal of the tangent function, so this can be rewritten as $\left(\sin\dfrac{\pi}{3}\right)\left(\dfrac{1}{\tan\dfrac{\pi}{3}}\right) = \dfrac{\sin\dfrac{\pi}{3}}{\tan\dfrac{\pi}{3}}$. Use a calculator to find the values of the numerator and denominator separately. This becomes approximately $\dfrac{0.866}{1.732} = 0.5$. This does match the value of $\cos\dfrac{\pi}{3}$, so eliminate (F). Choice (G) becomes $\dfrac{1}{\sec\dfrac{\pi}{3}}$. The secant function is the reciprocal of the cosine function, so this can be rewritten as $\cos\dfrac{\pi}{3}$. This has already

been calculated as 0.5, so eliminate (G). Choice (H) becomes $\dfrac{\sin\frac{\pi}{3}}{\tan\frac{\pi}{3}}=\dfrac{0.866}{1.732}=0.5$, so eliminate

(H). Choice (J) becomes $\dfrac{\cot\frac{\pi}{3}}{\csc\frac{\pi}{3}}$. The cosecant function is the reciprocal of the sine function, so

this can be rewritten as $\dfrac{\frac{1}{\tan\frac{\pi}{3}}}{\frac{1}{\sin\frac{\pi}{3}}}=\dfrac{1}{\tan\frac{\pi}{3}}\times\dfrac{\sin\frac{\pi}{3}}{1}=\dfrac{\sin\frac{\pi}{3}}{\tan\frac{\pi}{3}}=0.5$. Eliminate (J). Choice (K) becomes

$\dfrac{\csc\frac{\pi}{3}}{\tan\frac{\pi}{3}}=\dfrac{\frac{1}{\sin\frac{\pi}{3}}}{\tan\frac{\pi}{3}}=\dfrac{1}{\sin\frac{\pi}{3}}\times\dfrac{1}{\tan\frac{\pi}{3}}=\dfrac{1}{(0.866)(1.732)}\approx 1.5$. This is the one that does not match 0.5, so the

correct answer is (K).

43. **C** The question asks for the number of points Everett has compared to James. Since the question asks for a specific value and the answers contain numbers in increasing order, plug in the answers. Begin by labeling the answers as "Everett more than James" and start with (C), 19.5 points. The question states that Everett has 97.5 points. If this is 19.5 *more points than James,* then James has 97.5 − 19.5 = 78 points. Everett's points are *25% more* than James's points, so take 25% of James's points. *Percent* means to divide by 100, and *of* means to multiply. Thus, Everett has $\dfrac{25}{100}\times 78 = 19.5$ points more than James. This matches the value given in (C), so stop here. The correct answer is (C).

44. **G** The question asks for the value of a logarithmic function. When working with logs, remember that $\log_b n = x$ can be rewritten as $b^x = n$. Substituting the numbers from the question, $\log_2(8^3) = 3a$ can be rewritten as $2^{3a} = 8^3$. When working with exponents, the MADSPM rules apply only when the two numbers have the same base. Convert 8 into 2^3 and the equation is now $2^{3a} = (2^3)^3$. The PM part of the MADSPM acronym indicates that taking a base with an exponent to a Power means to Multiply the exponents. Do this on the right side of the equation to get $2^{3a} = 2^9$. Because the numbers have the same base, the exponents can be set equal to get $3a = 9$. Divide both sides by 3 to get $a = 3$. The correct answer is (G).

45. **B** The question asks for the area of the shaded region on a figure. Use the Geometry Basic Approach. Start by labeling the figure with the given information. The semicircles have a radius of 1, so the diameter is $2r = 2(1) = 2$. Label *MN* and *LO* as 2. *LMNO* is a square, so also label *LM* and *NO* as

2. The area of the shaded region will be the area of the square minus the areas of the two semicircles, which have the same radius and thus add up to one whole circle. Write out the formulas needed. The formula for the area of a square is $A = s^2$, and the formula for the area of a circle is $A = \pi r^2$. The area of the square becomes $A = 2^2 = 4$. Eliminate (D) and (E) because these answers give the area of the square as 8. The area of the circle created by the two semicircles is $A = \pi(1^2) = \pi$. The area of the shaded region is $4 - \pi$. The correct answer is (B).

46. **G**   The question asks for a probability, which is defined as $\dfrac{want}{total}$. Read the question carefully to find the numbers to make the probability. There are 30 tickets, one for each member of the club, so that is the *total*. Of these tickets, 3 will be drawn to win a prize. The question asks for the probability that Tanja will *NOT* win a prize, and there are 27 tickets that will not be drawn. Therefore, 27 is the *want*, and the probability is $\dfrac{27}{30}$. This reduces to $\dfrac{9}{10}$. The correct answer is (G).

47. **E**   The question asks for a probability, which is defined as $\dfrac{want}{total}$. Read the table carefully to find the numbers to make the probability. To find the total number of students in the class, add up all the numbers in the right column to get 25; that is the *total*. Of these students, 6 had *exactly 2 first cousins*, so that is the *want*. Therefore, the probability is $\dfrac{6}{25} = 0.24$. The correct answer is (E).

48. **F**   The question asks for a graph that represents a real-life situation. To find the best representation, read the question and compare features of the graphs in the answer choices. The image shows that the dot on the wheel begins below the surface, and the question defines *y* as the distance the dot is *below or above the surface*. Therefore, the graph for this situation would have a negative *y*-intercept to indicate that the dot started below the surface. Eliminate answer choices that do not match this information. Choices (G), (H), (J), and (K) all show the dot started at the surface or above it, so they can be eliminated. The correct answer is (F).

49. **B**   The question asks for the number of edges on a 3D block. There are 7 edges shown in the figure, and there will be more edges on the back that are not visible. Eliminate (A), which is too small. There are 3 of the 6 triangular faces showing, so the image shows half the figure and there can be at most 14 edges. Eliminate (D) and (E), which are too big. To determine the exact number of remaining edges, sketch the sides on the back of the block. It will look like this:

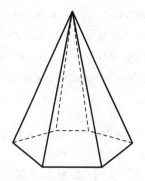

There are five more edges that are not visible, so the total number of edges is 7 + 5 = 12. If visualizing this is difficult, find the sum of all the edges of all the faces. There are 6 triangles with 3 edges each, so the edges of the triangles add up to 3(6) = 18. The hexagonal base has 6 sides, so this makes the number of edges 18 + 6 = 24. This sum counts each shared edge twice, so divide this number by 2 to correct for that. The number of edges is $\frac{24}{2} = 12$, Either way, the correct answer is (B).

50. **H** The question asks for the area of one triangular face on a figure. Use the Geometry Basic Approach. Start by labeling the figure with the given information. Label the short edge as 1.4 and the long edges as 2.5. Write out the formula for the area of a triangle, which is $A = \frac{1}{2}bh$. No height is drawn, so draw a line from the vertex at the top of the center triangle to the middle of that triangle's base. This will divide the base in half, creating two right triangles that each have a base of 0.7 and a hypotenuse of 2.5. To find the measurement of the height, use Pythagorean Theorem or Pythagorean triples (this is a 7:24:25 triangle with each side divided by 10) to find that the height is 2.4. The area of the triangular face becomes $A = \frac{1}{2}(1.4)(2.4) = 1.68$. The correct answer is (H).

51. **E** The question asks for the maximum number of groupings possible. This is also known as a *combination*. First calculate the total number of outcomes by finding the number of possibilities for each outcome and multiplying the results. There will be 4 contestants chosen, so there are 4 separate outcomes. For the first contestant chosen, it can be any of the 16 in the competition. Once that first person is chosen, there are only 15 remaining for the second one chosen. There are then only 14 for the third one chosen and only 13 for the fourth one chosen. Therefore, the total number of outcomes is (16)(15)(14)(13). The question asks for the number of *groupings,* though, and this calculation for the number of outcomes counts groups containing the same members multiple times. For example, it counts the outcome with contestants 1, 2, 3, 4 chosen in order as a different outcome with contestants 2, 4, 3, 1 chosen in order, when those two outcomes really result in the same *group*. To get rid of duplicates when trying to find the number of groups, divide by a factorial of the number of choices made. There were four contestants chosen, so the factorial is (4)(3)(2)(1). Thus, the number of groupings is $\frac{(16)(15)(14)(13)}{(4)(3)(2)(1)}$. The correct answer is (E).

52. **J** The question asks for an expression to represent the length of Amy's professional career in relation to the length of Rachel's professional career. There is a variable in the answer choices, so plug in. Make $R = 7$ to make the math simpler. If Rachel's career is 7 years and she has spent $\frac{5}{7}$ of it in her current job, then she has been in her current job for $\frac{5}{7}(7) = 5$ years. The question states that Amy and Rachel

began their current jobs at the same time, which means Amy has also been in her current job for 5 years. This is $\frac{2}{3}$ the length of her career, which can be called A. This means that $\frac{2}{3}A = 5$. Solve for A by multiplying both sides by the reciprocal of the fraction: $A = \frac{3}{2}(5) = \frac{15}{2}$ or 7.5 years. This is the target value; circle it. Now plug $R = 7$ into the answer choices to see which one matches the target value. Choice (F) becomes $\frac{10}{21}(7) = \frac{70}{21} = \frac{10}{3} = 3.\overline{33}$. This does not match the target, so eliminate (F). Choice (G) becomes $\frac{5}{7}(7) = \frac{35}{7} = 5$. Eliminate (G). Choice (H) becomes $\frac{14}{15}(7) = \frac{98}{15} = 6.5\overline{33}$. Eliminate (H). Choice (J) becomes $\frac{15}{14}(7) = \frac{105}{14} = 7.5$. Keep (J) but check (K) just in case. Choice (K) becomes $\frac{7}{5}(7) = \frac{49}{5} = 9.8$. Eliminate (K). The correct answer is (J).

53. **C** The question asks about the average time for all participants in the first heat of a race. Start by ballparking—the average time of all participants must be somewhere between the averages for each group. Eliminate (A) and (E), as these times represent the average times of the two separate groups. Use the formula $T = AN$, in which T is the total, A is the average, and N is the number of things. The *Average* for the runners was 31 minutes and the *Number of things* was 64, so *Total time* = (31)(64) = 1,984 minutes for the runners. The *Average* for the walkers was 59 minutes and the *Number of things* was 48, so *Total time* = (59)(48) = 2,832 minutes for the walkers. To find the average for all participants, add the total times and the total number of participants. The time adds up to 1,984 + 2,832 = 4,816, and the number of participants adds up to 64 + 48 = 112, so 4,816 = A(112). Divide both sides of the equation by 112 to get $A = 43$. The correct answer is (C).

54. **J** The question asks for the maximum score Bob received in 3 bowling games based on some statistical data. The table gives the mean (average), the minimum, and the median. The median of a list of numbers is the middle number when all values are arranged in order. Therefore, Bob's middle score must be 218. Bob's minimum score is listed as 178. Use the formula $T = AN$, in which T is the total, A is the average, and N is the number of things, to calculate the total points Bob received in his 3 games. The *Average* is 207 and the *Number of things* is 3, so *Total* = (207)(3) = 621. The two scores already known add up to 218 + 178 = 396. To find the third score, subtract this from 621 to get 621 − 396 = 225. The correct answer is (J).

55. **D** The question asks for the number Alex can use to count by as she knocks over all the ducks in a row. Since the question asks for a specific value and the answers contain numbers in increasing order, plug in the answers. Begin by labeling the answers as "n" and start with (C), 4. If Alex knocks over every 4th duck, she will knock over ducks 4, 8, 12, 16, 20, 24, 28, 32, 36, 40, 44, and 48. Then she will start counting back at the first duck, spraying water where the 4th duck was. She will end up trying to knock over the exact same ducks on the second pass down the row. This will not end up knocking over every duck, so eliminate (C). Another even number will have the same result, so eliminate (A) and (E) as well. Try 5 next. If Alex knocks over every 5th duck, she will knock over ducks 5, 10, 15, 20, 25, 30, 35, 40, and 45. Then she will count duck 46 as 1, 47 as 2, and 48 as 3. She will start

counting back at duck 1 as 4, then knock over ducks 2, 7, 12, 17, 22, 27, 32, 37, 42, and 47. In the next pass, she will knock over ducks 4, 9, 14, 19, etc. If she continues, she will end up knocking over all the ducks. Using 3 as n won't work because 48 is divisible by 3. The correct answer is (D).

56. **G**   The question asks for the digit in the ones place of a very large number. Trying to find 18^{55} on a calculator will not work, so instead look for a pattern in the units digits of powers of 18. Write the powers out starting with 18^1.

$18^1 = 18$ $18^2 = 324$ $18^3 = 5,832$ $18^4 = 104,976$
$18^5 = 1,889,568$ $18^6 = 34,012,224$ $18^7 = 612,220,032$ $18^8 = 11,019,960,576$

At this point the pattern has started to repeat, so stop and write down the pattern of the units digits. The pattern of the units digits is 8, 4, 2, 6. Eliminate (F), as none of these units digits is 0. Following the pattern, every 4th power will have a units digit of 6. Find a multiple of 4 that is near 55, such as 52. This means that 18^{52} ends in 6. Start back at the beginning of the pattern to find that 18^{53} ends in 8, 18^{54} ends in 4, and 18^{55} ends in 2. The correct answer is (G).

57. **B**   The question asks for the coordinates of two points on a figure. Use the Geometry Basic Approach. Start by ballparking. The points F and J are on the same horizontal line, so they will have the same y-coordinates when the figure is graphed in the coordinate plane. Eliminate (A) and (C), as these pairs of points do not have matching y-coordinates. In the formula for an ellipse, $\dfrac{(x-h)^2}{a^2} + \dfrac{(y-k)^2}{b^2} = 1$, the point (h, k) is the center, $2a$ is the width, and $2b$ is the height. For this ellipse, the center is at $(-2, 0)$. The value of a is 5, because $a^2 = 25$, so the width is $2(5) = 10$. The value of b is 2, because $b^2 = 4$, so the height is $2(2) = 4$. Use this information to sketch the coordinate plane on the figure. It will look like this:

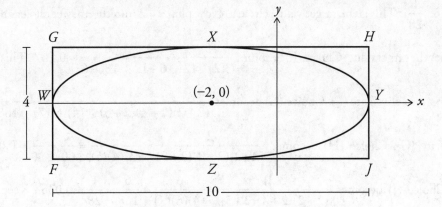

The x-coordinate of F is 5 units to the left of the center, so it is at $-2 - 5 = -7$. Eliminate (D) and (E), which do not have this x-coordinate for F. The correct answer is (B).

58. **F**   The question asks for an equivalent form of an expression with fractional exponents. Although there are variables in the answer choices, plugging in on this question would be difficult, given all the exponents and roots. Instead, use exponent rules to convert the fractional exponents to roots. Start by

getting a common denominator for the fractional exponents. The lowest common denominator of 5 and 2 is 10. The expression becomes $a^{\frac{14}{10}}b^{\frac{5}{10}}$. With fractional exponents, the numerator is the power and the denominator is the root. The expression can be rewritten as $\sqrt[10]{a^{14}b^5}$. The powers of a and b do not match, so eliminate (G) and (K). The term a^{14} under the root means that there are 14 a's all multiplied together. Taking the 10th root means that one a can come out for every 10 under the root symbol. This leaves 4 a's under the root, so the expression becomes $a\sqrt[10]{a^4b^5}$. The correct answer is (F).

59. **D**   The question asks for the combined height of the boxes in the short stack. Translate the English to math in Bite-Sized Pieces. Each stack cannot be more than 72 centimeters tall, and each box is 13.5 centimeters tall. Divide 72 by 13.5 to find that there can be $5.\overline{33}$ boxes in each stack. Round this down to 5 boxes in a stack because there cannot be fractions of boxes. There are 48 shoe boxes total, so there will be $\frac{48}{5}$ stacks, meaning 9 full stacks of 5 boxes with 3 boxes left over. Therefore, the short stack will have only 3 boxes in it. The height of the short stack will be $3(13.5) = 40.5$ centimeters. The correct answer is (D).

60. **J**   The question asks for an equivalent form of an expression. There is a variable in the answer choices, so plug in. Make $x = 2$. The expression becomes $\frac{5}{2^2 + 9(2) + 20} - \frac{2}{2^2 + 6(2) + 8}$. This simplifies to $\frac{5}{4 + 18 + 20} - \frac{2}{4 + 12 + 8} = \frac{5}{42} - \frac{2}{24}$. Use a calculator to find that this is approximately $0.119 - 0.083 \approx 0.036$ or $\frac{1}{28}$. This is the target value; circle it. Now plug $x = 2$ into the answer choices to see which one matches the target value. Choice (F) becomes $\frac{3}{3(2) + 12} = \frac{3}{6 + 12} = \frac{3}{18} = \frac{1}{6} \approx 0.167$. This does not match the target, so eliminate (F). Choice (G) becomes $\frac{3}{(2 + 2)(2 + 4)(2 + 5)} = \frac{3}{(4)(6)(7)} = \frac{3}{168} = \frac{1}{56} \approx 0.018$. Eliminate (G). Choice (H) becomes $\frac{2}{(2 + 1)(2 + 2)(2 + 3)} = \frac{2}{(3)(4)(5)} = \frac{2}{60} = \frac{1}{30} \approx 0.033$. Eliminate (H). Choice (J) becomes $\frac{3(2)}{(2 + 2)(2 + 4)(2 + 5)} = \frac{6}{(4)(6)(7)} = \frac{6}{168} = \frac{1}{28} \approx 0.036$. Keep (J), but check (K) just in case. Choice (K) becomes $\frac{3(2) + 20}{(2 + 2)^2(2 + 5)} = \frac{6 + 20}{(4)^2(7)} = \frac{26}{16(7)} = \frac{26}{112} = \frac{13}{56} \approx 0.232$. Eliminate (K). The correct answer is (J).

Chapter 10
Practice Test 2

ACT MATHEMATICS TEST

60 Minutes—60 Questions

DIRECTIONS: Solve each problem, choose the correct answer, and then darken the corresponding oval on your answer document.

Do not linger over problems that take too much time. Solve as many as you can; then return to the others in the time you have left for this test.

You are permitted to use a calculator on this test. You may use your calculator for any problems you choose, but some of the problems may best be done without using a calculator.

Note: Unless otherwise stated, all of the following should be assumed:

1. Illustrative figures are NOT necessarily drawn to scale.

2. Geometric figures lie in a plane.

3. The word *line* indicates a straight line.

4. The word *average* indicates arithmetic mean.

---

1. In a geometric sequence, the quotient of any two consecutive terms is the same. If the third term of a geometric sequence is 8 and the fourth term is 16, then what is the second term?

   A. −8
   B. −4
   C. 2
   D. 4
   E. 8

DO YOUR FIGURING HERE.

2. If the function $f(a,b)$ is defined as $f(a,b) = 2ab - (a+b)$, then $f(3,4) = ?$

   F. 7
   G. 17
   H. 21
   J. 24
   K. 31

3. The Korean BBQ taco truck sells short rib tacos for 99¢. Christine has only pennies, nickels, dimes, and quarters in her purse. If she wants to pay with exact change, then what is the fewest number of coins Christine can use to buy a 99¢ taco?

   (Note: Assume any sales tax is included in the price.)

   A. 6
   B. 7
   C. 8
   D. 9
   E. 10

4. What is the area, in square inches, of a square with a side length of 8 inches?

   F. 8
   G. 16
   H. 24
   J. 32
   K. 64

GO ON TO THE NEXT PAGE.

5. If $x = 3$, then the expression $\dfrac{(x+1)^2}{x^2-1}$ is equal to:

   A.   2

   B. $\dfrac{1}{2}$

   C.   0

   D. $-\dfrac{1}{2}$

   E. -8

6. Which of the following is NOT a factor of 1,776 ?

   F.   12
   G.   16
   H.   18
   J.   24
   K.   37

7. Lauren's world history teacher needs to select one of his 19 students to lead the class in song. Lauren's teacher decides that the song leader, who will be chosen at random, CANNOT be any of the 4 seniors in the class. What is the probability that Lauren, who is NOT a senior, will be chosen?

   A.   0

   B. $\dfrac{1}{19}$

   C. $\dfrac{1}{15}$

   D. $\dfrac{4}{19}$

   E. $\dfrac{15}{19}$

8. If $4(x-5) + x = 45$, then $x = ?$

   F.   5
   G.   8
   H.   9
   J.   10
   K.   13

9. Joe rents a car to drive across the state to visit his family for Thanksgiving. The car rental company charges Joe $112 for the weekend rental, plus $0.99 for each mile he drives. If Joe drives the rental car m miles, then which of the following expressions gives Joe's total cost, in dollars, for renting the car?

   A. $0.99m - 112$
   B. $0.99m + 112$
   C. $49.95m$
   D. $112m + 0.99$
   E. $112.99m$

GO ON TO THE NEXT PAGE.

10. Stella wants to buy a scooter for $4,800. A loan company offers to finance the purchase in return for payments of $130 a month for 4 years. If Stella were to finance the scooter, then how much more than the purchase price of the scooter will Stella have paid at the end of the 4-year period?

F. $ 520
G. $ 780
H. $1,040
J. $1,300
K. $1,440

DO YOUR FIGURING HERE.

11. The expression $\dfrac{20y^8}{4y^2}$ is equivalent to:

A. $5y^4$
B. $5y^6$
C. $5y^8$
D. $16y^4$
E. $16y^6$

12. Which of the following is equal to $\dfrac{3-\dfrac{1}{2}}{2+\dfrac{3}{4}}$?

F. $\dfrac{10}{11}$

G. 2

H. 12

J. 20

K. $\dfrac{55}{2}$

13. Point C is at 3.5 on the real number line. If Point D is also on the real number line and is 8.5 units from C, then which of the following are the possible locations of D ?

A. −12 and −5
B. −12 and 5
C. −5 and 5
D. 12 and −5
E. 12 and 5

14. The mean of 4 numbers in a data set is 7. If 3 of these numbers are 2, 4, and 10, then which of the following is the fourth number?

F. 4
G. 7
H. 8
J. 10
K. 12

GO ON TO THE NEXT PAGE.

DO YOUR FIGURING HERE.

15. Motorcars, Inc. made $1,489,000 in net profit in 2007. In 2009, Motorcars, Inc. made $1,725,000 in net profit. If the net profit increased linearly from 2007 through 2009, then what was the net profit earned in 2008 ?

   A. $1,607,000
   B. $1,698,000
   C. $1,724,000
   D. $1,779,000
   E. $1,842,000

16. The art teacher at Valley High School is decorating her classroom by reproducing famous pictures on her walls. She has a picture 8 inches wide and 10 inches tall that she wants to replicate to scale on the wall. If the painting on the wall will be 6 feet tall, then approximately how wide will the painting be, in feet?

   F. 5
   G. 7
   H. 9
   J. 11
   K. 13

17. The equation of line l in standard form is $5x - y = 2$. Which of the following gives the formula for line l in slope-intercept form?

   A. $y = 5x + 2$
   B. $y = 5x - 2$
   C. $y = 2x - 5$
   D. $y = -5x - 2$
   E. $y = -5x + 2$

18. The expression $|2 - 14| - |-25|$ is equal to:

   F. 41
   G. 37
   H. 13
   J. −13
   K. −37

19. In △JKL the measure of ∠J is exactly 37° and the measure of ∠K is less than or equal to 63°. Which of the following phrases best describes the measure of ∠L ?

   A. Exactly 120°
   B. Exactly 100°
   C. Exactly 80°
   D. Greater than or equal to 80°
   E. Less than or equal to 80°

GO ON TO THE NEXT PAGE.

20. If $3x - 1 > 26$, then which of the following is the least possible integer value of x?

F.　6
G.　7
H.　8
J.　9
K.　10

21. Paul is tying red and white ribbons around a gift box. He begins by tying the white ribbon and one red ribbon around the box. These two ribbons intersect on one face of the box at a 62° angle, as shown in the figure below. Now Paul wants to tie a second red ribbon onto the box so that the two red ribbons are parallel. What is the degree measure of the angle, indicated below, between the white ribbon and the bottom red ribbon?

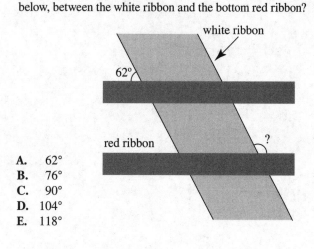

A.　62°
B.　76°
C.　90°
D.　104°
E.　118°

22. In right triangle *PRS* shown below, Q is the midpoint of $\overline{PR}$. What is the length of $\overline{QR}$, to the nearest inch?

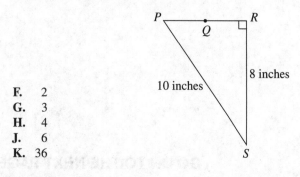

F.　2
G.　3
H.　4
J.　6
K.　36

GO ON TO THE NEXT PAGE.

DO YOUR FIGURING HERE.

> Use the following information to answer questions 23–24.

Katie notices that the textbooks for her past 3 math courses have the same length and width, but each year's textbook has more pages and weighs more than the previous year's textbook. Katie weighs the textbooks, to the nearest 0.1 ounce, for her past 3 math courses and wonders about the relationship between the number of pages in math textbooks and the weights of those textbooks. She graphs the number of pages and corresponding weights of her 3 math textbooks in the standard (x, y) coordinate plane, as shown below, and discovers a linear relationship among these 3 points. She concludes that the equation of the line that passes through these 3 points is $y = 0.1x + 2.2$.

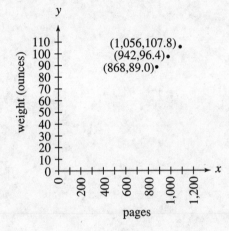

23. How much more, in ounces, does a math textbook with 1,056 pages weigh than one with 868 pages?

    A. 18.8
    B. 19.8
    C. 54.1
    D. 77.3
    E. 107.8

24. According to Katie's equation, how much would a math textbook with 1,338 pages weigh, in pounds?

(Note: 16 ounces = 1 pound)

    F. 7.4
    G. 8.5
    H. 10.2
    J. 13.6
    K. 14.1

GO ON TO THE NEXT PAGE.

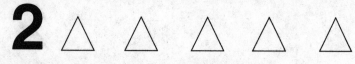

25. All line segments that intersect in the polygon below do so at right angles. If the dimensions given are in centimeters, then what is the area of the polygon, in square centimeters?

DO YOUR FIGURING HERE.

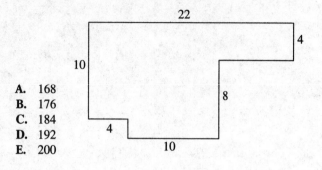

A. 168
B. 176
C. 184
D. 192
E. 200

26. Mr. Baylor spent 6 days grading 996 essays. He averaged 178 essays per day for the first 3 days. Which of the following is closest to his average speed, in essays graded per day, for the final 3 days?

F. 154
G. 157
H. 160
J. 163
K. 166

27. For all values of y, which of the following is equivalent to $(y+1)(y^2 - 3y + 2)$?

A. $y^3 + y^2 - y - 2$
B. $y^3 + y^2 + 2y + 2$
C. $y^3 - 2y^2 - y + 2$
D. $y^3 - 2y^2 + y - 2$
E. $y^3 + 2y + 2$

28. For $\angle D$ in $\triangle DEF$ below, which of the following trigonometric expressions has value $\dfrac{4}{5}$?

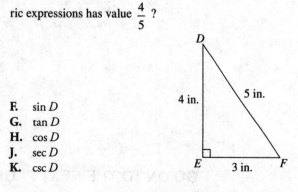

F. $\sin D$
G. $\tan D$
H. $\cos D$
J. $\sec D$
K. $\csc D$

GO ON TO THE NEXT PAGE.

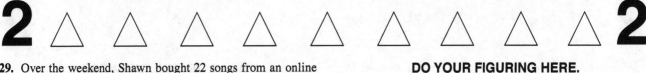

29. Over the weekend, Shawn bought 22 songs from an online music store. He spent a total of $17.90 on contemporary and classical songs. If contemporary songs cost $0.95 each and classical songs cost $0.75 each, then how many contemporary songs did Shawn buy?

(Note: There is no sales tax charged on these songs because they were purchased online.)

A. 7
B. 9
C. 10
D. 13
E. 15

DO YOUR FIGURING HERE.

30. If the operation # is defined as $x \# y = \dfrac{x^2 - y^2}{x + y}$, where x and y are real numbers such that $x \neq -y$, then what is the value of $(-3)\#(-7)$?

F. 10
G. 4
H. 1
J. −4
K. −10

31. Esther is making $2\frac{1}{4}$ gallons of punch for a large party. While mixing the punch, she uses $\frac{1}{2}$ gallon of pineapple juice. What fraction of the punch consists of pineapple juice?

A. $\dfrac{1}{9}$

B. $\dfrac{1}{6}$

C. $\dfrac{2}{9}$

D. $\dfrac{1}{3}$

E. $\dfrac{2}{3}$

32. Point O is the center of the circle shown below, and $\overline{XZ}$ is the diameter of the circle. If $\overline{XZ} = 8$ ft, Y lies on the circle, and $\overline{OX} = \overline{XY}$, then what is the area, in square feet, of XYZ?

F. $4\sqrt{2}$
G. $8\sqrt{3}$
H. 16
J. 32
K. 64

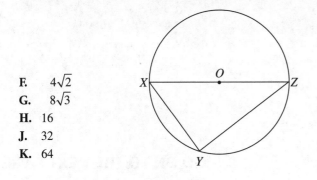

GO ON TO THE NEXT PAGE.

33. Which of the following values provides one of the roots for the equation $y^2 - 4y - 5 = 7$?

   A. −12
   B. −6
   C. −2
   D. −1
   E. 5

DO YOUR FIGURING HERE.

34. The plastic model house shown below consists of a right pyramid atop a right rectangular prism. The length and width of the prism and of the pyramid are 20 millimeters. The height of the prism is 16 millimeters and the height of the pyramid is 12 millimeters. Which of the following is closest to the volume of the plastic model house, in cubic millimeters?

(Note: The volume of a right pyramid is given by $\frac{1}{3}lwh$, where l is the length, w is the width, and h is the height. The volume of a right rectangular prism is given by lwh, where l is the length, w is the width, and h is the height.)

   F. 6,900
   G. 8,000
   H. 9,100
   J. 12,300
   K. 25,600

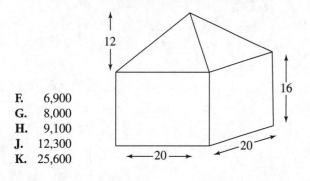

35. An isosceles trapezoid has bases of length 5 inches and 11 inches. The area of the trapezoid is 40 square inches. What is the height of the trapezoid, in inches?

   A. 4
   B. 5
   C. 7.5
   D. 17.5
   E. 35

GO ON TO THE NEXT PAGE.

36. What is the slope of the line that passes through the points (–2,6) and (3,–9) in the standard (x,y) coordinate plane?

DO YOUR FIGURING HERE.

F. $\frac{1}{15}$
G. $-\frac{1}{3}$
H. $-\frac{3}{5}$
J. –3
K. –5

37. Right triangle ΔWXY is isosceles and has its right angle at Point *X*. Point *Z* is collinear with points *X* and *Y*, with *Y* between *X* and *Z*. What is the measure of $\angle WYZ$?

A. 45°
B. 90°
C. 120°
D. 135°
E. 145°

38. The decimal construction of $\frac{5}{13}$ repeats and can be written as $0.384615384615\cdots$. What is the 99th digit to the right of the decimal point in this decimal construction?

F. 1
G. 3
H. 4
J. 5
K. 6

GO ON TO THE NEXT PAGE.

39. Points $W(-2,2)$, $X(2,2)$, and $Y(2,-2)$ lie in the standard (x,y) coordinate plane and are 3 of the vertices of square $WXYZ$. What is the length, in coordinate units, of $\overline{XZ}$?

A.   2

B.   4

C.   16

D. $2\sqrt{2}$

E. $4\sqrt{2}$

40. The equation $y = x^2$ is graphed in the standard (x,y) coordinate plane, then reflected across the x-axis. Which of the following is the equation of this reflection?

F. $y = x^2$

G. $y = -x^2$

H. $y = (-x)^2$

J. $y = |x|$

K. $|y| = |x|$

41. In the figure below, $\overline{JK} \parallel \overline{MN}$, and $\overline{JM}$ and $\overline{KN}$ intersect at L. Which of the following statements must be true?

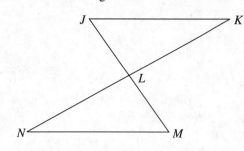

A. $\overline{JK} \cong \overline{MN}$

B. $\overline{JL} \cong \overline{LM}$

C. $\triangle JKL \cong \triangle MNL$

D. $\triangle JKL$ is similar to $\triangle MNL$

E. $\overline{JM}$ bisects $\overline{KN}$

GO ON TO THE NEXT PAGE.

DO YOUR FIGURING HERE.

Use the following information to answer questions 42–44.

The Wildcat athletic department at Wilson High School needs to raise $3,000.00 to fill a gap in its annual budget. The athletic department can choose 1 of the 2 options below to raise the needed funds.

Sell "Wildcat baseball caps" option: After paying a one-time fee of $23.00 to rent the necessary equipment, the athletic department can sell baseball caps featuring the school's logo. The athletic department will buy plain caps and print the school logo on each, at a cost of $3.50 per cap. The athletic department will sell each cap for $5.00.

Sell "Wildcat T-shirts" option: After paying a one-time fee of $19.00 to rent the necessary equipment, the athletic department can sell T-shirts featuring the school's logo. The athletic department will buy plain T-shirts and print the school logo on each, at a cost of $2.25 per T-shirt. The athletic department will sell each T-shirt for $4.00.

42. For the "Wildcat baseball caps" option, at least how many baseball caps must be sold in order to cover the one-time fee of renting the necessary equipment?

   F. 14
   G. 15
   H. 16
   J. 17
   K. 23

43. The Wildcat athletic department sold 540 tickets to Friday's football game. Of those tickets, 60% were adult tickets and the remainder were student tickets. The revenue from these ticket sales had already been factored into the annual budget. Jordan suggested raising the price of the adult tickets $2.00 to help fill the budget gap. If the athletic department had raised the price of each adult ticket $2.00, then by approximately what percent would the budget gap have been filled?

   A. 22%
   B. 23%
   C. 24%
   D. 25%
   E. 26%

GO ON TO THE NEXT PAGE.

44. The Wildcat athletic department chose the "Wildcat T-shirt" option and successfully filled the budget gap. What is the minimum number of T-shirts the athletic department must have sold?

F. 1,480
G. 1,664
H. 1,709
J. 1,726
K. 1,812

DO YOUR FIGURING HERE.

45. The graph of $y^2 = x$ is shown in the standard (x,y) coordinate plane below for values of x such that $0 \leq x \leq 4$. The x-coordinates of points D and E are both 4. What is the area of $\triangle DEO$, in square coordinate units?

A. $\dfrac{5}{2}$

B. 4

C. 8

D. 12

E. 16

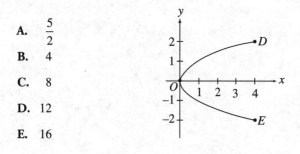

46. In $\triangle XYZ$ below, the length of $\overline{XY}$ is 12 centimeters. How long is $\overline{YZ}$, to the nearest tenth of a centimeter?

(Note: The law of sines states that in $\triangle ABC$ with sides length a, b, and c opposite $\angle A$, $\angle B$, and $\angle C$, respectively, $\dfrac{\sin A}{a} = \dfrac{\sin B}{b} = \dfrac{\sin C}{c}$.)

(Note: $\sin 53° \approx 0.799$, $\sin 59° \approx 0.857$, $\sin 68° \approx 0.927$)

F. 9.6
G. 10.3
H. 11.1
J. 12.9
K. 13.9

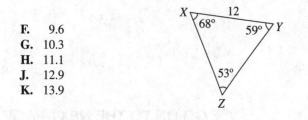

GO ON TO THE NEXT PAGE.

DO YOUR FIGURING HERE.

47. Jacob used the quadratic equation to find that the solutions to an equation are $x = 3 \pm \sqrt{-16c^2}$, where c is a positive real number. Which of the following expressions gives these solutions as complex numbers?

    A. $3 \pm 1ci$
    B. $3 \pm 2ci$
    C. $3 \pm 4ci$
    D. $3 \pm 8ci$
    E. $3 \pm 16ci$

48. Points C and D are on the circle with center O as shown in the figure below. The length of $\overline{CD}$ is 12 millimeters and the measure of $\overset{\frown}{CD}$ is 60°. What is the length of the diameter of this circle?

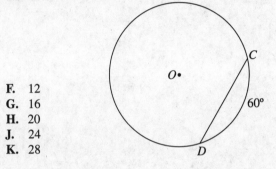

    F. 12
    G. 16
    H. 20
    J. 24
    K. 28

49. A nylon cord is stretched from the top of a vertical playground pole to the ground. The cord is 25 feet long and makes a 19° angle with the ground. Which of the following expressions gives the horizontal distance, in feet, between the pole and the point where the cord touches the ground?

    A. $\dfrac{\sin 19°}{25}$

    B. $\dfrac{\cos 19°}{25}$

    C. $25 \tan 19°$

    D. $25 \sin 19°$

    E. $25 \cos 19°$

50. What are the coordinates of the center of the circle with the equation $x^2 + 8x + y^2 - 2y + 8 = 0$ in the standard (x, y) coordinate plane?

    F. $(-4, 1)$
    G. $(-1, -4)$
    H. $(1, -4)$
    J. $(4, -1)$
    K. $(4, 1)$

GO ON TO THE NEXT PAGE.

51. Scott's swimming pool has a depth of 8 feet and holds 13,000 gallons of water when full. Because of the warm weather, 10% of the water in the pool evaporates each day. Scott fills the pool with water and comes back the next day to measure the amount of water remaining in the pool. He considers this "Day 1" because it was taken 1 day after the pool was filled, and labels his measurement as such. The next day, he measures the amount of water again, and labels the results "Day 2" because it is now 2 days after he filled the pool. If Scott continues, on which day will he measure the pool that it is less than half full?

   A. 5
   B. 6
   C. 7
   D. 8
   E. 9

52. If $\begin{vmatrix} a & b \\ c & d \end{vmatrix} = ad - bc$, then $\begin{vmatrix} 2d & 2c \\ 2a & 2b \end{vmatrix} = ?$

   F. $2da - 2cb$
   G. $2db - 2ca$
   H. $4da - 4cb$
   J. $4db - 4ca$
   K. $ad - bc$

53. The figure below shows 4 congruent circles, each tangent to 2 other circles and to 2 sides of the square. If the length of a side of the square is 24 inches, then what is the area, in square inches, of 1 circle?

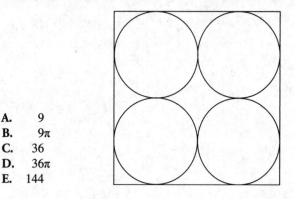

   A. 9
   B. 9π
   C. 36
   D. 36π
   E. 144

54. Andy has 30 collectible comic books, which he bought in 2005 for $28.95 each. These comic books are currently valued at $34.35 each. Andy will sell these 30 comic books when their combined value is exactly $600.00 more than he paid for them. How much more will the average value per comic book have risen when Andy sells these 30 comic books?

   F. $14.60
   G. $12.72
   H. $10.05
   J. $ 7.84
   K. $ 5.40

GO ON TO THE NEXT PAGE.

55. Circles with centers G and K intersect at points C and F, as shown below. Points B, G, H, J, K, and D are collinear. The lengths of $\overline{AC}$, $\overline{CE}$, and $\overline{HJ}$ are 18 cm, 10 cm, and 3 cm, respectively. What is the length, in centimeters, of $\overline{BD}$?

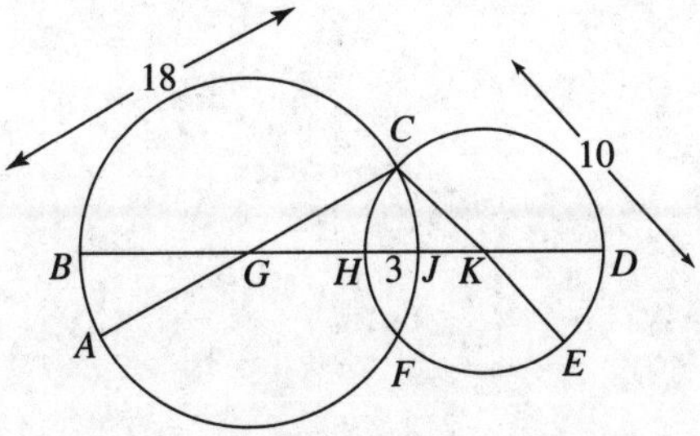

DO YOUR FIGURING HERE.

A. 22
B. 25
C. 26
D. 28
E. 29

56. A parabola with vertex $(-3,-2)$ and axis of symmetry $y = -2$ crosses the y-axis at $\left(0, -2 + 3\sqrt{3}\right)$. At what other point does the parabola cross the y-axis?

F. No other point

G. $\left(0, 2 + 3\sqrt{3}\right)$

H. $\left(0, 2 - 3\sqrt{3}\right)$

J. $\left(0, -2 - 3\sqrt{3}\right)$

K. Cannot be determined from the given information

57. If $z \neq 4$ and $z \neq -4$, then which of the following is equivalent to the expression $\dfrac{3z}{4-z} + \dfrac{3z}{z^2 - 16}$?

A. $\dfrac{3z^2 + 15z}{z^2 - 16}$

B. $\dfrac{9z^2 - 12z}{z^2 - 16}$

C. $\dfrac{-12z}{z^2 - 16}$

D. $\dfrac{-3z^2}{z^2 - 16}$

E. $\dfrac{-3z^2 - 9z}{z^2 - 16}$

GO ON TO THE NEXT PAGE.

58. The sides of the angle with measure θ are the positive x-axis and a portion of the line $y = -x$, as shown in the standard (x, y) coordinate plane below. What is the value of tan θ ?

F. 1

G. $\dfrac{\sqrt{2}}{2}$

H. $\dfrac{1}{2}$

J. $-\dfrac{\sqrt{2}}{2}$

K. -1

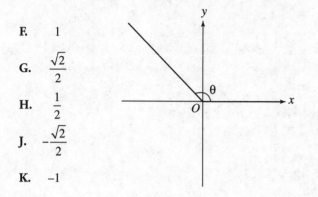

59. The nth term of an arithmetic sequence, a_n, is given by $a_n = a_1 + dn - d$, where a_1 is the 1st term and d is the common difference between terms. Which of the following expressions gives d in terms of a_n, a_1, and n ?

A. $\dfrac{a_n - a_1}{n - 1}$

B. $\dfrac{n - 1}{a_n - a_1}$

C. $\dfrac{a_n - a_1}{n}$

D. $\dfrac{a_n}{a_1 + n}$

E. $a_n - a_1 - n$

GO ON TO THE NEXT PAGE.

DO YOUR FIGURING HERE.

60. For all real positive values of x and y, $2\sqrt{x} \times 3\sqrt{y} = 12y$.
What is x in terms of y ?

   F. $2y$

   G. $3y$

   H. $4y$

   J. $6y$

   K. $7y$

END OF TEST.
STOP! DO NOT TURN THE PAGE UNTIL TOLD TO DO SO.

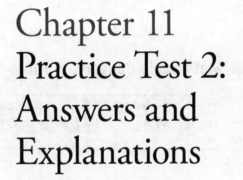

Chapter 11
Practice Test 2:
Answers and
Explanations

SCORE YOUR PRACTICE TEST

Step A

Count the number of correct answers: _____. This is your *raw score*.

Step B

Use the score conversion table below to look up your raw score. The number to the left is your *scale score*: _____.

Math Scale Conversion Table

Scaled Score	Raw Score	Scaled Score	Raw Score	Scaled Score	Raw Score
36	58–60	27	41–43	18	24–25
35	56–57	26	39–40	17	21–23
34	54–55	25	37–38	16	17–20
33	53	24	35–36	15	13–16
32	51–52	23	33–34	14	10–12
31	49–50	22	31–32	13	8–9
30	48	21	30	12	6–7
29	46–47	20	28–29	11	5
28	44–45	19	26–27	10	4

MATH PRACTICE TEST 2 ANSWER KEY

1.	D	31.	C
2.	G	32.	G
3.	D	33.	C
4.	K	34.	G
5.	A	35.	B
6.	H	36.	J
7.	C	37.	D
8.	K	38.	H
9.	B	39.	E
10.	K	40.	G
11.	B	41.	D
12.	F	42.	H
13.	D	43.	A
14.	K	44.	J
15.	A	45.	C
16.	F	46.	K
17.	B	47.	C
18.	J	48.	J
19.	D	49.	E
20.	K	50.	F
21.	E	51.	C
22.	G	52.	J
23.	A	53.	D
24.	G	54.	F
25.	D	55.	B
26.	F	56.	J
27.	C	57.	E
28.	H	58.	K
29.	A	59.	A
30.	G	60.	H

MATH PRACTICE TEST 2 EXPLANATIONS

1. **D** The question asks for the second term in a geometric sequence. The question states that, in such a sequence, *the quotient of any two consecutive terms is the same*. The third term is 8 and the fourth term is 16. The *quotient* is the result of division, so $\frac{3rd}{4th} = \frac{8}{16}$. This reduces to $\frac{1}{2}$, and this will also be the quotient of the second and third terms. This becomes $\frac{2nd}{3rd} = \frac{1}{2}$ or $\frac{x}{8} = \frac{1}{2}$. Cross-multiply to get $2x = 8$, then divide both sides by two to get $x = 4$. It is also possible to plug in the answers to see which gives the quotient of $\frac{1}{2}$ when the answer is divided by 8. Either way, the correct answer is (D).

2. **G** The question asks for the value of a function. In function notation, the number inside the parentheses is the *x*-value that goes into the function, and the value that comes out of the function is the *y*-value. This function is defined in terms of *a* and *b* and the question asks for the value of $f(3,4)$. Plug 3 for *a* and 4 for *b* into the *f* function to get $f(3,4) = 2(3)(4) - (3 + 4)$. This simplifies to $24 - 7 = 17$. The correct answer is (G).

3. **D** The question asks for the fewest number of coins that can be used to make a purchase. In order to minimize the number of coins, Christine must use as many high-value coins as she can. The highest value coins she has are quarters, worth 25 cents each. Find the greatest multiple of 25 that is less than 99: $25 \times 1 = 25$; $25 \times 2 = 50$; $25 \times 3 = 75$; $25 \times 4 = 100$. Thus, Christine can use at most 3 quarters, for a total of 75 cents. She now has $99 - 75 = 24$ cents left to pay. The next highest value coins she has are dimes, worth 10 cents each. Find the greatest multiple of 10 that is less than 24: $10 \times 2 = 20$. Thus, she can use at most 2 dimes, for an additional 20 cents. She needs $99 - 75 - 20 = 4$ more cents to get to the 99 cents she needs, so she cannot use any nickels. She must use 4 pennies, bringing her number of coins to $3 + 2 + 4 = 9$. The correct answer is (D).

4. **K** The question asks for the area of a square with a side length of 8 inches. Use the Geometry Basic Approach. Start by drawing a square and labeling it with the given information. Label all four sides as 8. Then write out the formula for the area of a square: $A = s^2$. Plug in $s = 8$ to get $A = 8^2 = 64$. The correct answer is (K).

5. **A** The question asks for the value of the expression if $x = 3$. Plug $x = 3$ into the expression to get $\frac{(3+1)^2}{3^2-1}$. This simplifies to $\frac{4^2}{9-1} = \frac{16}{8} = 2$. The correct answer is (A).

6. **H** The question asks for the choice that is NOT a factor of 1,776. The question asks for a specific value and the answers contain numbers in increasing order, so plug in the answers. A factor divides evenly into the given number, so go through the choices and determine whether the result of dividing 1,776 by that choice results in an integer. Choice (F) becomes $1,776 \div 12 = 148$. This means that 12 is a factor of 1,776, so eliminate (F). Choice (G) becomes $1,776 \div 16 = 111$. Eliminate (G). Choice (H) becomes $1,776 \div 18 = 98.\overline{66}$. This is not an integer, so 18 is not a factor of 1,776. The correct answer is (H).

7. **C**   The question asks for a probability, which is defined as $\dfrac{want}{total}$. Read the question carefully to find

the numbers for *want* and *total*. There is only one student, Lauren, that the probability refers to, so

the number for *want* is 1. The student selected must NOT be a senior. Of the students in the class, 4

are seniors, so 19 – 4 = 15 are NOT seniors. Lauren is NOT a senior, so the *total* is 15. Therefore, the

probability that Lauren is chosen is $\dfrac{1}{15}$. The correct answer is (C).

8. **K**   The question asks for the value of *x*. Since the question asks for a specific value and the answers
contain numbers in increasing order, Plugging In the Answers is an option. Begin by labeling the
answers as "*x*" and start in the middle with (H), 9. The equation becomes 4(9 – 5) + 9 = 45. Simplify
the left side of the equation to 4(4) + 9 = 45, then to 16 + 9 = 45, and finally 25 = 45. This is not true,
so eliminate (H). Because the result was too small, try a larger number like (K), 13. The equation
becomes 4(13 – 5) + 9 = 45, which simplifies to 4(8) + 13 = 45, and then to 32 + 13 = 45. This is true,
so stop here. Another way to answer this is to solve for *x* algebraically. Start by distributing on the left
side of the equation to get 4*x* – 20 + *x* = 45. Then combine like terms to get 5*x* – 20 = 45. Add 20 to
both sides of the equation to get 5*x* = 65; then divide both sides by 5 to get *x* = 13. Either way, the
correct answer is (K).

9. **B**   The question asks for an expression that models a specific situation. Translate the English to math in
Bite-Sized Pieces and eliminate after each piece. The number of miles will be represented as *m*, and
Joe pays *$0.99 for each mile he drives*. Therefore, the cost for the miles can be represented as 0.99*m*.
Eliminate (C), (D), and (E), because these don't include this expression. The question also states that
there is a charge of *$112 for the weekend*, so that must be added to the cost. Choice (A) subtracts 112
instead of adding it, so eliminate (A). The correct answer is (B).

10. **K**   The question asks how much more than the purchase price Stella will pay with the payment plan.
Calculate her cost with the plan, on which she pays *$130 a month for 4 years*. There are 12 months in
a year, so Stella will make payments for 4 × 12 = 48 months. Multiply the amount per month by the
number of months to get a total payment of $130(48) = $6,240. The phrase *how much more* means
to subtract, so subtract the purchase price from the amount Stella pays with the payment plan. This
results in a difference of $6,240 – $4,800 = $1,440. The correct answer is (K).

11. **B**   The question asks for an equivalent expression with exponents. Work in Bite-Sized Pieces and use
Process of Elimination. Start with the coefficients. The 20 in the numerator will be divided by the
4 in the denominator to get a coefficient of 5. Eliminate (D) and (E), because those do not include
5. Now work with the exponents, remembering the MADSPM rules. The DS part of the acronym
indicates that Dividing matching bases means to Subtract the exponents. The *y* term becomes $y^{8-2} = y^6$.
Eliminate (A) and (C). The correct answer is (B).

12. **F**   The question asks for a value that is equal to the given fraction. The most accurate way to handle this is to turn the fractions within the numerator and the denominator into decimals and use a calculator to find the value of the fraction. The $\frac{1}{2}$ in the numerator can be written as 0.5, and the $\frac{3}{4}$ in the denominator can be written as 0.75. The entire fraction becomes $\frac{3-0.5}{2+0.75} = \frac{2.5}{2.75}$. Use a calculator to find that this is equal to $0.\overline{90}$. This is less than 1, so the answer must be (F). To verify that (F) is less than 1, calculate $\frac{10}{11}$, which does equal $0.\overline{90}$. The correct answer is (F).

13. **D**   The question asks for the possible locations of D on a number line. Use the Geometry Basic Approach. Start by drawing a number line and labeling it with Point C at 3.5. Add 8.5 to find the point to the right of C at 3.5 + 8.5 = 12. Eliminate (A), (B), and (C), because these do not contain the value 12. Now subtract 8.5 from 3.5 to find the point to the left of C at 3.5 − 8. 5 = −5. Eliminate (E). The correct answer is (D).

14. **K**   The question asks for the fourth number in a set with a mean of 7. Since the question asks for a specific value and the answers contain numbers in increasing order, Plugging In the Answers is an option. Begin by labeling the answers as "fourth number" and start in the middle with (H), 8. Use the formula $T = AN$, in which T is the total, A is the average, and N is the number of things to calculate the average with the answer choice as the fourth number. If the four numbers are 2, 4, 8, and 10, the total is 2 + 4 + 8 + 10 = 24. There are 4 numbers, so the formula becomes 24 = A(4). Divide both sides of the equation by 4 to get A = 6. According to the question, the average is 7, so this is wrong. Eliminate (H). The result was too small, so try a larger number, like (K), 12. Now the total becomes 2 + 4 + 10 + 12 = 28. The number of things is still 4, so the formula becomes 28 = A(4). Divide both sides by 4 to get A = 7. This matches the value given in the question, so stop here. Another option is to use $T = AN$ to find the total. The average is 7, and the number of things is 4, so T = (7)(4) = 28. The three numbers already on the list are 2, 4, and 10, which add up to 16. The fourth number must be the difference between the total of the given three numbers and the total of all four numbers, so the fourth number is 28 − 16 = 12. Either way, the correct answer is (K).

15. **A**   The question asks for the net profit in 2008 given the trend from 2007 to 2009. The net profit in 2007 was $1,489,000, and the net profit in 2009 was $1,725,000. If the net profit *increased linearly*, then the net profit for 2008 must be between these two values. Eliminate (D) and (E), both of which are greater than $1,725,000. Now find the value exactly in between the given ones by adding those together and dividing the sum by 2. This becomes $\frac{\$1,489,000 + \$1,725,000}{2} = \frac{\$3,214,000}{2} = \$1,607,000$. The correct answer is (A).

16. **F**   The question asks for a measurement and gives conflicting units. When dealing with scale maps or models, make a proportion, being sure to match up dimensions. The proportion is $\dfrac{10 \text{ inches tall}}{6 \text{ feet tall}} = \dfrac{8 \text{ inches wide}}{x \text{ feet wide}}$. Cross-multiply to get $10x = 48$. Divide both sides of the equation by 10 to get $x = 4.8$ feet wide. The question asks for the approximate width, so round to 5 feet. The correct answer is (F).

17. **B**   The question asks for the equation of a line in *slope-intercept form*. In this form, $y = mx + b$, so solve the given equation for y. Start by adding y to both sides of the equation to get $5x = y + 2$. Subtract 2 from both sides to get $5x - 2 = y$, and then switch the sides of the equation to get $y = 5x - 2$. The correct answer is (B).

18. **J**   The question asks for a value equal to the given expression, so simplify the expression. With absolute values, work inside the absolute value symbol first. The expression becomes $|-12| - |-25|$. Next, make the values inside the absolute values positive. This becomes $12 - 25 = -13$. The correct answer is (J).

19. **D**   The question asks for the best descriptor of an angle in a triangle. Use the Geometry Basic Approach. Start by drawing a triangle and labeling it with the given information. Make $\angle K$ exactly 63° for simplicity. It will look like this:

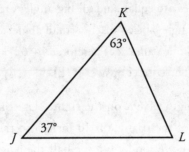

There are 180° in a triangle, so the measure of $\angle L$ is $180° - 37° - 63° = 80°$. Eliminate (A) and (B) based on this calculation. Choices (C), (D), and (E) all include the possibility that $\angle L$ is 80°, so try a different measure for $\angle K$, such as 60°. The new measure of $\angle L$ is $180° - 37° - 60° = 83°$. Eliminate (C) and (E). The correct answer is (D).

20. **K**   The question asks for the least possible integer value of *x*. One option is to solve the inequality for *x*. Start by adding 1 to both sides of the inequality to get $3x > 27$. Divide both sides by 3 to get $x > 9$. The only choice that is greater than 9 is 10, which is (K). Since the question asks for a specific value and the answers contain numbers in increasing order, Plugging In the Answers is also an option. Begin by labeling the answers as "*x*" and start with (F), 6, because that is the least value. The inequality becomes $3(6) - 1 > 26$, which simplifies to $18 - 1 > 26$ or $17 > 26$. This is not true, so eliminate (F). The value on the left of the inequality was much too small, so consider skipping (G) and trying a greater number next, such as 8 in (H). The inequality becomes $3(8) - 1 > 26$, which becomes $24 - 1 > 26$, or $23 > 26$. This is not true and is still too small on the left side, so try (J) next. If $x = 9$, the inequality becomes $3(9) - 1 > 26$, then $27 - 1 > 26$, or $26 > 26$. This is still not true, so the value of *x* must be greater than 9. Try 10 just to be certain: the inequality becomes $3(10) - 1 > 26$, then $30 - 1 > 26$, and finally $29 > 26$. This is true. Either way, the correct answer is (K).

21. **E**   The question asks for the measure of an angle on a figure. Use the Geometry Basic Approach. Start by ballparking. The angle labeled 62° is smaller than the one asked for, so the answer must be greater than 62. Eliminate (A). The angle in question also looks to be obtuse, or greater than 90°, so it is likely safe to eliminate (B) and (C) as well. Next, label the figure with the given information, which is that the two gray bars representing red ribbons are parallel. When parallel lines are cut by a third line (or a set of parallel lines such as the edges of the white ribbon), two kinds of angles are created: big and small. All small angles are equal, and all big angles are equal. The sum of any big angle and any small angle is 180°. The angle labeled 62° is a small angle, and the angle labeled with the question mark is a big angle, which can be called *x*. Therefore, $x + 62° = 180°$. Subtract 62° from both sides of the equation to get $x = 118°$. The correct answer is (E).

22. **G**   The question asks for the length of $\overline{QR}$ on the figure. Use the Geometry Basic Approach. Start by ballparking: the hypotenuse of the triangle is 10 inches, so the length of $\overline{PR}$ must be less than that. Eliminate (J) and (K), as both are too long to be half the length of one leg on the triangle. Use the Pythagorean Theorem ($a^2 + b^2 = c^2$) or recognize that this triangle is a Pythagorean triple (6:8:10) to find that $\overline{PR}$ is 6 inches long. Label $\overline{PR}$ as 6. Because point *Q* is the midpoint of $\overline{PR}$, it divides this length in half, so $\overline{QR} = 6 \div 2 = 3$. The correct answer is (G).

23. **A**   The question asks for the difference in the weights of two textbooks. Look up the values on the graph. The number of pages is on the *x*-axis, and the weight in ounces is on the *y*-axis. For a book with an *x*-value of 1,056 pages, the corresponding *y*-value is 107.8 ounces. For a book with an *x*-value of 868 pages, the corresponding *y*-value is 89 ounces. The phrase *how much more* means to subtract, so this becomes $107.8 - 89 = 18.8$ ounces. The correct answer is (A).

24. **G**   The question asks for the weight of a textbook in pounds given an equation relating the number of pages to the weight in ounces. Start by plugging the number of pages into the equation $y = 0.1x + 2.2$ to get the weight in ounces. The *x*-value is the number of pages, so the equation becomes $y = 0.1(1,338) + 2.2 = 133.8 + 2.2 = 136$ ounces. The question asks for the weight in pounds, so

convert ounces to pounds. The note below the question states that there are 16 ounces in a pound, so set up a proportion, being sure to match the units: $\frac{16 \text{ ounces}}{1 \text{ pound}} = \frac{136 \text{ ounces}}{x \text{ pounds}}$. Cross-multiply to get $16x = 136$; then divide by 16 to get $x = 8.5$. The correct answer is (G).

25. **D** The question asks for the area of a polygon. Use the Geometry Basic Approach. There is a figure provided and it is labeled, so use the formulas for area. There is no formula for the area of an irregular shape like this, so divide the figure into rectangles. One way to do it is like this:

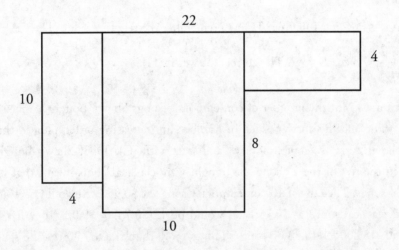

Then write out the formula for the area of a rectangle: $A = lw$. For the rectangle on the left side of the figure, the formula becomes $A = (10)(4) = 40$. Now figure out the other dimensions. The length across the top of the figure is 22. Since all lines meet at right angles, the horizontal lengths across the lower part of the figure must all be parallel to the top and must cover the same distance. Therefore, for the rectangle on the right side of the figure, the width will be $22 - 4 - 10 = 8$. Label the figure with this information. For that rectangle, the area formula becomes $A = (8)(4) = 32$. Now find the missing dimension on the rectangle in the middle of the figure. Just as the horizontal dimensions of the overall figure were the same, the vertical dimensions will all be the same. Therefore, the sum of the vertical sides on the right have the same measurement as the missing side of the middle rectangle. This becomes $4 + 8 = 12$, and the area of that rectangle becomes $A = (12)(10) = 120$. Now add the areas of all three rectangles to get the total area as $40 + 32 + 120 = 192$. The correct answer is (D).

26. **F** The question asks for the average speed for part of the time Mr. Baylor spent grading essays. Use the formula $T = AN$, in which T is the total, A is the average, and N is the number of things. For the first 3 days, the average is 178 and the number of things is 3, so $T = (178)(3) = 534$. The total for all 6 days is 996, so subtract the total he graded over the first 3 days to find that he graded $996 - 534 = 462$ essays in the final 3 days. Use the average formula again with a total of 462 and a number of things of 3 to get $462 = A(3)$; then divide both sides of the equation by 3 to get $A = 154$. The correct answer is (F).

27. **C** The question asks for an equivalent expression. Although there are variables in the answer choices, plugging in on this question might be difficult, given several terms and negative signs. Instead, distribute each term in the first set of parentheses to each in the second set, being careful with the signs. The result is $y^3 - 3y^2 + 2y + y^2 - 3y + 2$. Combine like terms to get $y^3 - 2y^2 - y + 2$. The correct answer is (C).

28. **H** The question asks for a trigonometric expression that relates to angle D and has a value of $\frac{4}{5}$. In relation to angle D, the side labeled as 4 is the adjacent side, and the side labeled as 5 is the hypotenuse. Write out SOHCAHTOA to remember the trig functions. The CAH part defines cosine as $\frac{adjacent}{hypotenuse}$, so $\cos D = \frac{4}{5}$. The correct answer is (H).

29. **A** The question asks for the number of contemporary songs Shawn bought. Since the question asks for a specific value and the answers contain numbers in increasing order, plug in the answers. Begin by labeling the answers as "contemporary" and start with (C), 10. If Shawn bought 10 contemporary songs, then the rest of the 22 songs he bought were classical. This means that he bought $22 - 10 = 12$ classical songs. The cost of 10 contemporary songs at \$0.95 each would be $10(\$0.95) = \$9.50$. The cost of 12 classical songs at \$0.75 each would be $12(\$0.75) = \$9.00$. Together, Shawn would have spent $\$9.50 + \$9.00 = \$18.50$ on songs. This is more than the \$17.90 that he spent, so eliminate (C). To bring Shawn's total cost down, he needs to buy more of the cheaper songs, which means more classical and fewer contemporary. Eliminate (D) and (E), as these will only increase Shawn's cost. Try (B), 9. If Shawn bought 9 contemporary songs, then he bought $22 - 9 = 13$ classical songs. The cost of 9 contemporary songs would be $9(\$0.95) = \$8.55$. The cost of 13 classical songs would be $13(\$0.75) = \$9.75$. Together, Shawn would have spent $\$8.55 + \$9.75 = \$18.30$ on songs. This is still more than the \$17.90 that he spent, so eliminate (B). Because the result of (B) was less than the result of (C), a smaller starting value is needed. Only one smaller answer remains. The correct answer is (A).

30. **G** The question asks for the value of operation $(-3)\#(-7)$ as defined as $x \# y = \frac{x^2 - y^2}{x + y}$. Because the x value is to the left of the # sign and the y value is to the right, $x = -3$ and $y = -7$. Plug these values into the operation to get $\frac{(-3)^2 - (-7)^2}{(-3) + (-7)}$, which simplifies to $\frac{9 - 49}{-10} = \frac{-40}{-10} = 4$. The correct answer is (G).

31. **C** The question asks for the fraction of the punch that is pineapple juice. To make this fraction, put the quantity of pineapple juice in the numerator and the quantity of punch in the denominator. Making a fraction with mixed numbers and fractions in both the numerator and denominator can be tricky, so convert both numbers to decimals. The quantity of pineapple juice can be written as 0.5 gallons, and the quantity of punch can be written as 2.25 gallons. The fraction becomes $\frac{0.5}{2.25}$. Use a calculator

to find that this is $0.\overline{2}$. Now use the calculator to see which answer choice also has this value. Choice (A) becomes $0.\overline{1}$, so eliminate (A). Choice (B) becomes $0.\overline{16}$, so eliminate (B). Choice (C) becomes $0.\overline{2}$. This matches the calculation above, so stop here. The correct answer is (C).

32. **G**   The question asks for the area of a triangle inscribed in a circle. Use the Geometry Basic Approach. Start by labeling the figure with the given information. Label $\overline{XZ}$ as 8 and $\overline{OX}$ as equal to $\overline{XY}$. Next, write the formula for the area of a triangle: $A = \frac{1}{2}bh$. A base and a height are needed for the triangle, so try to determine some of the other measurements. If $\overline{XZ}$ is a diameter, then $\overline{OX}$ is a radius and is half the diameter, or 4. Label $\overline{OX}$ and $\overline{XY}$ as 4. When a triangle is drawn in a circle such that one side of the triangle is also the diameter of the circle, and the point opposite that side is on the circle, a right triangle is created with the diameter as the hypotenuse. This means that angle Y is 90° and, because $\overline{XY}$ and $\overline{YZ}$ meet at a right angle, they can be used as the base and the height of the triangle. $\overline{XY}$ has already been marked with a length of 4, so the height is 4. The hypotenuse $\overline{XZ}$ has also been marked with a length of 8. Use the Pythagorean Theorem ($a^2 + b^2 = c^2$) or the fact that the measures of $\overline{XY}$ and $\overline{XZ}$ indicate that this is a 30°-60°-90° triangle to find that the length of $\overline{YZ}$ is $4\sqrt{3}$. The area formula becomes $A = \frac{1}{2}(4\sqrt{3})(4) = 8\sqrt{3}$. The correct answer is (G).

33. **C**   The question asks for one of the roots of the quadratic equation, or the value of y that will make the equation true. Since the question asks for a specific value and the answers contain numbers in increasing order, Plugging In the Answers is an option. Begin by labeling the answers as "y" and start with (C), –2. The equation becomes $(-2)^2 - 4(-2) - 5 = 7$. This simplifies to $4 + 8 - 5 = 7$ or $7 = 7$. This is true, so stop here. Another option is to get the equation into the standard form, $ax^2 + bx + c = 0$, and then solve it. Subtract 7 from both sides of the equation to get $y^2 - 4y - 12 = 0$. To factor this, look for a pair of numbers that multiply to –12 and add to –4. These values are –6 and 2. The equation becomes $(y - 6)(y + 2) = 0$. Setting each binomial equal to 0 and solving results in roots of $y = 6$ and $y = -2$. Only one of these is an answer choice. Either way, the correct answer is (C).

34. **G**   The question asks for the volume of a plastic model of a house. Use the Geometry Basic Approach. There is a figure provided and it is labeled, so use the formulas for volume. There is not a formula for this shape, but formulas are given for the shape of the pyramid and the rectangular prism it sits on. Start with the rectangular prism, for which $V = lwh$. The length and width are both 20, and the height is 16, so the formula becomes $V = (20)(20)(16) = 6,400$. Now focus on the pyramid, for which

$V = \frac{1}{3}lwh$. For this shape, the length and width are also 20, and the height is 12, so the formula

becomes $V = \frac{1}{3}(20)(20)(12) = 1,600$. The volume of the model will be the sum of the volumes of the

rectangular prism and the pyramid, so this becomes $6,400 + 1,600 = 8,000$. The correct answer is (G).

35. **B**   The question asks for the area of a trapezoid. Use the Geometry Basic Approach. Start by drawing a
trapezoid and labeling it with the given information. It will look like this:

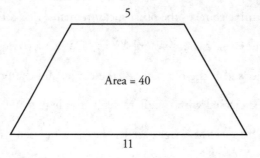

Solve for the area by dividing the trapezoid into a rectangle and two triangles. The base that is 11
inches long can be divided into 3 + 5 + 3 inches. It will look like this:

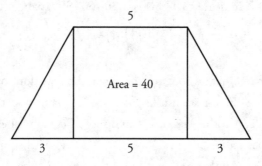

The formula for the area of a rectangle is $A = lw$ or bh, and the formula for the area of a triangle

is $A = \frac{1}{2}bh$. The area of the trapezoid will be the area of the rectangle plus the area of the two

triangles. Both the rectangle and the triangles have the same height. Plug in the known information

to get $40 = 5h + \frac{1}{2}(3)h + \frac{1}{2}(3)h$. This simplifies to $40 = 5h + 3h$ or $40 = 8h$. Divide both sides of the

equation by 8 to get $h = 5$. Either way, the correct answer is (B).

36. **J**   The question asks for the slope of a line in the coordinate plane given two points (–2, 6) and (3, –9).

Use the formula $slope = \frac{y_2 - y_1}{x_2 - x_1}$ with the given points to get $slope = \frac{6 - (-9)}{-2 - 3} = \frac{15}{-5} = -3$. The correct

answer is (J).

37. **D** The question asks for the measure of an angle in a triangle. Use the Geometry Basic Approach. Start by drawing an isosceles right triangle, which has two equal legs. Label it with the given information. The question states that there is a right angle at X, so legs $\overline{WX}$ and $\overline{XY}$ are equal. The figure will look like this:

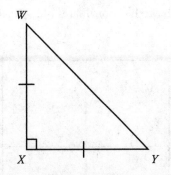

The question states that point Z is *collinear with points X and Y*. The word *collinear* means "on the same line," and the question states that Y is *between X and Z*. Add point Z to the figure.

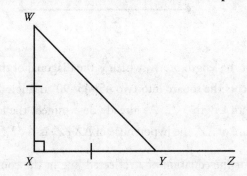

The question asks for the measure of $\angle WYZ$, which makes up a straight line with $\angle XYW$. There are 180° in a line, so find the measure of $\angle XYW$ and subtract it from 180°. Because ΔWXY is isosceles, the two smaller angles are equal and measure 45° each. Therefore, $\angle XYW$ is 45° and $\angle WYZ = 180° - 45° = 135°$. The correct answer is (D).

38. **H** The question asks for a certain digit in a repeating decimal. Determine the pattern of the repeating decimal rather than trying to write it out to the 99th place to the right of the decimal. There are 6 numbers before the pattern repeats: 384615. This pattern of 6 numbers will repeat, so every 6th digit will be the last number in the pattern: 5. Look for a multiple of 6 that is near 99. The closest one is 96, so the 96th digit is 5. Following the pattern, the 97th digit is 3, the 98th digit is 8, and the 99th digit is 4. The correct answer is (H).

39. **E** The question asks for the length of a line segment in the coordinate plane. Use the Geometry Basic Approach. Start by drawing a coordinate plane and plotting the given points. Use the coordinates of the three given points to find the location of point Z, the fourth vertex of the square. Using points X and W, the side of the square is $2 - (-2) = 2 + 2 = 4$. Thus, point Z must be 4 units away from both point W and point Y and will have the coordinates $(-2, -2)$. The figure will look like this:

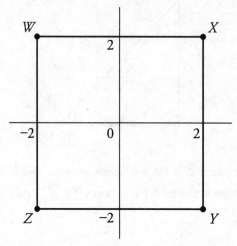

The question asks for the length of $\overline{XZ}$, which is the diagonal of the square. Draw this line on the figure. A square's diagonal cuts the square into two 45°-45°-90° triangles, each of which has legs with length s and a hypotenuse with length $s\sqrt{2}$. As already determined, the length of s, the side of the square, is 4. Therefore, the measure of $\overline{XZ}$, the hypotenuse of $\triangle XYZ$, is $4\sqrt{2}$. The correct answer is (E).

40. **G** The question asks for the equation of a reflected line in the coordinate plane. Start by sketching the original graph or graphing it on a graphing calculator. It will look like this:

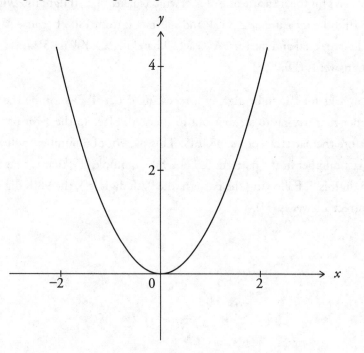

A graph that is *reflected* over the *x*-axis is flipped over that axis as if that axis were a mirror. The new graph will look like this:

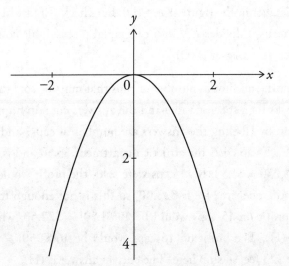

The shape of the new graph is still a parabola, so it must still have an x^2 term. Eliminate (J) and (K), which do not contain that term. The equation in (F) is the same as the original equation, so that cannot represent the reflected graph. Eliminate (F). To decide between (G) and (H), plug in points or graph the equations on a graphing calculator. Since the graph represents the equation $y = x^2$, it contains the point (1, 1). The new graph, therefore, contains the point (1, –1). Plug $x = 1$ into the remaining answers to see which results in a *y*-value of –1. Choice (G) becomes $y = -(1^2) = -1$, and (H) becomes $y = (-1)^2 = 1$. Only (G) provides the correct value for *y*. The correct answer is (G).

41. **D**   The question asks for a true statement based on a geometric figure. Use the Geometry Basic Approach. A figure is provided, but when determining what *must be true*, it is often necessary to redraw it based on the information given. The question states that $\overline{JK}$ is parallel to $\overline{MN}$. A new figure with the same information could look like this:

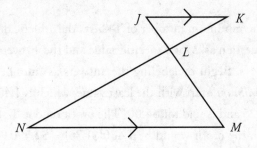

When parallel lines are cut by a third line, two kinds of angles are created: big and small. All small angles are equal, and all big angles are equal. Because $\overline{JK}$ is parallel to $\overline{MN}$, $\angle K$ is equal to $\angle N$, and $\angle J$ is equal to $\angle M$. The remaining angles in the two triangles are also equal, because they are opposite one another. Now use Process of Elimination on the answer choices. Choice (A) says that $\overline{JK}$ and $\overline{MN}$ are equal. Though they appear to be in the original drawing, the new drawing shows that they are not necessarily equal. Eliminate (A). Choice (B) says that $\overline{JL}$ and $\overline{LM}$ are equal, but this is not necessarily true either. Eliminate (B). Choice (C) says that the two triangles are congruent. Again, the new drawing shows that while they could be, they don't have to be. Eliminate (C). Choice (D) says that the two triangles are *similar*. Similar triangles have the same angles and proportional sides, and this is true of the triangles in the figure. Keep (D), but check (E) just in case. Choice (E) says that $\overline{JM}$ bisects $\overline{KN}$, which means it divides $\overline{KN}$ into two equal pieces. This could be true but could be false. Eliminate (E). The correct answer is (D).

42. **H**   The question asks for the minimum number of caps that must be sold to cover the one-time rental fee. Since the question asks for a specific value and the answers contain numbers in increasing order, plug in the answers. Begin by labeling the answers as "number of caps" and start with the smallest value, which is 14 in (F). Each cap costs the athletic department $3.50 and is sold for $5.00. The profit on one hat is $5.00 − $3.50 = $1.50. If 14 caps were sold, the profit would be 14($1.50) = $21.00. The question states that the one-time fee is $23.00, so this is not enough to cover the fee. Eliminate (F). Try (G) next. The profit on 15 caps would be 15($1.50) = $22.50, which is still not quite enough. Eliminate (G). Try (H). The profit on 16 caps would be 16($1.50) = $24, which makes the profit enough to cover the $23 fee, so stop here. The correct answer is (H).

43. **A**   The question asks for the percent by which the budget gap would have been filled if the price of each adult ticket had been raised by $2.00. Translate the English to math, reading carefully, and use Bite-Sized Pieces. The department sold 540 tickets, and 60% of those were adult tickets. Take 60% of 540 to find that the number of adult tickets sold was $\frac{60}{100}(540) = 324$. An increase of $2 per ticket would result in increased revenue of $2(324) = $648. The question states that the budget gap was $3,000. To find the percent that 648 is out of 3,000, divide the numbers and multiply by 100 to get $\frac{648}{3,000} \times 100 = 21.6\%$. The question asks for an approximate percent, so round this to 22%. The correct answer is (A).

44. **J**   The question asks for the minimum number of T-shirts the athletic department sold if they filled the budget gap. Since the question asks for a specific value and the answers contain numbers in increasing order, plug in the answers. Begin by labeling the answers as "number of T-shirts" and, because the question asks for the *minimum*, start with the least value, which is 1,480 in (F). Each T-shirt costs the athletic department $2.25 and is sold for $4.00. The profit on one T-shirt is $4.00 − $2.25 = $1.75. If 1,480 T-shirts were sold, the profit would be 1,480($1.75) = $2,590.00. The question states that the budget gap is $3,000, and they must also pay the one-time rental fee of $19.00. This is not enough to fill the gap and cover the fee. Eliminate (F). Because the result using the value in (F) is much too small, consider skipping (G) and trying the value in (H) next. If 1,709 T-shirts were sold, the profit would be 1,709($1.75) = $2,990.75, which is still not enough. Eliminate (G) and (H). Try (J). If 1,726 T-shirts were sold, the profit would be 1,726($1.75) = $3,020.50, which is enough to cover the budget gap and the fee, so stop here. The correct answer is (J).

45. **C** The question asks for the area of a triangle formed within a parabola in the coordinate plane. Use the Geometry Basic Approach. A figure is provided, but the triangle is not drawn, so start by connecting points *D, E,* and *O.* Then write out the formula for the area of a triangle: $A = \frac{1}{2}bh$. The base and height must be perpendicular, so make $\overline{DE}$ the base, and make the distance on the *x*-axis from *O* to $\overline{DE}$ the height. The base goes from $y = 2$ to $y = -2$, so the base is $2 - (-2) = 2 + 2 = 4$. Points *D* and *E* appear to have *y*-coordinates of 2 and –2, respectively, but check by plugging $x = 4$ into the equation. If $y^2 = 4$, then $y = \pm 2$. Thus, the height is also $2 - (-2) = 2 + 2 = 4$. Now plug the values for the base and height into the formula to get $A = \frac{1}{2}(4)(4) = 8$. The correct answer is (C).

46. **K** The question asks for the length of $\overline{YZ}$ in the triangle. Use the Geometry Basic Approach. There is a figure provided and it is labeled, so move on to the formula. The Law of Sines is provided, so use it to find the length of $\overline{YZ}$, which is opposite angle *X.* The length of $\overline{XY}$ is given, so use that and the measure of its opposite angle *Z* to set up the proportion. This becomes $\frac{\sin X}{YZ} = \frac{\sin Z}{XY}$. Plug in the information from the figure to get $\frac{\sin 68°}{YZ} = \frac{\sin 53°}{12}$; then use the note to plug in the values for the numerators. This becomes $\frac{0.927}{YZ} = \frac{0.799}{12}$. Cross-multiply to get $0.799(YZ) = 11.124$; then divide both sides of the equation by 0.799 to get $YZ = 13.9224$. This rounds to 13.9. The correct answer is (K).

47. **C** The question asks for solutions to $x = 3 \pm \sqrt{(-1)(16c^2)}$ expressed as complex numbers. Use Bite-Sized Pieces and Process of Elimination to tackle this question. All the answers start with $3 \pm$, so focus on the square root. To make it easier to see what can come out from under the root, factor the expression under the root symbol to $\sqrt{(-1)(16)(c^2)}$. The 16 and the c^2 are perfect squares, so these become 4 and *c*, respectively. Eliminate any answer that does not contain 4 and *c*, and only (C) remains. To check, bring those two terms in front of the root to leave $4c\sqrt{-1}$. The imaginary number *i* is defined as $\sqrt{-1}$, so this becomes $4ci$. The correct answer is (C).

48. **J** The question asks for the length of the diameter of a circle. Use the Geometry Basic Approach. Start by labeling the figure with the given information. Label *CD* as 12. It may be difficult to determine how to find the diameter, but this value is equal to 2 times the radius. The most useful radii to draw will be the ones that connect *O* to *C* and *O* to *D*, as this creates a triangle. To solve difficult Geometry questions, it is often necessary to use the information about one shape to determine the measurements of another shape. For the new triangle, the measure of the central angle *COD* equals the measure of the arc it creates, so $\angle COD = 60°$. The radii *CO* and *DO* are equal, so angles *OCD* and *ODC* are equal. There are 180° in a triangle, so there are $180° - 60° = 120°$ left for angles *OCD* and *ODC*. Because the angles are equal, each angle is $120° \div 2 = 60°$, so triangle *COD* is equilateral. Therefore, $CD = CO = DO = 12$. If the radius is 12, then the diameter is $2(12) = 24$. The correct answer is (J).

49. **E** The question asks for the distance between the pole and the point where the cord touches the ground. Use the Geometry Basic Approach. Start by drawing a pole and the cord and labeling it with the given information. Label the length of the cord as 25 feet and the angle it makes with the ground as 19°. It will look like this:

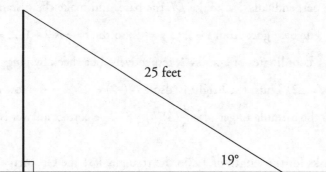

The question asks for the distance between the pole and the cord on the ground, so this is the base of the triangle. Label that as x. There are trigonometric expressions in the answer choices, so write out SOHCAHTOA to remember the trig functions. In relation to the angle that is 19°, the base of the triangle is the adjacent side, and the side labeled as 25 is the hypotenuse. The CAH part defines cosine as $\frac{adjacent}{hypotenuse}$, so $\cos 19° = \frac{x}{25}$. Multiply both sides of the equation by 25 to get $25 \cos 19° = x$. The correct answer is (E).

50. **F** The question asks for the coordinates of the center of a circle in the coordinate plane. The equation of a circle in standard form is $(x - h)^2 + (y - k)^2 = r^2$, in which (h, k) is the center and r is the radius. To get the given equation into this form, it is necessary to complete the square for the x terms and the y terms. Start by moving the constant 8 to the right side by subtracting it from both sides of the equation to get $x^2 + 8x + y^2 - 2y = -8$. To complete the square for x, take half the coefficient on the x term, square it, and then add it to both sides. The coefficient is 8, half that is 4, and the square of that is 16. Adding 16 to both sides results in $x^2 + 8x + 16 + y^2 - 2y = -8 + 16$. The x terms can now be written as $(x + 4)^2$. Set this equal to $(x - h)^2$ to find the x-coordinate of the center, h. This becomes $(x - h)^2 = (x + 4)^2$, so take the square root of both sides to get $x - h = x + 4$. Subtract x from both sides to get $-h = 4$, so $h = -4$. Eliminate (G), (H), (J), and (K), which do not have this as the x-coordinate. The correct answer is (F).

51. **C** The question asks for the day on which the measurement of the pool will indicate that it is less than half full. For long word problems, read carefully and use Bite-Sized Pieces. The question states that the depth of the pool is 8 feet and the volume of the pool is 13,000 gallons. Either measurement can be used to determine when the pool is *half full*: it will be when the water is at a depth of 4 feet or when the volume is 6,500 gallons. It may be easier to use smaller numbers, so focus on the depth. When Scott

measures it on Day 1, it is 10% less than it was when full, so the depth is $8 - \dfrac{10}{100}(8) = 8 - 0.8 = 7.2$ feet. Another way to think about this is that each day, the depth of the pool is 90% of the depth from the previous day. This can simplify the calculation that needs to be made for each day. When Scott measures it on Day 2, the depth is $(7.2)(0.9) = 6.48$ feet. On Day 3, the depth is $(6.48)(0.9) = 5.832$ feet. On Day 4, the depth is $(5.832)(0.9) = 5.2488$ feet. On Day 5, the depth is $(5.2488)(0.9) = 4.72392$ feet. This is still not *less than half full*, so eliminate (A), which indicates Day 5. On Day 6, the depth is $(4.72392)(0.9) = 4.251528$ feet. Eliminate (B). On Day 7, the depth is $(4.251528)(0.9) = 3.8263752$ feet. This is the first value less than 4, so the pool is *less than half full* on Day 7. The correct answer is (C).

52. **J**   The question asks for the value of a matrix. Although there are variables in the answer choices, plugging in on this question would be difficult, given four variables and complicated relationships among them. Instead, follow the definition given in the question to find the correct answer. In the equation $\begin{vmatrix} a & b \\ c & d \end{vmatrix} = ad - bc$, the values in the upper left and lower right are multiplied together, and then the product of the values in the upper right and lower left is subtracted from that. Doing the same with the expression $\begin{vmatrix} 2d & 2c \\ 2a & 2b \end{vmatrix}$ results in $(2d)(2b) - (2c)(2a)$. This simplifies to $4db - 4ca$. The correct answer is (J).

53. **D**   The question asks for the area of one circle within the figure. Use the Geometry Basic Approach. Start by labeling the figure with the given information. Label all four sides of the square as 24. Then write out the formula for the area of a circle: $A = \pi r^2$. To solve difficult Geometry questions, it is often necessary to use the information about one shape to determine the measurements of another shape. The circles are tangent to the square, which means that the length of a side of the square is equivalent to the sum of the diameters of two circles. All the circles are congruent, so each has a diameter of $24 \div 2 = 12$. The radius is half the diameter, so the radius is $12 \div 2 = 6$. Plug $r = 6$ into the area formula to get $A = \pi(6)^2 = 36\pi$. The correct answer is (D).

54. **F**   The question asks *how much more* one average value will be than another. For long word problems, read carefully and use Bite-Sized Pieces. The question says that Andy bought 30 comics at $28.95 each. The total he paid for them was $30(\$28.95) = \$868.50$. He will sell them when the value is *$600 more than he paid for them*. Add this to the total he paid to get $\$868.50 + \$600 = \$1,468.50$. To find the average value at that time, use the formula $T = AN$, in which T is the total, A is the average, and N is the number of things. The total is $1,468.50$, and the number of things is 30, so $\$1,468.50 = A(30)$. Divide both sides of the equation by 30 to get $\$48.95 = A$. Finally, to find *how much more* the average value has risen, find the difference between this and the current value of $34.35. The result is $\$48.95 - \$34.35 = \$14.60$. The correct answer is (F).

55. **B**   The question asks for the length of $\overline{BD}$ on the figure. Use the Geometry Basic Approach. There is a figure provided and it is labeled, so see what else can be determined from the figure. Since B, D, and all the points between them are *collinear*, $\overline{BD}$ is a straight line. This line is made up of the diameter of circle G and the diameter of circle K, but there is some overlap in the middle. For circle G, diameter $\overline{AC}$ is labeled as 18, so diameter $\overline{BJ}$ is also 18. Label this on the figure. For circle K, diameter $\overline{CE}$ is labeled as 10, so diameter $\overline{HD}$ is also 10. Label this on the figure as well. Now it is possible to see that the overlap is the length of $\overline{HJ}$, which has a length of 3. Therefore, the length of $\overline{BD}$ is the sum of the length of $\overline{BJ}$ and only the part of $\overline{HD}$ that is not already contained in $\overline{BJ}$. This second part is $10 - 3 = 7$, so $\overline{BD} = 18 + 7 = 25$. The correct answer is (B).

56. **J**   The question asks for the other point at which the parabola crosses the y-axis. Start by drawing a coordinate plane and plotting the given points. Use a calculator to determine that $\left(0, -2 + 3\sqrt{3}\right)$ is approximately $(0, 3.2)$. Connect the points and use them to sketch the parabola. Also draw the line of symmetry at $y = -2$. It will look like this:

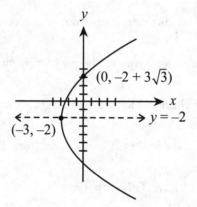

As shown in the sketch, the other point at which the parabola crosses the y-axis has a negative y-value. Eliminate (F), which indicates that there is not another y-intercept, and (G), which makes the second y-intercept positive. Choice (K) also cannot be correct, because there is a line of symmetry and both y-intercepts will be an equal distance from that line. Eliminate (K). Rather than trying to calculate the exact value of the missing y-intercept, use a calculator to estimate the locations of the points in the remaining answers. Choice (H) becomes approximately $(0, -3.2)$. Eliminate (H). Choice (J) becomes approximately $(0, -7.2)$. This is the only point that could work. The correct answer is (J).

57. **E**   The question asks for an equivalent expression to the one given. There is a variable in the answer choices, so plug in. Make $z = 2$. The expression becomes $\dfrac{3(2)}{4-2} + \dfrac{3(2)}{2^2 - 16}$, which simplifies to $\dfrac{6}{2} + \dfrac{6}{-12}$. To combine the fractions, move the negative in the second denominator to the front of that fraction and reduce that fraction. The expression becomes $\dfrac{6}{2} - \dfrac{1}{2} = \dfrac{5}{2}$. This is the target value; circle it. Now plug $z = 2$ into the answer choices to see which one matches the target value. Choice (A) becomes $\dfrac{3(2)^2 + 15(2)}{2^2 - 16} = \dfrac{12 + 30}{4 - 16} = \dfrac{42}{-12} = -\dfrac{14}{4}$. This does not match the target value. Eliminate (A).

The remaining choices all have the same denominator, so focus on the numerators. The numerator in (B) becomes $9(2)^2 - 12(2) = 9(4) - 24 = 36 - 24 = 12$. With a denominator of -12, this becomes $\frac{12}{-12} = -1$. Eliminate (B). The numerator in (C) becomes $-12(2) = -24$. With a denominator of -12, this becomes $\frac{-24}{-12} = 2$. Eliminate (C). The numerator in (D) becomes $-3(2)^2 = -3(4) = -12$. With a denominator of -12, this becomes $\frac{-12}{-12} = 1$. Eliminate (D). The numerator in (E) becomes $-3(2)^2 - 9(2) = -3(4) - 18 = -12 - 18 = -30$. With a denominator of -12, this becomes $\frac{-30}{-12} = \frac{5}{2}$, which matches the target value. The correct answer is (E).

58. **K**   The question asks for the value of tan θ. Use the Geometry Basic Approach. Start by labeling the figure with the given information, which is that the equation of the line is $y = -x$. Because this is the only information given, it must be the way to find the measurement of θ. The measure of θ plus the measure of the angle below the line and above the negative x-axis form a straight line and will add up to 180°. To find the measure of that smaller angle, draw a vertical line from a point on the line $y = -x$ down to the x-axis to form a triangle. Label the missing angle as *a*. It will look like this:

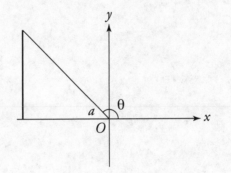

To find the lengths of the legs, find a point that is on the line $y = -x$ by plugging in for x. If $x = -2$, then $y = -(-2) = 2$. The point $(-2, 2)$ could be the top vertex of the triangle. With this point, the base of the triangle is 2 and the height is 2. The triangle is an isosceles right triangle, so angle *a* is 45°. This means that θ is $180° - 45° = 135°$. Now use a calculator in degree mode to find that tan 135° = −1. The correct answer is (K).

59. **A**   The question asks for the expression that gives *d* in terms of the other variables. Although there are variables in the answer choices, plugging in on this question would be difficult, given the four different variables. Solve this algebraically by isolating *d* instead. Start by subtracting a_1 from both sides of the equation to get $a_n - a_1 = dn - d$. Factor *d* out of both terms on the right side to get $a_n - a_1 = d(n - 1)$; then divide both sides by $(n - 1)$ to get $\frac{a_n - a_1}{n - 1} = d$. The correct answer is (A).

60. **H** The question asks for the equation to be solved for x in terms of y. There is a variable in the answer choices, so plug in for y and solve for x. Make $y = 4$ to make the square root on the left side of the equation easy to work with. The equation becomes $2\sqrt{x} \times 3\sqrt{4} = 12(4)$. This simplifies to $2\sqrt{x} \times 3(2) = 48$ or $12\sqrt{x} = 48$. Divide both sides of the equation by 12 to get $\sqrt{x} = 4$, and then square both sides to get $x = 16$. This is the target value; circle it. Now plug $y = 4$ into the answer choices to see which one matches the target value. Choice (F) becomes $2(4) = 8$. This does not match the target, so eliminate (F). Choice (G) becomes $3(4) = 12$. Eliminate (G). Choice (H) becomes $4(4) = 16$. Keep (H) but check the remaining answers just in case. Choice (J) becomes $6(4) = 24$ and (K) becomes $7(4) = 28$. Eliminate (J) and (K). The correct answer is (H).

Chapter 12
Practice Test 3

ACT MATHEMATICS TEST
60 Minutes—60 Questions

DIRECTIONS: Solve each problem, choose the correct answer, and then darken the corresponding oval on your answer document.

Do not linger over problems that take too much time. Solve as many as you can; then return to the others in the time you have left for this test.

You are permitted to use a calculator on this test. You may use your calculator for any problems you choose, but some of the problems may best be done without using a calculator.

Note: Unless otherwise stated, all of the following should be assumed:

1. Illustrative figures are NOT necessarily drawn to scale.

2. Geometric figures lie in a plane.

3. The word *line* indicates a straight line.

4. The word *average* indicates arithmetic mean.

---

1. Bob's Burgers charges $8 dollars for a hamburger and $5 for an order of French fries. Last month, h hamburgers and f orders of fries were purchased. Which of the following expressions gives the total amount of money, in dollars, Bob's Burgers earned on hamburgers and fries last month?

   A. $5h + 8f$
   B. $8h + 5f$
   C. $13(h + f)$
   D. $40(h + f)$
   E. $8(h + f) + 5f$

2. If $a = 8$, $b = -2$, and $c = 3$, what does $(a - b + c)(b + c)$ equal?

   F. -65
   G. -13
   H.   9
   J.   13
   K.   65

3. An artist at the State Fair paints 40 portraits per day. A second artist paints 50 portraits per day. The second artist opens for business three days after the first. Both remain open until the Fair closes, which is 11 days after the first artist began. How many total portraits will the two artists have painted when the Fair closes?

   A. 400
   B. 440
   C. 720
   D. 840
   E. 900

4. Josh has been a professional baseball player for four years. His home run totals each year have been 30, 39, 51, and 44, respectively. In order to maintain his current average number of home runs per season, how many home runs must Josh hit next year?

   F. 31
   G. 39
   H. 41
   J. 44
   H. 51

DO YOUR FIGURING HERE.

GO ON TO THE NEXT PAGE.

DO YOUR FIGURING HERE.

5. A craftswoman is paid $9.00 per necklace for making up to 30 necklaces per week. For each necklace over 30 that she is asked to make in a week, she is paid 1.5 times her regular pay. How much does she earn in a week in which she is asked to make 34 necklaces?

   A. $162
   B. $270
   C. $306
   D. $324
   E. $459

6. Which of the following mathematical expressions is equivalent to the verbal expression "The square root of a number, n, is 19 less than the value of 5 divided by n" ?

   F. $n^2 = \dfrac{5}{n} - 19$

   G. $n^2 = \dfrac{n}{5} - 19$

   H. $\sqrt{n} = 19 - \dfrac{n}{5}$

   J. $\sqrt{n} = \dfrac{y}{n} - 19$

   K. $\sqrt{n} = \dfrac{5}{n} - 19$

7. If $12(y - 3) = -7$, then $y = ?$

   A. $-\dfrac{43}{12}$

   B. $-\dfrac{10}{12}$

   C. $-\dfrac{7}{12}$

   D. $\dfrac{29}{12}$

   E. $\dfrac{43}{12}$

8. At a department store, purses sell for $12 each during a one-day sale. Rita spent $84 on purses during the sale, $38.50 less than if she had bought the purses at the regular price. How much does each purse cost at the regular price?

   F. $ 5.50
   G. $15.50
   H. $16.00
   J. $17.50
   K. $20.00

GO ON TO THE NEXT PAGE.

9. $(2a - 5b^2)(2a + 5b^2) =$

   A. $4a^2 - 25b^4$
   B. $4a^2 - 10b^4$
   C. $4a^2 + 25b^4$
   D. $2a^2 - 25b^4$
   E. $2a^2 - 10b^4$

DO YOUR FIGURING HERE.

10. A rectangle's perimeter is 18 feet, and its area is 18 square feet. What is the length of the longest side of the rectangle?

    F. 10
    G. 8
    H. 6
    J. 3
    K. 2

11. In $\triangle XYZ$, $\angle X$ is 64°. What is the sum of $\angle Y$ and $\angle Z$?

    A. 26°
    B. 64°
    C. 116°
    D. 126°
    E. 128°

12. Each morning, a glee club member chooses her outfit among 4 plaid skirts, 5 pairs of argyle socks, 3 sweaters, and 4 head-bands. How many different outfits can she put together on any given morning that consist of one skirt, one pair of socks, one sweater, and one headband?

    F. 4
    G. 15
    H. 16
    J. 120
    K. 240

13. Positive integers x, y, and z are consecutive such that $x < y < z$. The sum of x, $2y$, and $\frac{z}{2}$ is 59. What are the values of x, y, and z, respectively?

    A. 10, 11, 12
    B. 11, 12, 13
    C. 14, 15, 16
    D. 16, 17, 18
    E. 18, 19, 20

14. A function $h(x)$ is defined as $h(x) = -5x^3$. What is $h(-2)$?

    F. −1,000
    G. −40
    H. 30
    J. 40
    K. 1,000

GO ON TO THE NEXT PAGE.

DO YOUR FIGURING HERE.

15. If $z = \sqrt[4]{97}$, then which of the following must be true?

A. $2 < z < 3$
B. $3 < z < 4$
C. $4 < z < 5$
D. $5 < z < 6$
E. $6 < z$

16. What is the greatest common factor of 96, 108, and 144 ?

F. 12
G. 18
H. 24
J. 36
K. 48

17. Cowan Cola is holding a contest to develop a new, more environmentally efficient can for its soft drink. The winning can is a cylinder ten inches tall, with a volume of 40π cubic inches. What is the radius, in inches, of the can?

A. 1
B. 2
C. 4
D. 5
E. 8

18. A clock has 12 numbered points. Four points W, X, Y, Z lie on the clock representing certain numbers. W represents 3:00. X is 4 units clockwise from W. Y is 9 units counterclockwise from W. Z is 5 units counterclockwise from W and 7 units clockwise from W. What is the order of points, starting with W and working clockwise around the circle?

F. W, X, Y, Z
G. W, X, Z, Y
H. W, Y, X, Z
J. W, Y, Z, X
K. W, Z, Y, X

19. Tribbles reproduce at a rate described by the function $f(a) = 12(3)^a$, where a represents the number of days and $f(a)$ represents the number of tribbles. At this rate, how many tribbles will there be at the end of Day Four?

A. 48
B. 96
C. 240
D. 972
E. 1,296

GO ON TO THE NEXT PAGE.

20. The height of a triangle is half the height of a larger triangle. The two triangles have the same base. The area of the larger triangle is Y square feet. The area of the smaller triangle is xY square units. Which of the following is the value of x ?

F. $\dfrac{1}{4}$

G. $\dfrac{1}{2}$

H. 1

J. 2

K. 4

21. $(2x + 3y + 4z) - (6x - 7y + 8z)$ is equivalent to:

A. $-4x + 10y - 4z$
B. $-4x + 10y + 12z$
C. $-4x - 4y - 4z$
D. $-8x + 10y + 12z$
E. $-8x - 4y + 12z$

22. The right triangle shown below has lengths measured in inches. What is $\cos \theta$?

F. $\dfrac{x}{y}$

G. $\dfrac{x}{z}$

H. $\dfrac{y}{x}$

J. $\dfrac{y}{z}$

K. $\dfrac{z}{y}$

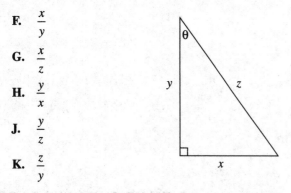

DO YOUR FIGURING HERE.

GO ON TO THE NEXT PAGE.

23. On a dead-end street, 8 houses are evenly spaced around a circular cul-de-sac. A newspaper delivery person bikes around the cul-de-sac and tosses the newspapers onto the driveway of each house. The delivery person bikes rapidly enough that the person can only toss to every third house. On which lap around the cul-de-sac will the delivery person have delivered newspapers to all 8 houses on the street?

- A. 2nd
- B. 3rd
- C. 4th
- D. 8th
- E. 11th

24. Lines q and m are in the standard (x,y) coordinate plane. The equation for line q is $y = 23x + 500$. The y-intercept of line m is 10 less than the y-intercept of line q. What is the y-intercept of line m ?

- F. 2.3
- G. 13
- H. 50
- J. 490
- K. 510

25. The expression $-9a^5(8a^7 - 4a^3)$ is equivalent to:

- A. $-36a^9$
- B. $-72a^{12} + 36a^8$
- C. $-72a^{12} - 36a^8$
- D. $-72a^{35} + 36a^{15}$
- E. $-72a^{35} - 36a^{15}$

26. $-4|-9 + 2| = ?$

- F. -44
- G. -28
- H. 3
- J. 28
- K. 44

GO ON TO THE NEXT PAGE.

27. In right triangle $\triangle WYZ$ shown below, $\overline{XV}$ is perpendicular to $\overline{WZ}$ at point V and is parallel to $\overline{YZ}$. Line segments $\overline{WY}$, $\overline{XV}$, and $\overline{WV}$ measure 30 inches, 6 inches, and 8 inches, respectively. What is the measurement, in inches, of $\overline{YZ}$?

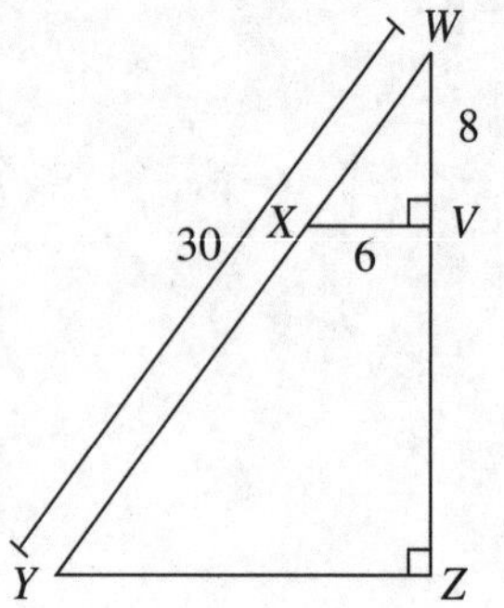

DO YOUR FIGURING HERE.

A. 15
B. 18
C. 20
D. 24
E. 27

28. As an experiment in botany class, students tracked a plant growing at a constant rate upward, perpendicular to the ground. As shown in the table below, they measured the height, h inches, of the plant at 1-week intervals from $w = 0$ weeks to $w = 4$ weeks.

w	0	1	2	3	4
h	7	10	13	16	19

Which of the following equations expresses this data?

F. $h = w + 7$
G. $h = 3w + 4$
H. $h = 3w + 7$
J. $h = 7w + 3$
K. $h = 10w$

29. The inequality $4(n-3) < 5(n+2)$ is equivalent to which of the following inequalities?

A. $n > -22$
B. $n > -14$
C. $n > -13$
D. $n > -2$
E. $n > 2$

GO ON TO THE NEXT PAGE.

30. The sides of an equilateral triangle are 4 inches long. One vertex of the triangle is at (1,1) on a coordinate graph labeled in inch units. Which of the following could give the coordinates of another vertex of the triangle?

   F. (–4, 1)
   G. (0, 1)
   H. (2, 3)
   J. (1,–3)
   K. (5,–3)

31. For △*LMN*, shown below, which of the following expresses the value of *m* in terms of *n* ?

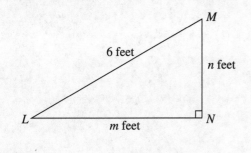

   A. $6 - n$
   B. $\sqrt{6 - n}$
   C. $\sqrt{12 + n^2}$
   D. $\sqrt{36 - n^2}$
   E. $\sqrt{36 + n^2}$

32. A jar holds 10 pear jellybeans, 16 cherry jellybeans, and 19 watermelon jellybeans. How many extra pear jellybeans must be added to the 45 jellybeans currently in the jar so that the probability of randomly selecting a pear jellybean is $\frac{3}{8}$?

   F. 9
   G. 11
   H. 21
   J. 35
   K. 45

GO ON TO THE NEXT PAGE.

33. The graph of the equation $6x + 3y = 12$ is found in which quadrants of the standard (x,y) coordinate plane below?

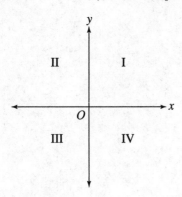

A. II and IV only
B. I, II, and III only
C. I, II, and IV only
D. I, III, and IV only
E. II, III, and IV only

34. The graph of $y = -2x^2 + 10$ contains the point $(3,4n)$ in the standard (x,y) coordinate plane. What is the value of n ?

F. 7
G. 1
H. -2
J. -4
K. -8

35. Jennifer, Kelly, and Meredith split their apartment rent. Jennifer paid $\frac{2}{3}$ of the rent, Kelly paid $\frac{1}{4}$ of the rent, and Meredith paid the rest. What is the ratio of Jennifer's contribution to Kelly's contribution to Meredith's contribution?

A. 1:3:8
B. 3:8:1
C. 3:1:8
D. 8:3:1
E. 8:1:3

GO ON TO THE NEXT PAGE.

36. In the standard (x,y) coordinate plane, a circle has an equation of $x^2 + (y+4)^2 = 28$. Which of the following gives the center and radius of the circle, in coordinate units?

	Center	Radius
F.	(0,–4)	$\sqrt{28}$
G.	(0,–4)	14
H.	(0,–4)	28
J.	(0, 4)	$\sqrt{28}$
K.	(0, 4)	14

37. An equilateral triangle and 2 semicircles have dimensions as shown in the figure below. What is the perimeter, in inches, of the figure?

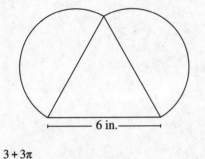

— 6 in. —

A. $3 + 3\pi$
B. $6 + 6\pi$
C. $6 + 12\pi$
D. $18 + 6\pi$
E. $18 + 12\pi$

38. In the figure below, points H, J, K, and L bisect the sides of rhombus $DEFG$, and point M is the intersection of $\overline{HK}$ and $\overline{JL}$. The area enclosed by $DEFG$ except the area enclosed by $HEFM$ is shaded. What is the ratio of the area of $HEFM$ to the area of the shaded area?

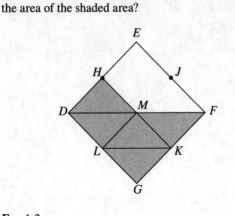

F. 1:2
G. 3:4
H. 3:5
J. 3:8
K. Cannot be determined from the given information

GO ON TO THE NEXT PAGE.

39. In the standard (x,y) coordinate plane, the endpoints of $\overline{FG}$ lie on the coordinates $(-6,10)$ and $(8,-2)$. What is the y-coordinate of the midpoint of $\overline{FG}$?

A. 1
B. 2
C. 4
D. 6
E. 8

40. What is the volume, in cubic feet, of a cube with a side of length 9 feet?

F. 729
G. 486
J. 243
H. 81
K. 27

41. The system below has linear equations, in which r, s, t, and v are positive integers.

$$rx + sy = t$$
$$rx + sy = v$$

Which of the following best describes a possible graph of such a system of equations in the standard (x,y) coordinate plane?

   I.   2 lines intersecting at only 1 point
  II.   1 single line
 III.   2 parallel lines

A. I only
B. III only
C. I and II only
D. II and III only
E. I and III only

GO ON TO THE NEXT PAGE.

42. Given the dimensions in the figure below, which of the following expresses the distance, in feet, from the tree to the house?

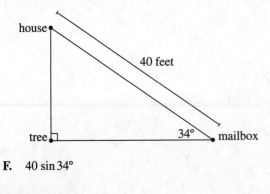

DO YOUR FIGURING HERE.

F. $40 \sin 34°$

G. $40 \cos 34°$

H. $40 \tan 34°$

J. $\dfrac{40}{\sin 34°}$

K. $\dfrac{40}{\cos 34°}$

43. The chart below shows the percentage of students, by grade, enrolled in a school. A student is picked randomly in a lottery to win a new graphing calculator. What are the odds (in the grade:not in the grade) that the winning student is in Grade 6 ?

Grade	5	6	7	8	9
Percentage of total number of students	12	22	25	27	14

A. 1:4
B. 1:5
C. 7:25
D. 11:39
E. 11:50

GO ON TO THE NEXT PAGE.

Use the following information to answer questions 44–46.

The figure below shows the pattern of a square tile mosaic to decorate the wall of Chelsea's Mexican Café. Grout fills the small spaces between individual tile pieces. All white triangular tiles are equilateral and share a vertex with each adjacent triangular piece. A green square piece is at the center of the mosaic. The length of the mosaic is 3 meters.

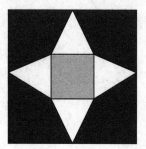

44. How many lines of symmetry in the plane does the pattern of the tile mosaic have?

F. 2
G. 3
H. 4
J. 8
K. Infinitely many

45. What is the length of the diagonal of the mosaic, to the nearest 0.1 meters?

A. 2.4
B. 3.0
C. 3.4
D. 4.2
E. 5.7

46. Joe wanted to put a tile mosaic on the wall of his office using a pattern identical to that in the restaurant. However, Joe realized that the length of the office wall is 20% shorter than the length of the mosaic. How many meters long is the office wall?

F. 0.6
G. 2.4
H. 2.8
J. 3.6
K. 6.0

GO ON TO THE NEXT PAGE.

47. In the figure below, $\overline{DE} \parallel \overline{FG}$, $\overline{DG}$ bisects $\angle HDE$, and $\overline{HG}$ bisects $\angle FGD$. If the measure of $\angle EDG$ is 68°, what is the measure of $\angle DHG$?

DO YOUR FIGURING HERE.

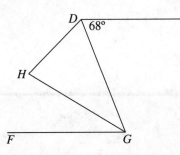

A. 68°
B. 78°
C. 80°
D. 82°
E. Cannot be determined from the given information

48. In the figure shown below, points A, B, and C lie on the circle with an area of 16π square meters and center O (not shown). $\overline{AC}$ is the longest chord in the circle, and the measure of $\overline{AB}$ is 4 meters. What is the degree measure of minor arc BC ?

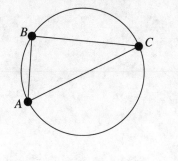

F. 60°
G. 90°
H. 120°
J. 145°
K. Cannot be determined from the given information

49. For which of the following values of b would the system of equations below have no solutions?

$$12x + 8y = 16$$

$$3x + by = 2$$

A. 2
B. 4
C. 8
D. 16
E. 32

GO ON TO THE NEXT PAGE.

Use the following information to answer questions 50–52.

Rebecca and Scott make and sell pies and cookies for school bake sales. It takes them 1 hour to make a dozen cookies and 3 hours to make a pie. The shaded triangular region shown below is the graph of a system of inequalities representing weekly constraints Rebecca and Scott have on their baking. For making and selling d dozen cookies and p pies, they make a profit of $12d + 25p$ dollars. They sell all the goods they bake.

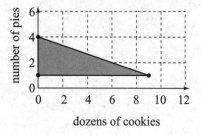

50. The constraint represented by the horizontal line segment containing (9,1) means that each school-week, Rebecca and Scott make a minimum of:

   F. 1 pie
   G. 9 pies
   H. 1 dozen cookies
   J. 9 dozen cookies
   K. 10 dozen cookies

51. What is the maximum profit Rebecca and Scott can earn from the baking they do in 1 school-week?

   A. $100
   B. $109
   C. $122
   D. $133
   E. $237

52. During the third week of October each year, school is closed for Fall Break, and Rebecca and Scott have more time than usual to bake. During that week, for every hour that they spend baking, they donate $2 to the school's fund for after-school reading programs. This year, they baked 5 pies and 3 dozen cookies during Fall Break. Which of the following is closest to the percent of that week's profit they donated to the reading program fund?

   F. 5%
   G. 9%
   H. 15%
   J. 18%
   K. 22%

GO ON TO THE NEXT PAGE.

DO YOUR FIGURING HERE.

53. The *determinant* of a matrix $\begin{bmatrix} a & c \\ b & d \end{bmatrix}$ equals $ad - bc$. What must be the value of w for the matrix $\begin{bmatrix} w & w \\ w & 10 \end{bmatrix}$ to have a determinant of 25 ?

   A. 5

   B. $\dfrac{10}{3}$

   C. $\dfrac{5}{2}$

   D. $-\dfrac{5}{3}$

   E. -5

54. Henry discovers that the population of the bacterial colony in his lab can be calculated using the equation $x = B(1 + 0.2g)^n$, where x is the current population, B is the original number of bacteria, g is a growth rate constant for that species, and n is the number of days elapsed. Which of the following is an expression for B in terms of g, n, and x ?

   F. $x - 0.2g^n$

   G. $x + 0.2g^n$

   H. $\left(\dfrac{x}{1 + 0.2g}\right)^n$

   J. $\dfrac{x}{(1 - 0.2g)^n}$

   K. $\dfrac{x}{(1 + 0.2g)^n}$

55. If m and n are real numbers such that $m < -1$ and $n > 1$, then which of the following inequalities *must* be true?

   A. $\dfrac{n}{m} > 1$

   B. $|n|^2 > |m|$

   C. $\dfrac{n}{7} + 2 > \dfrac{m}{7} + 2$

   D. $n^2 + 1 > m^2 + 1$

   E. $n^{-2} > m^{-2}$

GO ON TO THE NEXT PAGE.

56. Triangles *TVW* and *XYZ* are shown below. The given side lengths are in inches. The area of △*TVW* is 45 square inches. What is the area of △*XYZ* in square inches?

DO YOUR FIGURING HERE.

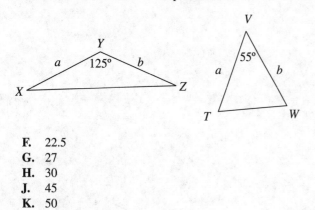

    F. 22.5

    G. 27

    H. 30

    J. 45

    K. 50

57. Triangle *JKL* is shown in the figure below. The measure of ∠*K* is 50°, *JK* = 9 cm, and *KL* = 6 cm. Which of the following is the length, in centimeters, of *LJ* ?

(Note: For a triangle with sides of length *a*, *b*, and *c* opposite angles ∠*A*, ∠*B*, and ∠*C*, respectively, the Law of Sines states $\dfrac{\sin \angle A}{a} = \dfrac{\sin \angle B}{b} = \dfrac{\sin \angle C}{c}$, and the Law of Cosines states $c^2 = a^2 + b^2 - 2ab\cos \angle C$.)

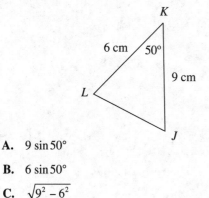

    A. $9 \sin 50°$

    B. $6 \sin 50°$

    C. $\sqrt{9^2 - 6^2}$

    D. $\sqrt{9^2 + 6}$

    E. $\sqrt{9^2 + 6^2 - 2(9)(6)\cos 50°}$

GO ON TO THE NEXT PAGE.

58. What is the sum of the first 3 terms of the arithmetic sequence in which the 7th term is 13.5, and the 11th term is 18.3 ?

- **F.** 15.9
- **G.** 22.5
- **H.** 25.5
- **J.** 32.4
- **K.** 43.5

DO YOUR FIGURING HERE.

59. In the equation $w^2 - pw + q = 0$, p and q are integers. The *only* possible value for w is 8. What is the value of p ?

- **A.** −16
- **B.** −8
- **C.** 8
- **D.** 16
- **E.** 64

60. The solution set of which of the following equations is the set of real numbers that are 4 units from −1 ?

- **F.** $|x+1| = 4$
- **G.** $|x-1| = 4$
- **H.** $|x+4| = 1$
- **J.** $|x-4| = 1$
- **K.** $|x+4| = -1$

END OF TEST.
STOP! DO NOT TURN THE PAGE UNTIL TOLD TO DO SO.

Chapter 13
Practice Test 3:
Answers and
Explanations

SCORE YOUR PRACTICE TEST

Step A

Count the number of correct answers: _____ . This is your *raw score*.

Step B

Use the score conversion table below to look up your raw score. The number to the left is your *scale score*: _____ .

Math Scale Conversion Table

Scaled Score	Raw Score	Scaled Score	Raw Score	Scaled Score	Raw Score
36	58–60	27	41–43	18	24–25
35	56–57	26	39–40	17	21–23
34	54–55	25	37–38	16	17–20
33	53	24	35–36	15	13–16
32	51–52	23	33–34	14	10–12
31	49–50	22	31–32	13	8–9
30	48	21	30	12	6–7
29	46–47	20	28–29	11	5
28	44–45	19	26–27	10	4

MATH PRACTICE TEST 3 ANSWER KEY

1. B		31. D	
2. J		32. G	
3. D		33. C	
4. H		34. H	
5. D		35. D	
6. K		36. F	
7. D		37. B	
8. J		38. H	
9. A		39. C	
10. H		40. F	
11. C		41. D	
12. K		42. F	
13. D		43. D	
14. J		44. H	
15. B		45. D	
16. F		46. G	
17. B		47. B	
18. H		48. H	
19. D		49. A	
20. G		50. F	
21. A		51. D	
22. J		52. K	
23. B		53. A	
24. J		54. K	
25. B		55. C	
26. G		56. J	
27. B		57. E	
28. H		58. G	
29. A		59. D	
30. J		60. F	

MATH PRACTICE TEST 3 EXPLANATIONS

1. **B** The question asks for an expression that represents the total amount of money, in dollars, earned on hamburgers and fries last month. Translate the information in Bite-Sized Pieces and eliminate after each piece. One piece of information says that Bob's Burgers charges $8 for a hamburger. Since the number of hamburgers is represented by h, the correct answer should contain the expression $8h$. Eliminate (A), (C), and (D). Compare the remaining answer choices. Both (B) and (E) contain the expression $5f$, which is the correct way to show that Bob's Burgers sold f fries for $5 each. However, (E) includes an additional and unnecessary expression with f. Eliminate (E). The correct answer is (B).

2. **J** The question asks for the value of an expression. Plug in the values given in the question. The expression becomes $(8 - (-2) + 3)(-2 + 3)$. This simplifies to $(8 + 2 + 3)(1)$ or $(13)(1) = 13$. The correct answer is (J).

3. **D** The question asks for the number of portraits painted by the two artists together. Translate the English to math in Bite-Sized Pieces and eliminate after each piece. The first artist paints 40 portraits per day and paints for 11 days, so the first artist paints $(40)(11) = 440$ portraits. Since the second artist's portraits will increase that total, eliminate (A) and (B). The second artist starts painting three days after the first one, so the second artist paints for $11 - 3 = 8$ days. Since the second artist paints 50 portraits per day, that artist paints $(50)(8) = 400$ portraits. Adding the numbers of portraits painted by the two artists gives $440 + 400 = 840$. The correct answer is (D).

4. **H** The question asks how many home runs Josh must hit next year to maintain his current average number of home runs per season. First calculate Josh's current average number of home runs per season. For averages, use the formula $T = AN$, in which T is the total, A is the average, and N is the number of things. The total is $30 + 39 + 51 + 44 = 164$. Since there are 4 values in the set, the formula becomes $164 = A(4)$. Divide both sides of the equation by 4 to get $A = 41$. Hitting more or fewer home runs than his average in the next season would raise or lower Josh's average. Since the question asks for the number of home runs Josh must hit to maintain his average, he must hit exactly 41 home runs. If this is not intuitive, use the answer choices to verify. Since the question asks for the number of home runs Josh must hit next year, which is a specific value, and the answers contain numbers in increasing order, plug in the answers. Begin by labeling the answers as "number of home runs" and start with (H), 41. If Josh hits 41 home runs next year, his total runs over five years will be $30 + 39 + 51 + 44 + 41 = 205$. The formula becomes $205 = A(5)$, so $A = 41$. This matches his current average number of home runs, so stop here. The correct answer is (H).

5. **D** The question asks how much a craftswoman would earn if she made 34 necklaces. Read the question carefully and use Bite-Sized Pieces. One piece of information says the craftswoman is paid $9.00 per necklace for the first 30 necklaces she makes. This means she would make $(\$9.00)(30) = \$270.00$ for the first 30 necklaces. Since she would make more money for the remaining necklaces the answer must be larger than this, so eliminate (A) and (B). She is asked to make 34 necklaces total, and 30 have been accounted for, so calculate her earnings for the remaining $34 - 30 = 4$ necklaces. The question says she would make 1.5 times her regular pay for these necklaces. Therefore, she would make $(\$9.00)(1.5) = \$13.50$ for each of these necklaces. That means she would make $(\$13.50)(4) = \$54.00$ for the remaining necklaces. Add these two amounts to get a total of $\$270.00 + \$54.00 = \$324.00$ The correct answer is (D).

6. **K**   The question asks which mathematical expression represents a given verbal expression. Translate the English to math in Bite-Sized Pieces and eliminate after each piece. The verbal expression doesn't mention variable y, so eliminate (J). The verbal expression includes the square root of n, $\sqrt{n}$, not the square of n, n^2, so eliminate (F) and (G). The verbal expression asks for *19 less than the value of 5 divided by n*. This means subtracting 19 from 5 divided by n, which translates to $\frac{5}{n} - 19$. Choice (H) has both the subtraction and the division in the wrong order, so eliminate (H). The correct answer is (K).

7. **D**   The question asks for the value of y that satisfies an equation. The question asks for a specific value and the answers contain numbers in increasing order, so Plugging In the Answers is an option. However, with the fractions and negatives that may be time-consuming, so solve the equation algebraically instead. Distribute the 12 on the left side of the equation to get $12y - 36 = -7$. Add 36 to both sides of the equation to get $12y = 29$. Divide both sides of the equation by 12 to get $y = \frac{29}{12}$. The correct answer is (D).

8. **J**   The question asks for the cost of a purse at a department store at regular price. Since the question asks for a specific value and the answers contain numbers in increasing order, plug in the answers. Begin by labeling the answers as "regular price of a purse" and start with (H). To determine Rita's total cost if each purse cost $16, use other information in the question. The question says that Rita spent $84 on purses during the sale when they were on sale for $12 each. This means she bought $84 \div 12 = 7$ purses. Had Rita bought 7 purses for $16 each, she would have spent $16 \times 7 = \$112$. The question also says that Rita spent $38.50 less than she would have spent if the purses had been regular price. Because $112 - \$84 = \$28$ and not $38.50, (H) is incorrect. Because $28 is less than $38.50, try a larger number, such as (J) $17.50. Plug in $17.50 and Rita would have spent $17.50 \times 7 = \$122.50$ at regular price. The difference in cost, $\$122.50 - \$84.00 = \$38.50$, matches the value given in the question, so stop here. The correct answer is (J).

9. **A**   The question asks for an equivalent form of the provided expression. Although there are variables in the answer choices, plugging in on this question might be time-consuming given that there are two variables and exponents. Instead, use Bite-Sized Pieces and Process of Elimination to tackle this question. Begin with the first term, $2a$, and multiply it by the like term in the second set of parentheses: $(2a)(2a) = 4a^2$. Choices (C) and (D) do not contain this term, so eliminate them. Next take the second term, $-5b$, and multiply it by the like term in the second set of parentheses: $(-5b)(5b) = -25b^2$. The only remaining choice that includes this term is (A). The correct answer is (A).

10. **H** The question asks for the longest side of a rectangle. Since the question asks for a specific value and the answers contain numbers in decreasing order, plug in the answers. Begin by labeling the answers as "longest side" and start with the middle value, (H). The formula for the area of a rectangle is $A = lw$. Substitute the given value for the area, 18, and the value in (H), 6, for one of the sides, and the equation becomes $18 = 6(w)$. Dividing both sides by 6 gives the other side of the rectangle as $w = 3$. Since the question specifies that the answer represents the "longest side" and 6 is greater than 3, this is a possible value for the width of the rectangle. Check if these numbers give the correct perimeter. The formula for the perimeter of a rectangle is $P = 2(l) + 2(w)$. Substituting the current values for the two sides gives: $P = 2(6) + 2(3)$. This simplifies to $12 + 6 = 18$. This matches the value for the perimeter of the rectangle given in the question, so stop here. The correct answer is (H).

11. **C** The question asks for the sum of $\angle Y$ and $\angle Z$, two of the angles in a triangle. The sum of the angles in any triangle is 180°. Therefore, $\angle X + \angle Y + \angle Z = 180$. Substituting 64 for $\angle X$ gives $64 + \angle Y + \angle Z = 180$. Subtract 64 from both sides of the equation to get $\angle Y + \angle Z = 180 - 64 = 116$. The correct answer is (C).

12. **K** The question asks for the number of possible outfits given the number of available selections for each type of clothing in the outfit. The question states that there are 5 possible choices for socks, so eliminate (F) because there must be at least 5 possible outfits. Create a blank for each type of clothing that must be selected. Fill in each blank with the number of choices for that type:

$$\underline{\quad 4 \quad} \quad \underline{\quad 5 \quad} \quad \underline{\quad 3 \quad} \quad \underline{\quad 4 \quad}$$
$$\text{Skirts} \qquad \text{Socks} \qquad \text{Sweaters} \quad \text{Headbands}$$

Since the choices are independent and do not affect each other, multiply these numbers together to get $(4)(5)(3)(4) = 240$. The correct answer is (K).

13. **D** The question asks for the values of three positive, consecutive integers. Since the question asks for specific values and the answers contain sets of numbers in increasing order, plug in the answers. Begin by labeling the answers "x, y, z" and start with (C). Using the numbers in (C), $x = 14$, $2y = 2(15) = 30$, and $\frac{z}{2} = \frac{16}{2} = 8$. Add these together to get $14 + 30 + 8 = 52$. Since this does not equal 59, eliminate (C). Since larger numbers are needed, eliminate (A) and (B) as well. Try (D). In (D), $x = 16$, $2y = 2(17) = 34$, and $\frac{z}{2} = \frac{18}{2} = 9$. Add these together to get $16 + 34 + 9 = 59$, which matches the value given in the question. The correct answer is (D).

14. **J** The question asks for the value of a function. In function notation, the number inside the parentheses is the x-value that goes into the function, and the value that comes out of the function is the y-value. Plug $x = -2$ into the function to get $h(-2) = -5(-2)^3$. This simplifies to $-5(-8) = 40$. The correct answer is (J).

15. **B** The question gives an expression and asks which range contains the value of that expression. Use the integer values in the answer choices to estimate the value of z. Because $3^4 = 81$, $\sqrt[4]{81} = 3$, and because $4^4 = 256$, $\sqrt[4]{256} = 4$. Since $81 < 97 < 256$, $\sqrt[4]{81} < \sqrt[4]{97} < \sqrt[4]{256}$. Thus, z must be between 3 and 4. Alternatively, use a calculator to evaluate $\sqrt[4]{97} = 3.13$, which is between 3 and 4. Either way, the correct answer is (B).

16. **F** The question asks for the greatest common factor of three numbers. Since the question asks for a specific value and the answers contain numbers in increasing order, plug in the answers. The question asks for the greatest common factor, so start with the largest value, (K). Divide each of the three numbers by 48. If 48 is a common factor of all three numbers, each number divided by 48 will result in an integer. $96 \div 48 = 2$, which is an integer, but $108 \div 48 = 2.25$, which is not. Thus, 48 is not a common factor of all three numbers. Eliminate (K). Try (J): $96 \div 36 = 2.67$, which is not an integer, so eliminate (J). Continue with (H): $108 \div 24 = 4.5$, which is not an integer, so eliminate (H). Try (G): $96 \div 18 = 5.33$, which is not an integer, so eliminate (G). The only remaining answer is (F) but, to check, divide all three numbers by 12: $96 \div 12 = 8$, $108 \div 12 = 9$, and $144 \div 12 = 12$. Each calculation results in an integer. Thus, 12 is a factor of all three numbers. The correct answer is (F).

17. **B** The question asks for the radius of a cylinder given its volume and its height. Since the question asks for a specific value and the answers contain numbers in increasing order, plug in the answers. Begin by labeling the answers as "radius" and start in the middle with (C). The formula for the volume of a cylinder is $V = \pi r^2 h$. The question states that the height of the cylinder is 10 inches, so plug in 4 for r and 10 for h. The volume can now be represented by $V = \pi(4^2)(10)$, which simplifies to $V = \pi(16)(10)$ or 160π. This is not equal to 40π, so eliminate (C). A smaller volume is required, so try (B). Plug in 2 for the radius. This gives a volume of $V = \pi(2)^2(10)$. This simplifies to $V = \pi(4)(10)$ or 40π. That matches the value given in the question, so stop here. The correct answer is (B).

18. **H** The question asks for the order of certain points placed around the circle of a clock. To help visualize this question, draw a circle containing the numbers 1 through 12 to represent a simple clock. The question states that point W is at 3:00, so put a W on the drawing at 3:00. The question states that X is 4 units clockwise from W. Count 4 units clockwise from 3:00 to reach 7:00. Add an X to the drawing at 7:00. The question states that Y is 9 units counterclockwise from W. Count 9 units counterclockwise from 3:00 to reach 6:00. Add a Y to the drawing at 6:00. The question states that Z is 5 units counterclockwise from W. Count 5 units counterclockwise from 3:00 to reach 10:00. Add a Z to the drawing at 10:00. Start at W and move clockwise, writing down each letter in order. The ordered list is W, Y, X, Z. The correct answer is (H).

19. **D** The question asks for the value of a function. In function notation, the number inside the parentheses is the value that goes into the function. The question states that the variable a represents the number of days and asks for the number of tribbles there will be at the end of day 4, so $a = 4$. Plug this number into the equation, $f(a) = 12(3)^a$. This becomes $f(4) = 12(3)^4$. This simplifies to 12(81) or 972. The correct answer is (D).

20. **G**   The question asks for the value of x, which when multiplied by the area of a larger triangle gives the area of a smaller triangle. Because the question asks for one variable in relation to another, plug in values. Make the height of the larger triangle equal 4. Make the base of the larger triangle equal 3. The formula for the area of a triangle is $A = \frac{1}{2}bh$. Substituting the values for the larger triangle gives $A_L = \frac{1}{2}(3)(4) = 6$. Therefore, $Y = 6$. The question states that the height of the smaller triangle is half the height of the larger triangle, so the height of the smaller triangle is $\frac{4}{2} = 2$. The question states that the triangles have the same base, so the base of the smaller triangle is 3. Substituting the values for the smaller triangle gives $A_S = \frac{1}{2}(3)(2) = 3$. Therefore, $xY = 3$. Substitute the value for Y to get $x(6) = 3$. Dividing both sides of this equation by 6 gives $x = \frac{3}{6} = \frac{1}{2}$. The correct answer is (G).

21. **A**   The question asks for an equivalent form of the provided expression. Although there are variables in the answer choices, plugging in on this question would be time-consuming, given the number of variables. Instead, use Bite-Sized Pieces and Process of Elimination to tackle this question. Begin by gathering the x terms: $2x - 6x = -4x$. Eliminate (D) and (E). Next gather the y terms: $3y - (-7y) = 10y$. Eliminate (C). Lastly gather the z terms: $4z - 8z = -4z$. Eliminate (B). The correct answer is (A).

22. **J**   The question asks for the cosine of an angle in a given triangle. Write out SOHCAHTOA to remember the trig functions. The CAH part defines the cosine as $\frac{adjacent}{hypotenuse}$. In the given triangle, the length of the side adjacent to θ is y, and the length of the hypotenuse is z. Therefore, $\cos(\theta) = \frac{y}{z}$. The correct answer is (J).

23. **B**   The question asks on which lap around a cul-de-sac will newspapers have been delivered to all 8 houses on a street. Draw a circle with 8 points to represent the cul-de-sac and houses. Start at any house and mark every third house to represent a paper being delivered there. On the first trip around the cul-de-sac, papers are delivered to the first, fourth, and seventh houses. On the second trip around, papers are delivered to the second, fifth, and eighth houses. On the third trip around, papers are delivered to the third and sixth houses. It will look like this:

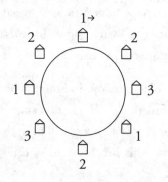

Since all houses have had a paper delivered, the delivery was completed on the third lap around the cul-de-sac. The correct answer is (B).

24. **J** The question asks for the y-intercept of line m. First find the y-intercept of line q. The equation for line q is in $y = mx + b$ form, in which m is the slope and b is the y-intercept. The equation for line q is $y = 23x + 500$, so the y-intercept of line q is 500. The question states that the y-intercept of line m is 10 less than the y-intercept of line q, so the y-intercept of line m is $500 - 10 = 490$. The correct answer is (J).

25. **B** The question asks for an equivalent form of the provided expression. Although there are variables in the answer choices, plugging in on this question would be difficult, given the large exponents. Instead, use Bite-Sized Pieces and Process of Elimination to tackle this question. Begin by multiplying out the first term. When dealing with questions about exponents, remember the MADSPM rules. The MA part of the acronym indicates that Multiplying matching bases means to Add the exponents. This means $-9a^5(8a^7) = -72a^{12}$. Eliminate (A), (D), and (E). Compare the remaining choices, (B) and (C), and note that the only difference between them is the sign of the last term. Multiply the second term to get $-9a^5(-4a^3) = 36a^8$. Since this term is positive, eliminate (C). The correct answer is (B).

26. **G** The question asks for the value of an expression with absolute values. When working with absolute values, do the calculations inside the absolute value symbols as if they are parentheses, and then take the absolute value. The expression $-4|-9 + 2|$ becomes $-4|-7|$. Applying the absolute value gives $-4(7)$, or -28. The correct answer is (G).

27. **B** The question asks for the length of line $\overline{YZ}$ in a figure with triangles. When given two or more triangles with angles in common, look for similar triangles. $\angle XWV$ is congruent to $\angle YWZ$ because they are the same angle. $\angle WVX$ is congruent to $\angle WZY$ because they are both right angles. Therefore, $\triangle WXV$ is similar to $\triangle WYZ$ and their sides are proportional. Create two proportions using corresponding sides from each triangle and set those proportions equal to each other. Because the question asks for the length of $\overline{YZ}$ on $\triangle WYZ$, one of the proportions should relate that value with the corresponding side on $\triangle WXV$, which is $\overline{XV}$. Placing the value corresponding to $\triangle WYZ$ on top, the first proportion is $\dfrac{YZ}{XV}$. Look for one more pair of corresponding sides to set up a second proportion. Another value given on $\triangle WYZ$ is the length of $\overline{WY}$, so use that in the second proportion. Relate it to the corresponding side on $\triangle WXV$, which is $\overline{WX}$. Still putting the value for $\triangle WYZ$ on top, the second proportion is $\dfrac{WY}{WX}$. The equation should now look like $\dfrac{YZ}{XV} = \dfrac{WY}{WX}$. Plug in the known values and it becomes $\dfrac{YZ}{6} = \dfrac{30}{WX}$.

The length of $\overline{WX}$ needs to be determined. Use the Pythagorean Theorem. The Pythagorean Theorem states that $a^2 + b^2 = c^2$, where c is the length of the hypotenuse. Since $\overline{WX}$ is the hypotenuse, the equation becomes $WV^2 + VX^2 = WX^2$. Substitute the given values to get $8^2 + 6^2 = WX^2$. This simplifies to $64 + 36 = WX^2$ or $100 = WX^2$. Take the square root of both sides to get $\overline{WX} = 10$. Put this value into the proportion equation to get $\dfrac{YZ}{6} = \dfrac{30}{10}$. Cross-multiply to get $YZ(10) = (30)(6)$. Divide both sides by 10 and simplify to get $\overline{YZ} = 18$. The correct answer is (B).

28. **H** The question asks for the relationship between two variables. When given a table of values and asked for the correct equation, plug values from the table into the answer choices to see which one works. Because the first set of points includes a 0 and the second includes a 1, use a different set of points. According to the table, $w = 2$ when $h = 13$. Choice (F) becomes $13 = 2 + 7$, or $13 = 9$. This is not true, so eliminate (F). Choice (G) becomes $13 = 3(2) + 4$, or $13 = 6 + 4$. This is not true, so eliminate (G). Choice (H) becomes $13 = 3(2) + 7$, or $13 = 6 + 7$. This is true, so keep (H) but check the remaining answers just in case. Choice (J) becomes $13 = 7(2) + 3$, and (K) becomes $13 = 10(2)$. Both statements are false, so eliminate (J) and (K). The correct answer is (H).

29. **A** The question asks for an equivalent form of an inequality. The answers are all in terms of n, so isolate n in the inequality in the question. Start by distributing the constants: $4(n - 3) < 5(n + 2)$ becomes $4n - 12 < 5n + 10$. Subtract $4n$ from both sides of the inequality to get $-12 < 5n - 4n + 10$, or $-12 < n + 10$. Subtract 10 from both sides to get $-22 < n$, or $n > -22$. The correct answer is (A).

30. **J** The question asks for a point that could be the vertex of an equilateral triangle given the coordinates of another vertex of the triangle. The question gives one vertex of the triangle as the point (1, 1) and states that the sides of the equilateral triangle are four inches long. This means that any other vertex of the triangle must be four units from the point (1, 1). Draw a sketch of the points, and then use Process of Elimination on answer choices that are not 4 units from (1, 1).

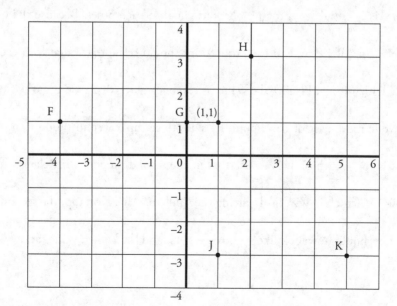

Try the easiest choices first. Choice (F) is 5 units to the left of (1, 1), so eliminate (F). Choice (G) is 1 unit below (1, 1), so eliminate (G). Checking (H) would involve using the distance formula, so skip it for now. Choice (J) is 4 units below (1, 1), so it could be the vertex of the triangle. Choice (K) is also difficult to check, but since (J) could work, there is no need. The correct answer is (J).

31. **D** The question asks for the relationship between two variables. There are variables in the answer choices, so plug in. Make $n = 3$. Since the triangle is a right triangle, use the Pythagorean Theorem. The Pythagorean Theorem says that the sides of a right triangle are related by the equation $a^2 + b^2 = c^2$ where c is the length of the hypotenuse. Substitute the value for n and the value for the hypotenuse given in the question to get $m^2 + (3)^2 = (6)^2$. Simplify to get $m^2 + 9 = 36$; then subtract 9 from both sides of the equation to get $m^2 = 27$. Take the square root of both sides to get $m = \sqrt{27}$. This is the target value; circle it. Now plug $n = 3$ into the answer choices to see which one matches the target value. Choice (A) becomes $6 - 3 = 3$. This does not match the target, so eliminate (A). Choice (B) becomes $\sqrt{6-3} = \sqrt{3}$. Eliminate (B). Choice (C) becomes $\sqrt{12+3^2} = \sqrt{12+9} = \sqrt{21}$. Eliminate (C). Choice (D) becomes $\sqrt{36-3^2} = \sqrt{36-9} = \sqrt{27}$. Keep (D) but check (E) just in case. Choice (E) becomes $\sqrt{36+3^2} = \sqrt{36+9} = \sqrt{45}$. Eliminate (E). Alternatively, since the algebra is not too complicated, this could also be solved by using the Pythagorean Theorem and algebraically solving for m. Substitute the values into the Pythagorean Theorem to get $m^2 + n^2 = (6)^2$ or $m^2 + n^2 = 36$. To isolate m, subtract n^2 from both sides to get $m^2 = 36 - n^2$. Then take the square root of both sides to get $m = \sqrt{36-n^2}$. Either way, the correct answer is (D).

32. **G** The question asks for the number of pear jellybeans that need to be added to a jar to make the probability that selecting a pear jellybean from the jar at random is $\frac{3}{8}$. Since the question asks for a specific value and the answers contain numbers in increasing order, plug in the answers. Begin by labeling the answers as "pear jellybeans added" and start with (H), 21. The jar already has 10 pear jellybeans, so after adding 21 it would have $10 + 21 = 31$. The jar has 45 jellybeans total, so after adding 21 the total number of jellybeans would be $45 + 21 = 66$. The probability of selecting a pear jellybean is the number of pear jellybeans in the jar divided by the total number of jellybeans in the jar, which is $\frac{45}{66}$ or about 0.68. Since this is larger than $\frac{3}{8}$, which is 0.375, eliminate (H). Since the resulting probability was too large, eliminate (J) and (K) as well. Try (G). For (G), the number of pear jellybeans in the jar is $10 + 11 = 21$. The total number of jellybeans in the jar is $45 + 11 = 56$. The probability of selecting a pear jellybean is now $\frac{21}{66}$, which simplifies to $\frac{3}{8}$. The correct answer is (G).

33. **C** The question asks through which quadrants of the coordinate plane a given line passes. Draw a sketch of the line by plotting two points. Try plugging in 1 for x. This gives $6(1) + 3(y) = 12$, which simplifies to $6 + 3y = 12$. Subtract 6 from both sides to get $3y = 6$. Divide both sides by 3 to get $y = 2$. This means that the point $(1, 2)$ is on the line. Mark that point on the coordinate plane. Since that point is in Quadrant I, eliminate (A) and (E). Try plugging in –1 for x. This gives $6(-1) + 3(y) = 12$, which simplifies to $-6 + 3y = 12$. Add 6 to both sides to get $3y = 18$. Divide both sides by 3 to get $y = 6$. This means that the point $(-1, 6)$ is on the line. Mark that point on the coordinate plane. Since that point is in Quadrant II, eliminate (D). Connect the points and extend the line to observe that the line also enters Quadrant IV but does not enter Quadrant III.

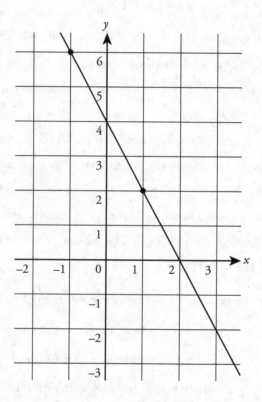

The correct answer is (C).

34. **H** The question asks what value of n will create a point that is contained in the graph of a given equation. Since the value of the x-coordinate of the point is given, plug it into the equation. The equation becomes $y = -2(3)^2 + 10$. This simplifies to $y = -2(9) + 10$, or $y = -8$. The y-coordinate of the point is given as $4n$, so $4n = -8$. Divide both sides of the equation by 4 to get $n = -2$. The correct answer is (H).

35. **D** The question asks for the ratio of the amount of rent paid by three people. The question involves a relationship between unknown numbers, so plug in. The amount of rent is not given, so plug in a value. Select a number that will make the arithmetic easier. Because there are fractions with 3 and 4 in the denominator, try plugging in 12 for the rent. The question states that Jennifer paid $\frac{2}{3}$ of the rent. Therefore, she paid $\frac{2}{3}(12) = 8$. The question states that Kelly paid $\frac{1}{4}$ of the rent. Therefore, she paid

$\frac{1}{4}(12) = 3$. The question states that Meredith paid the rest. Therefore, she paid $12 - 8 - 3 = 1$. The question asks for the ratio of Jennifer's contribution to Kelly's to Meredith's. This ratio is 8:3:1, which matches (D). The correct answer is (D).

36. **F** The question asks for the correct properties of the provided circle equation. Use Bite-Sized Pieces and Process of Elimination to tackle this question. The equation of a circle in standard form is $(x - h)^2 + (y - k)^2 = r^2$, where (h, k) is the center and r is the radius. Since $r^2 = 28$, the radius is $\sqrt{28}$. Eliminate (G), (H), and (K). Be careful of the sign changes in the equation when getting the center. In the equation $x^2 + (y + 4)^2$, the center is at $(0, -4)$. Eliminate (J). The correct answer is (F).

37. **B** The question asks for the perimeter of a figure. The perimeter of the figure consists of one side of the equilateral triangle and the arc lengths of two semicircles. Use Bite-Sized Pieces to calculate each part of the perimeter. The two semicircles make an entire circle, so the portion of the perimeter on the semicircles is just the circumference of one entire circle. The circumference of a circle is given by $C = 2\pi r$ where r is the radius of the circle. The diameter of the semicircles is a side of the equilateral triangle, which has sides of length 6. Therefore, the radius of the semicircles is $\frac{6}{2} = 3$. This gives $C = 2\pi(3)$, or $C = 6\pi$. The side of the triangle is given as 6, so the length of the entire perimeter of the figure is $6\pi + 6$. The correct answer is (B).

38. **H** The question asks for the ratio of the unshaded portion of a figure to the area of the shaded portion. Draw lines from point M to point J and from point H to point J as shown to divide the unshaded portion into triangles:

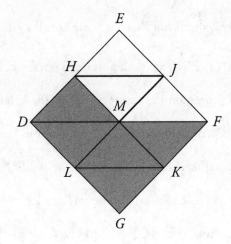

Because the question states that the figure is a rhombus, which has four equal sides, and all points are midpoints of the lines they are on, the triangles formed are all identical and have identical areas. Count the triangles in the unshaded and shaded portions. There are 3 triangles in the unshaded portion, and there are 5 in the shaded portion. Therefore, the ratio of the area of the unshaded portion to the area of the shaded portion is 3:5. The correct answer is (H).

39. **C** The question asks for the *y*-coordinate of the midpoint of a line segment given the coordinates of the endpoints of the line segment. The midpoint of a line segment is obtained by taking the average of the coordinates of the endpoints. Since the question asks only for the *y*-coordinate of the midpoint, calculate only the average of the *y*-coordinates of the endpoints. Sum the two values and divide by two to get $\dfrac{10+(-2)}{2}$. This simplifies to $\dfrac{8}{2}$, which equals 4. The correct answer is (C).

40. **F** The question asks for the volume of a cube given the length of one of its sides. The equation for the volume of a cube is $V = s^3$, where *s* is the length of a side. Plug in the length of the side to get $V = 9^3$, which is $V = 729$. The correct answer is (F).

41. **D** The question asks which of three descriptions could be a possible graph of a system of two linear equations. The equations are identical except for a constant term. Since parallel lines are mentioned in the question, look at the slopes of the lines. Since the line equations are in the standard form $Ax + By = C$, the slope for each is given by the expression $-\dfrac{A}{B}$. The first equation is $rx + sy = t$. Substitute the variables into the expression for slope to get $-\dfrac{r}{s}$. The second equation is $rx + sy = v$. Substitute the variables into the expression for slope to get $-\dfrac{r}{s}$. Both lines have a slope of $-\dfrac{r}{s}$. This means the lines are either two different, parallel lines or are the same line. Option (I) is not possible, so eliminate (A), (C), and (E). If $t = v$, then the two equations are identical and thus the same line. If $t \neq v$, then the lines are separate, parallel lines. Therefore, options (II) and (III) are both possible. The correct answer is (D).

42. **F** The question asks for an expression that corresponds to the length of a side of a triangle. Use the Geometry Basic Approach. Label the side of the triangle from the tree to the house as *x*. There are trigonometric expressions in the answer choices, so write out SOHCAHTOA to remember the trig functions. In relation to the angle that is 34°, the side labeled as *x* is the opposite side, and the side labeled as 40 is the hypotenuse. The SOH part defines the sine as $\dfrac{opposite}{hypotenuse}$, so $\sin 34° = \dfrac{x}{40}$. Multiply both sides of the equation by 40 to get $x = 40 \sin 34°$. The correct answer is (F).

43. **D** The question asks for the odds that a particular student is in Grade 6, represented as the ratio of *in the grade* to *not in the grade*. The table shows the percent of students in each grade, so plug in 100 for the number of students. The number of options for *in the grade* is simply the number of students in Grade 6, which is $\frac{22}{100} \times 100 = 22$. The number of options for *not in the grade* is the number of students not in Grade 6. The sum of the percentages of students in other grades is 12 + 25 + 27 + 14, which is equal to 78. When the total number of students is 100, 78% is the same as 78 students. Therefore, the required ratio of *in Grade 6* to *not in Grade 6* is 22:78, which reduces to 11:39. The correct answer is (D).

44. **H** The question asks for the number of lines of symmetry a figure has. Lines of symmetry must pass through the center and create identical, symmetrical halves. Draw lines passing through the center that divide the figure into identical halves. The only such possible lines are a line drawn vertically through the center, a line drawn horizontally through the center, and two lines drawn through the center on each of the diagonals. The correct answer is (H).

45. **D** The question asks for the length of the diagonal of a figure. The information for this set of questions states that the mosaic is a square and that the length of the mosaic is 3 meters. The Pythagorean Theorem could be used, but because this is a square, a diagonal divides the tile into two 45°-45°-90° triangles. This means that the hypotenuse is equal to $\sqrt{2}$ times the length of one of the square's sides. This is $3\sqrt{2}$. Use a calculator to find that this is approximately 4.24. The correct answer is (D).

46. **G** The question asks for the length of an office wall in meters. Because the office wall is shorter than the mosaic, which has a length of 3 meters, eliminate (J) and (K). The question states that the wall is 20% shorter than the mosaic. Start by finding 20% of the length of the mosaic. The question states that the mosaic has a length of 3 meters, so $\frac{20}{100} \times 3 = 0.6$. Because the question says the office wall is shorter than the mosaic, this must be subtracted from the length of the mosaic. This means the office wall is 3 − 0.6 = 2.4 meters. The correct answer is (G).

47. **B** The question asks for the value of an angle on a figure. Use the Geometry Basic Approach. Start by labeling the figure with the given information. Mark lines $\overline{DE}$ and $\overline{FG}$ as parallel. It may not be immediately obvious how to get the value of measure of $\angle DHG$, so see what else can be determined. The question states that $\overline{DG}$ bisects $\angle HDE$. This means $\angle EDG$ and $\angle GDH$ are equal, so label $\angle GDH$ as 68°. Also, when two parallel lines like $\overline{DE}$ and $\overline{FG}$ are cut by a third line, like $\overline{DG}$, two kinds of angles are created: big and small. All small angles are equal, and both $\angle EDG$ and $\angle DGF$ are small angles. Therefore $\angle DGF$ is 68°. Label the figure with this information. The question states that $\overline{HG}$ bisects $\angle FGD$. This means $\angle DGH$ and $\angle FGH$ are equal, so $\angle DGH$ is half of $\angle DGF$, and $\angle DGH$ = 34°. Label the figure with this information. Finally, because there are 180° in a triangle, $\angle GDH + \angle DGH + \angle DHG = 180$. Substitute the values for $\angle GDH$ and $\angle DGH$ to get 68 + 34 + $\angle DHG$ = 180, which means 102 + $\angle DHG$ = 180 and $\angle DHG$ = 78. The correct answer is (B).

48. **H** The question asks for the degree measure of a minor arc of a circle. Use the Geometry Basic Approach. Start by labeling the figure with the given information. Note that since $\overline{AC}$ is the longest chord in the circle, it is a diameter and therefore passes through the center of the circle, O. Mark O on the figure. The degree measure of minor arc BC is the angle measure of $\angle BOC$. Since the area of the circle is given, the equation for area of a circle can be used to find the circle's radius. The area of a circle is $A = \pi r^2$. Substitute in 16π for the area to get $16\pi = \pi r^2$. Divide both sides by π to get $16 = r^2$. Take the square root of both sides to get $r = 4$. Draw the line $\overline{BO}$. Note that $\overline{AO}$ and $\overline{BO}$ are both radii of the circle, and therefore have a length of 4. Label the length of both lines. Since the question states that the length $\overline{AB}$ is 4 as well, then all three sides of $\triangle ABO$ are the same length which means $\triangle ABO$ is an equilateral triangle. The angles in an equilateral triangle are all equal to 60°, so $\angle AOB$ is 60°. Add this information to the figure. Because $\overline{AB}$ is a straight line, $\angle AOB$ and $\angle BOC$ are supplementary. This means the measure of $\angle BOC$ is $180 - 60$, or 120°. Therefore, the degree measure of minor arc $\overset{\frown}{BC}$ is 120°. The correct answer is (H).

49. **A** The question asks for a value for a variable in a system of equations that would result in the system of equations having no solutions. Note that the equations are equations of lines. A system of equations with lines has no solutions only if the lines are parallel and not the same line. Parallel lines have the same slope, so find the slopes of the lines. Since the equations are in the standard form $Ax + By = C$, the slope for each is given by the expression $-\frac{A}{B}$. The first equation is $12x + 8y = 16$. Substitute the corresponding values into the expression for slope to get $-\frac{12}{8}$. The second equation is $3x + by = 2$. Substitute the corresponding values into the expression for slope to get $-\frac{3}{b}$. Because the lines must have the same slope, set these values for their slopes as equal. This gives $-\frac{12}{8} = -\frac{3}{b}$. Multiply both sides of the equation by -1 to get $\frac{12}{8} = \frac{3}{b}$. Cross-multiply to get $12(b) = 8(3)$. Simplify to $12(b) = 24$. Divide both sides by 12 to get $b = 2$. The correct answer is (A).

50. **F** The question asks about the graph of the data representing a certain situation. The point referenced, $(9, 1)$, represents 9 dozen cookies and 1 pie. Eliminate (G), (H), and (K) because they do not match this information. The question is asking about the horizontal line segment from $(0, 1)$ to $(9, 1)$. The points on this line have various values for the x-coordinate, but are always 1 on the y-coordinate. The y-coordinate corresponds to the number of pies, not cookies, so eliminate (J). The correct answer is (F).

51. **D** The question asks for the maximum value a quantity can reach in a given situation. Since the question asks about a maximum, check the endpoints or extremes of the graph. The question gives the expression representing profit as $12d + 25p$. For the point $(0, 4)$ this becomes $12(0) + 25(4)$, which is 100. The other extreme is at the point $(9, 1)$. At this point, the expression gives $12(9) + 25(1) = 133$, which is greater than 100. The correct answer is (D).

52. **K**   The question asks for the percentage of that week's profit that was donated to charity. Use Bite-Sized Pieces to tackle this question. The question states that they baked 5 pies and 3 dozen cookies. The expression given in the information above the question for their profit is $12d + 25p$. Substitute the number of pies and dozens of cookies baked into the expression to get $12(3) + 25(5)$, which is $36 + 125$ or $161. The question states that they donate $2 for each hour they spend baking, so figure out how many hours they spent baking. The information above the question states that it takes them 1 hour to make a dozen cookies and 3 hours to make a pie. Therefore, they baked for $1(3) + 3(5) = 18$ hours. Since they donate $2 for each hour, they donated $2(18) = \$36$. The question asks what percentage this is of the week's profit. The percent is $\frac{36}{161} \times 100$, which is approximately 22%. The correct answer is (K).

53. **A**   The question asks what value of w will give a certain matrix a determinant of 25. Since the question asks for a specific value and the answers contain numbers in increasing order, plug in the answers. Start by evaluating the determinant for the given matrix. The expression for determinant given in the question is $ad - bc$. The value of d is given in the question while a, b, and c are represented by w, so for the given matrix the determinant is $(w)(10) - (w)(w)$. Start with the answers without fractions because integers are often easier to plug in than fractions are. Plugging (A) into the expression in place of w gives $5(10) - (5)(5)$, which simplifies to $50 - 25$, or 25. The correct answer is (A).

54. **K**   The question asks for an expression which represents a variable in an equation. Although there are variables in the answer choices, plugging in on this question would be difficult, given the number of variables and the exponent. The question asks for the expression that represents B, so algebraically solve the equation for B. The original equation is $x = B(1 + 0.2g)^n$. Divide both sides of the equation by $(1 + 0.2g)^n$ to get $B = \dfrac{x}{(1 + 0.2g)^n}$. The correct answer is (K).

55. **C**   The question asks which equality must be true given certain conditions. There are variables in the answer choices, so plug in. Because the question asks for what *must be true*, it will likely be necessary to plug in more than once. Make $m = -2$, and $n = 3$. Start with (A). Choice (A) becomes $\dfrac{3}{-2} > 1$. This is false, so eliminate (A). Choice (B) becomes $\left|3\right|^2 > \left|-2\right|$, or $9 > 2$. This is true, so keep (B). Choice (C) becomes $\dfrac{3}{7} + 2 > \dfrac{-2}{7} + 2$, or $\dfrac{17}{7} > \dfrac{12}{7}$. This is true, so keep (C). Choice (D) becomes $3^2 + 1 > (-2)^2 + 1$, or $10 > 5$. This is true, so keep (D). Choice (E) becomes $3^{-2} > (-2)^{-2}$, or $\dfrac{1}{9} > \dfrac{1}{4}$. This is false, so eliminate (E). Because more than one choice remains, select new numbers to plug in. Notice that in each remaining answer choice, the expression containing n is greater than the expression containing m.

In order to eliminate more choices, the expression containing m needs to be greater than or equal to the expression containing n. Therefore, try plugging in a value for m with a greater absolute value than the absolute value of n. Try $m = -10$ and $n = 2$. Choice (B) becomes $\left|2\right|^2 > \left|-10\right|$, or $4 > 10$. This is false, so eliminate (B). Choice (C) becomes $\dfrac{2}{7} + 2 > \dfrac{-10}{7} + 2$, or $\dfrac{16}{7} > \dfrac{4}{7}$. This is true, so keep (C), but check (D). Choice (D) becomes $2^2 + 1 > (-10)^2 + 1$, or $5 > 101$. This is false, so eliminate (D). The correct answer is (C).

56. **J**   The question asks for the area of a triangle in inches given the area of a related triangle. Because the question is asking for information about one triangle but giving information about another, there should be a way to relate the two triangles to each other. One way is to realize that $125°$ and $55°$ add to $180°$, which is the sum of the angles in any triangle. In $\triangle XYZ$, $\angle X + \angle Z = 55°$. Therefore, $\triangle XYZ$ can be cut into two triangles and re-formed into a new triangle with one $55°$ angle consisting of $\angle X$ and $\angle Z$. Consider a line from Y to the midpoint of $\overline{XZ}$ which divides $\triangle XYZ$ into two triangles. Label the midpoint of $\overline{XZ}$ as M.

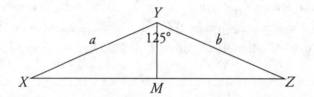

Dividing triangle XYZ along $\overline{MY}$ makes two triangles which can be rotated, flipped, and re-joined like this:

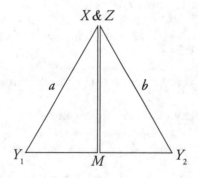

Because this new triangle has two sides and an included angle that are equivalent to those of $\triangle TVW$, the two triangles are equivalent, and thus have the same area. The question states the area of $\triangle TVW$ is 45, so the area of $\triangle XYZ$ is also 45. The correct answer is (J).

57. **E**   The question asks for the length of a side of a given triangle. The question gives an angle in a triangle and the length of two of the sides, and asks for the length of the third side. It also gives the Law of Sines, which defines a relationship between the sides and angles of a triangle, and the Law of Cosines, which defines a relationship between an angle in a triangle and the lengths of its three sides. Because more is known about sides than about angles, use the Law of Cosines. Let $\angle C$ represent the 50° angle and substitute the values from the figure into the Law of Cosines. This gives $c^2 = 9^2 + 6^2 - 2(9)(6) \cos 50°$. Taking the square root of both sides gives $c = \sqrt{9^2 + 6^2 - 2(9)(6)\cos 50°}$. The correct answer is (E).

58. **G**   The question asks for the sum of the first three terms of an arithmetic sequence given two other terms in the sequence. Solve using Bite-Sized Pieces. An arithmetic sequence has a common difference between each pair of terms, so find that difference. To go from the 7th term to the 11th term the common difference is added 4 times. That total difference is 18.3 − 13.5, which is 4.8. Divide this by 4 to get the common difference, which is 4.8 ÷ 4 = 1.2. To get from the 1st term to the 7th, the common difference was added 6 times. This means 1.2(6), or 7.2, is added to the 1st term to get to the 7th term. Therefore, the value of the 1st term is 13.5 − 7.2, which is 6.3. The 2nd term is 1.2 more than this, or 6.3 + 1.2 = 7.5. The 3rd term is 1.2 more than this, or 7.5 + 1.2 = 8.7. The sum of the first three terms is 6.3 + 7.5 + 8.7, which is 22.5. The correct answer is (G).

59. **D**   The question asks for the value of p that satisfies an equation with integer values. The question states that the only possible value of w is 8. This can be true only if the equation is equivalent to $(w - 8)(w - 8) = 0$. Use FOIL to multiply the expression out to the standard form $ax^2 + bx + c$ in order to match up coefficients with the equation in the question. The equation becomes $w^2 - 8w - 8w + 64 = 0$ or $w^2 - 16w + 64 = 0$. In this form, p is represented by the negative coefficient of w, which is 16. The correct answer is (D).

60. **F**   The question asks for an equation for which the solution set represents the numbers that are 4 units from −1. Absolute value never returns a negative number, so eliminate (K). The number 4 units to the left of −1 on a number line is −5. The number 4 units to the right of −1 on a number line is 3. Plug these values into the answer choices. Start with plugging in −5. Choice (F) becomes $|-5 + 1| = 4$, which simplifies to $|-4| = 4$, or 4 = 4. This is true, so keep (F), but check the remaining answers because the correct answer must work with both values. Choice (G) becomes $|-5 - 1| = 4$. This simplifies to $|-6| = 4$, or 6 = 4. This is false, so eliminate (G). Choice (H) becomes $|-5 + 4| = 1$. This simplifies to $|-1| = 1$, or 1 = 1. This is true, so keep (H). Choice (J) becomes $|-5 - 4| = 1$, which simplifies to $|-9| = 1$, or 9 = 1. This is false, so eliminate (J). Now try the other value, 3, in the two answers remaining. Choice (F) becomes $|3 + 1| = 4$. This simplifies to $|4| = 4$, or 4 = 4. This is true, so keep (F) but check (H). Choice (H) becomes $|3 + 4| = 1$. This simplifies to $|7| = 1$, or 7 = 1. This is false, so eliminate (H). The only remaining choice is (F). The correct answer is (F).

Chapter 14
Practice Test 4

ACT MATHEMATICS TEST
60 Minutes—60 Questions

DIRECTIONS: Solve each problem, choose the correct answer, and then darken the corresponding oval on your answer document.

Do not linger over problems that take too much time. Solve as many as you can; then return to the others in the time you have left for this test.

You are permitted to use a calculator on this test. You may use your calculator for any problems you choose, but some of the problems may best be done without using a calculator.

Note: Unless otherwise stated, all of the following should be assumed:

1. Illustrative figures are NOT necessarily drawn to scale.

2. Geometric figures lie in a plane.

3. The word *line* indicates a straight line.

4. The word *average* indicates arithmetic mean.

---

1. Four railroad lines, A, B, C, and D, are pictured below, such that the pair of lines A and B and C and D run parallel to each other, respectively. If the obtuse angle created by the intersection of line A and C measures 110°, what is the measure of the obtuse angle at which line B intersects line D ?

DO YOUR FIGURING HERE.

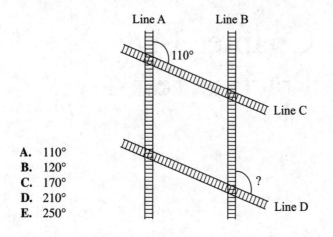

A. 110°
B. 120°
C. 170°
D. 210°
E. 250°

2. Which of the following is the simplified form of the expression $5(x - 3) - 3x + 10$?

F. $2x - 5$

G. $5x + 7$

H. $8x - 5$

J. $12x + 10$

K. $22x$

GO ON TO THE NEXT PAGE.

3. In the standard (x,y) coordinate plane, a point lies at $(4,-7)$. If the point is shifted up 4 units and left 10 units, what are the new coordinates of the point?

- **A.** $(-14,-9)$
- **B.** $(-3,-9)$
- **C.** $(-6,-9)$
- **D.** $(-6,-3)$
- **E.** $(0, 3)$

DO YOUR FIGURING HERE.

4. At a certain golf club, participants in a tournament must pay $13 if they belong to the club and $15 if they do not belong to the club. What is the total cost, in dollars, for x participants who belong to the club and 30 members who do not belong to the club?

- **F.** $13x + 15(30)$
- **G.** $(13 + 15)x$
- **H.** $13(x + 15)$
- **J.** $13(x + 30)$
- **K.** $x + 30$

5. If a new computer has its price increased from $500 to $650, by what percent did the computer's price increase?

- **A.** 5%
- **B.** 15%
- **C.** 23%
- **D.** 28%
- **E.** 30%

6. In the parallelogram $WXYZ$, $\angle W$ and $\angle Y$ are congruent, the measure of $\angle X$ is 112°. What is the measure of $\angle Y$?

- **F.** 56°
- **G.** 68°
- **H.** 90°
- **J.** 112°
- **K.** 136°

GO ON TO THE NEXT PAGE.

7. Nathan will choose one marble randomly from a sack containing 32 marbles that are in the colors and quantities shown in the table below. Each of the marbles is one color only.

Color	Quantity
White	5
Purple	1
Indigo	2
Cyan	8
Maroon	6
Tan	10

What is the probability that Nathan will choose a tan or maroon marble?

A. $\dfrac{3}{16}$

B. $\dfrac{5}{16}$

C. $\dfrac{7}{16}$

D. $\dfrac{1}{2}$

E. $\dfrac{1}{3}$

8. If a speedboat is traveling 100 miles in the span of $1\dfrac{1}{3}$ hours, what is the speedboat's average speed, in miles per hour?

F. 25
G. 33
H. 75
J. 100
K. 133

9. In order to calculate an employee's overall performance review value, Mr. Donovan removes the lowest value and then averages the remaining values. Shawna was evaluated 6 times with the following results: 22, 23, 26, 31, 35, and 43. What was Shawna's overall performance review value as determined by Mr. Donovan?

A. 27.4
B. 30.0
C. 31.0
D. 31.4
E. 31.6

DO YOUR FIGURING HERE.

GO ON TO THE NEXT PAGE.

10. Which of the following gives x in terms of p and q, given the equation $\dfrac{3x}{p} = q$?

   F. $\dfrac{q}{3p}$

   G. $\dfrac{p}{3q}$

   H. $\dfrac{pq}{3}$

   J. $pq - 3$

   K. $q + p - 3$

DO YOUR FIGURING HERE.

11. What is the value of $5x$ if $3x - 16 = 5$?

   A. 7
   B. 21
   C. 35
   D. 56
   E. 72

12. If the area of a square is 25 square feet, what is the perimeter of the square, in feet?

   F. 5
   G. 10
   H. 20
   J. 25
   K. 100

13. What is 11% of 3.22×10^4 ?

   A. 354,200
   B. 3,542
   C. 35.42
   D. 1.123
   E. 0.1123

14. Of the following expressions, which is a factor of the expression $x^2 + 3x - 18$?

   F. $x - 6$
   G. $x + 3$
   H. $x + 6$
   J. $x + 9$
   K. $x + 15$

15. Of the following real numbers, $v, w, x, y,$ and z such that $v < w$, $y > x$, $y < v$, and $z > w$, which of the numbers is the smallest?

   A. v
   B. w
   C. x
   D. y
   E. z

GO ON TO THE NEXT PAGE.

16. A new operation, ♣, is defined as follows: $(w,x) ♣ (y,z) = (wz - yx)(wx - yz)$. What is the value of $(3,2) ♣ (5,0)$?

F. −120
G. −60
H.   0
J.   6
K. 60

DO YOUR FIGURING HERE.

17. A team of artists requires 2 types of structures—spheres and pyramids—for a collaborative art piece. The 2 types of structures are created by overlapping 5-inch squares made of 3 different materials. The team will consist of three artists. The requirements for each structure type are provided in the tables below. The table with material types indicates how many squares are required for each type of structure, and the table with the artists indicates how many of each structure type each artist is to create.

	Wood	Iron	Plastic
Sphere	10	5	12
Pyramid	5	14	10

	Sphere	Pyramid
Suzuki	5	5
Mona	5	15
Jamilica	10	5

How many 5-inch squares of wood does Jamilica need to create her structures?

A. 150
B. 125
C.   52
D.   39
E.   29

18. Which of the following represents the least common multiple of 100, 60, and 20 ?

F.   80
G.   120
H.   300
J.   1,200
K.   120,000

GO ON TO THE NEXT PAGE.

19. The right triangle below represents three stores—Teddy's, ValuTime, and Burger Burger—as its vertices. The distances given on the triangle represent the numbers of miles required to travel between the stores on a road. Two customers leave Teddy's to shop at ValuTime. If the first customer travels from Teddy's to ValuTime on Coles St., while the second customer travels from Teddy's to Burger Burger on Monmouth St. before taking Brunswick Ave. to ValuTime, how many miles shorter is the first customer's trip than the second's?

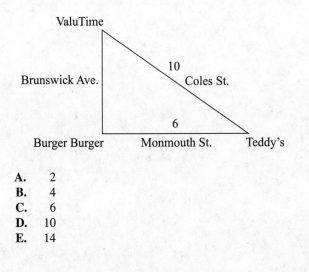

A. 2
B. 4
C. 6
D. 10
E. 14

20. Which of the following expressions is equivalent to $\left(y^6\right)^{12}$?

F. $72y$
G. $12y^6$
H. $6y^{12}$
J. y^{72}
K. y^{216}

21. Given the function $f(x) = 2x^3 + x^2$, which of the following represents the value of $f(-2)$?

A. −24
B. −20
C. −16
D. −13
E. −12

22. The Merry Mechanics Shop has just ended its discount program, raising the price of all repairs by 20%. Which of the following gives the price, in dollars, of any repair with price r ?

F. $0.2r$
G. $r + 0.2r$
H. $r - 0.2r$
J. $r + 0.2$
K. $r + 20r$

GO ON TO THE NEXT PAGE.

23. A local television advertisement offers 3 pairs of shoes for $30.97. Given the price of the shoes, how much would it cost to purchase 5 pairs of shoes?

A. $10.32
B. $10.33
C. $20.65
D. $51.61
E. $51.62

DO YOUR FIGURING HERE.

24. Terra is opening a store. Her monthly profit is calculated by subtracting her monthly expenses from the total amount she earns each day. If her monthly expenses are $500, and she earns $100 per day on a particular month, which of the following graphs represents her profit as a function of the number of days of business?

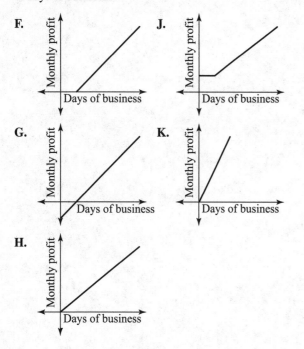

25. The positive integer $x!$ is defined as the product of all the positive integers less than or equal to x. For example, $4! = 1(2)(3)(4) = 24$. What is the value of the expression $\frac{6!4!}{5!}$?

A. 1
B. 2
C. 4
D. 72
E. 144

GO ON TO THE NEXT PAGE.

26. Alfred spent $25 to purchase 65 stamps. If each stamp costs either $0.20 or $0.45, how many of the more expensive stamps did he purchase?

    F.   17
    G.   48
    H.   56
    J.   65
    K.   125

DO YOUR FIGURING HERE.

27. A square with a side length of 2 feet is circumscribed, as shown below.

What is the area of the shaded region, in square feet?

    A. π
    B. $\pi - 4$
    C. $2\pi - 1$
    D. $2\pi - 2$
    E. $2\pi - 4$

28. Two similar triangles have corresponding sides that are in the ratio 3:4. The length of one of the sides of the larger triangle is 12 feet long. What is the length, in feet, of the corresponding side of the smaller triangle?

    F.   6
    G.   7
    H.   9
    J.   11
    K.   16

29. For the polygon below points V, Z, and Y are collinear. Which of the following represents the length, in inches, of $\overline{VZ}$?

    A.   10

    B. $10\cos 35°$

    C. $\cos 35°$

    D. $\dfrac{15}{\cos 35°}$

    E. $\dfrac{10}{\cos 35°}$

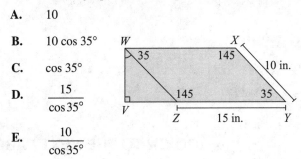

GO ON TO THE NEXT PAGE.

DO YOUR FIGURING HERE.

30. The perimeter of a rectangle is 144 feet, and one side measures 32 feet. If it can be determined, what are the lengths, in feet, of the other three sides?

F. 32, 40, 40
G. 32, 32, 46
H. 32, 48, 48
J. 32, 66, 66
K. Cannot be determined from the given information

31. If $9 + 4x < 2x - 7$, which of the following represents the solution?

A. $x > -12$
B. $x > -8$
C. $x < -8$
D. $x < -2$
E. $x < 8$

32. The drama team wants to post a triangular advertisement for its next play. The base of the advertisement will be 2.25 feet, and the height will be 3.5 feet. Which of the following is closest to the area, in square feet, of the advertisement?

F. 3.0
G. 3.9
H. 6.0
J. 7.9
K. 9.0

33. $-8|-2 - 7| = ?$

A. -112
B. -92
C. -72
D. 40
E. 72

34. In a local deli, some sandwiches have only one kind of meat, and other sandwiches have more than one kind of meat. Using the information given in the table below about the kinds of meat in the sandwiches, how many sandwiches have roast beef only?

Number of sandwiches	Meat
8	at least roast beef
10	at least chicken
12	at least turkey
5	both chicken and turkey, but no roast beef
1	both roast beef and turkey, but no chicken
3	chicken only
2	roast beef, chicken, and turkey

F. 9
G. 7
H. 5
J. 4
K. 2

GO ON TO THE NEXT PAGE.

Use the following information to answer questions 35–37.

The 4-H club at Arlington High School cares for various animals in the school's stockyards. The members of the club sell the animals in order to raise funds for the club, and Marcus and Jae are taking inventory of the animals. The table below gives the numbers of groups of animals. For example, there are 5 groups of pigs with 1 pig per group, 20 groups of chickens with 5 chickens per group, and 20 groups of rabbits with 10 rabbits per group. All of the animal groups have been counted except for the 5-animal groups of rabbits.

Animals	Number of 1-animal groups	Number of 5-animal groups	Number of 10-animal groups
Chickens	0	20	30
Rabbits	5	?	20
Pigs	5	10	0
Goats	22	10	0

35. Marcus finishes the inventory and afterward tells Jae that the number of rabbits is equal to the number of chickens. How many 5-animal groups of rabbits are in the stockyards?

A. 15
B. 25
C. 35
D. 39
E. 195

36. Mrs. Bradshaw purchased $\frac{1}{5}$ of the chickens for $1,200.00. What was the price of 1 chicken?

F. $10.00
G. $15.00
H. $20.00
J. $60.00
K. $120.00

37. Bethany takes all of the goats in the 1-animal groups and combines them to create as many 5-animal groups as possible. How many complete 5-animal groups of goats can Bethany create?

A. 22
B. 14
C. 10
D. 5
E. 4

GO ON TO THE NEXT PAGE.

Use the following information to answer questions 38–40

Isosceles triangle *DEF* is shown in the standard (*x,y*) coordinate plane below. The coordinates for two of its vertices are *D*(0,0) and *E*(*c,d*).

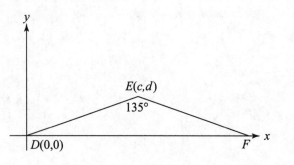

38. What are the coordinates of *F* ?

   F.   (0,   2*d*)
   G. (2*c*,   0)
   H. (*c* + *d*, 0)
   J.   (2*c*,   2*d*)
   K. (*c* + *d*,2*d*)

39. What is the measure of the angle formed by *DE* and the *y*-axis?

   A.   22.5°
   B.   30.0°
   C.   45.0°
   D.   60.0°
   E.   67.5°

40. Isosceles triangle *DEF* is rotated clockwise (↵) by 180° about the origin. If the new location of point *E* is called *E′*, what are the coordinates of *E′* ?

   F.   (–*c*, *d*)
   G. (*c*,–*d*)
   H. (–*d*,–*c*)
   J.   (–*c*,–*d*)
   K. (*d*, *c*)

GO ON TO THE NEXT PAGE.

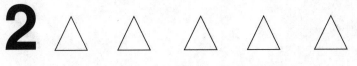

41. A gallon is 231 cubic inches. Which of the following is closest to the area of the base, in square inches, of a pyramid shaped container, shown below, with height 15 inches and volume 2 gallons?

(Note: The volume of a pyramid with base area B and height h is $\frac{1}{3}Bh$.)

DO YOUR FIGURING HERE.

A.   92
B.   132
C.   276
D.   432
E.   1,296

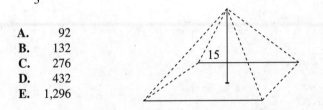

42. For law school, Aaron must read a book of legal cases in 6 months. He reads $\frac{1}{8}$ of the book in each of the first 2 months. For the remaining 4 months, what portion of the book, on average, must Aaron read per month?

F. $\frac{3}{16}$

G. $\frac{3}{32}$

H. $\frac{1}{16}$

J. $\frac{1}{32}$

K. $\frac{1}{64}$

43. Which of the following equations indicates the correct application of the quadratic formula to the equation $2x^2 + 3x - 10 = 10$?

A. $\dfrac{3 \pm \sqrt{9 - 4(2)(-10)}}{2(2)}$

B. $\dfrac{3 \pm \sqrt{9 + 4(2)(-10)}}{2(2)}$

C. $\dfrac{-3 \pm \sqrt{9 + 4(2)(-10)}}{2(2)}$

D. $\dfrac{-3 \pm \sqrt{9 - 4(2)(-10)}}{2(2)}$

E. $\dfrac{-3 \pm \sqrt{9 - 4(2)(10)}}{2(2)}$

GO ON TO THE NEXT PAGE.

44. In the standard (x,y) coordinate plane, the point $(-2,5)$ is the midpoint of the line segment with endpoints $(-7,3)$ and (c,d). What is (c,d) ?

 F. $(-19,8)$
 G. $(-12,1)$
 H. $(-12,7)$
 J. $(\ \ 3,1)$
 K. $(\ \ 3,7)$

DO YOUR FIGURING HERE.

45. A straight 4-meter-tall lamppost casts a shadow at an angle of 55°, as shown in the figure below. Which of the following expressions gives the length, in meters, of the shadow along the level ground?

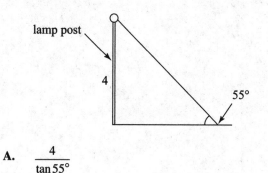

 A. $\dfrac{4}{\tan 55°}$

 B. $\dfrac{4}{\cos 55°}$

 C. $\dfrac{4}{\sin 55°}$

 D. $4\tan 55°$

 E. $4\sin 55°$

GO ON TO THE NEXT PAGE.

46. One of the following equations is graphed in the standard (*x,y*) coordinate plane below. Which one?

F. $y = 2x + 2$

G. $y = \dfrac{1}{2}x + 4$

H. $y = -\dfrac{1}{2}x + 2$

J. $y = -2x + 2$

K. $y = -2x - 4$

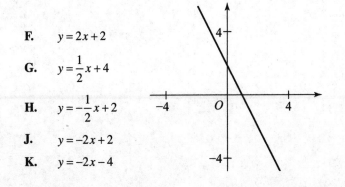

47. The vertices of *ABCD* have the (*x,y*) coordinates indicated in the figure below. What is the area, in square coordinate units, of *ABCD* ?

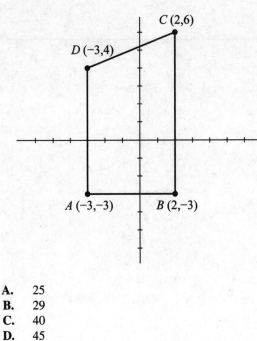

A.   25
B.   29
C.   40
D.   45
E.   81

GO ON TO THE NEXT PAGE.

48. Ms. Parker's economics class is reviewing slopes of lines. The class is tasked to graph the total expenditures, E, required for p products that cost 45¢ each. Ms. Parker instructs the class to characterize the slope between any 2 points (p,E) on the graph. Francine gives a correct answer that the slope between any 2 points on this graph must be:

F. two.
G. multiple positive values.
H. multiple negative values.
J. one positive value.
K. one negative value.

49. If the first four terms of a geometric sequence are 10, 15, 22.5, and 33.75, what is the fifth term in the sequence?

A. 35
B. 50.625
C. 56.25
D. 70.625
E. 75

50. The total surface area of a cube is 54 square inches. What is the volume, in cubic inches, of the cube?

F. 9
G. 18
H. 27
J. 81
K. 729

51. In the figure below, a region of a circle with a radius of 5 is shown shaded. The area of the shaded region is 15π. What is the measure of the central angle of the shaded region?

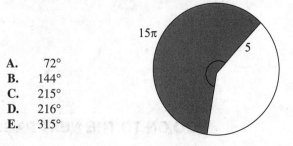

A. 72°
B. 144°
C. 215°
D. 216°
E. 315°

GO ON TO THE NEXT PAGE.

52. Which of the following equations represents the graph of a circle with center (2,–6) and radius 4 coordinate units in the standard (*x*,*y*) coordinate plane?

DO YOUR FIGURING HERE.

F. $(x-2)^2+(y+6)^2=4$
G. $(x+2)^2+(y-6)^2=4$
H. $(x-2)^2+(y-6)^2=16$
J. $(x-2)^2+(y+6)^2=16$
K. $(x+2)^2+(y-6)^2=16$

53. In ΔXYZ, the value of $\angle X$ is 53°, the value of $\angle Y$ is 88°, and the length of $\overline{YZ}$ is 11 inches. Which of the following is an expression for the length, in inches, of $\overline{XZ}$?

(Note: The Law of Sines states that for any triangle, the ratios of the lengths of the sides to the sines of the angles opposite those sides are equal.)

A. $\dfrac{(\sin 88°)(\sin 53°)}{11}$

B. $\dfrac{\sin 88°}{11 \sin 53°}$

C. $\dfrac{\sin 53°}{11 \sin 88°}$

D. $\dfrac{11 \sin 53°}{\sin 88°}$

E. $\dfrac{11 \sin 88°}{\sin 53°}$

54. The radius of a circle is *p* feet shorter than the radius of a second circle. How many feet shorter is the circumference of the first circle than the circumference of the second circle?

F. $\sqrt{p}$
G. p^2
H. πp
J. p
K. $2\pi p$

55. If $y \leq -3$, then $|y+3| = ?$

A. $y - 3$
B. $y + 3$
C. $-y - 3$
D. $-y + 3$
E. 0

GO ON TO THE NEXT PAGE.

56. There are 18 countries in the trade union. Of these 18 countries, 7 have fewer than 20 cities, 7 have more than 21 cities, and 2 have more than 22 cities. What is the total number of countries in the trade union that have 20, 21, or 22 cities?

- F. 15
- G. 11
- H. 9
- J. 7
- K. 4

57. If $\sin x = -\dfrac{3}{4}$, what is the value of $\cos 2x$?

(Note: $(\sin x)^2 = \dfrac{1-\cos 2x}{2}$)

- A. $-\dfrac{3}{4}$
- B. $-\dfrac{1}{4}$
- C. $-\dfrac{1}{8}$
- D. $\dfrac{1}{8}$
- E. $\dfrac{13}{4}$

58. Let $f(x) = x^3$ and $g(x) = \dfrac{x}{2} - k$. In the standard (x,y) coordinate plane, $y = f\big(g(x)\big)$ passes through $(-2,8)$. What is the value of k ?

- F. 2
- G. 1
- H. −3
- J. −8
- K. −9

59. A plane contains 7 vertical lines and 7 horizontal lines. These lines partition the plane into disjoint regions. How many of these disjoint regions have a finite, nonzero area?

- A. 12
- B. 14
- C. 25
- D. 36
- E. 49

60. Which of the following must be less than 0, if x, y, and z are real numbers and $x^3 y^4 z^6 < 0$?

- F. xy
- G. xy^2
- H. yz
- J. xyz
- K. $x^2 y^2 z^3$

END OF TEST.
STOP! DO NOT TURN THE PAGE UNTIL TOLD TO DO SO.

Chapter 15
Practice Test 4:
Answers and
Explanations

SCORE YOUR PRACTICE TEST

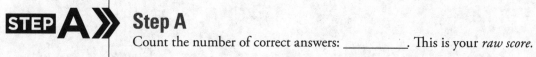

Step A

Count the number of correct answers: _____. This is your *raw score*.

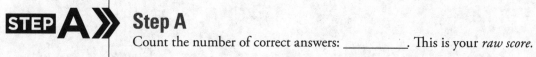

Step B

Use the score conversion table below to look up your raw score. The number to the left is your *scale score:* _____.

Math Scale Conversion Table

Scaled Score	Raw Score	Scaled Score	Raw Score	Scaled Score	Raw Score
36	58–60	27	41–43	18	24–25
35	56–57	26	39–40	17	21–23
34	54–55	25	37–38	16	17–20
33	53	24	35–36	15	13–16
32	51–52	23	33–34	14	10–12
31	49–50	22	31–32	13	8–9
30	48	21	30	12	6–7
29	46–47	20	28–29	11	5
28	44–45	19	26–27	10	4

MATH PRACTICE TEST 4 ANSWER KEY

1.	A		31.	C
2.	F		32.	G
3.	D		33.	C
4.	F		34.	H
5.	E		35.	D
6.	G		36.	G
7.	D		37.	E
8.	H		38.	G
9.	E		39.	E
10.	H		40.	J
11.	C		41.	A
12.	H		42.	F
13.	B		43.	D
14.	H		44.	K
15.	C		45.	A
16.	G		46.	J
17.	B		47.	C
18.	H		48.	J
19.	B		49.	B
20.	J		50.	H
21.	E		51.	D
22.	G		52.	J
23.	E		53.	E
24.	G		54.	K
25.	E		55.	C
26.	G		56.	H
27.	E		57.	C
28.	H		58.	H
29.	B		59.	D
30.	F		60.	G

MATH PRACTICE TEST 4 EXPLANATIONS

1. **A** The question asks for *the measure of the obtuse angle at which line B intersects line D*. Use the Geometry Basic Approach and label lines A and B and lines C and D parallel to each other as stated in the question. Notice that this creates a parallelogram. Where line A intersects line C, the obtuse angle is already labeled 110° so the acute, small angle below it and on the interior of the parallelogram must be 180° − 110° = 70° because these angles form a straight line. Since the small angles in a parallelogram are equal, that means that the small angle on the interior of the parallelogram where lines B and D intersect is also 70°. This angle and the angle that the question is asking about also form a straight line so the measure of the angle that the question asks about is 180° − 70° = 110°. The correct answer is (A).

2. **F** The question asks for *the simplified form of the expression* $5(x − 3) − 3x + 10$. There are variables in the question and answer choices. Plugging in is a viable option but will likely be more time consuming than the algebra, so simplify the expression. Start by distributing the 5 to the binomial in parentheses to get $5x − 15 − 3x + 10$; then combine like terms to get $2x − 5$. The correct answer is (F).

3. **D** The question asks for the *new coordinates of the point* $(4, −7)$ after it has been shifted. Drawing the coordinate plane and graphing the point can be helpful, so use the Geometry Basic Approach to draw the figure if needed. The question states that point $(4, −7)$ is *shifted up 4 units*; up-down shifts happen along the y-axis. Shifting up increases the y-coordinate so add to get $−7 + 4 = −3$. The new y-coordinate will be $−3$. Eliminate (A), (B), (C), and (E) because they do not contain a y-coordinate of $−3$. The correct answer is (D).

4. **F** The question asks for *the total cost, in dollars, for x participants who belong to the club and 30 members who do not belong to the club*. Use the Word Problem Basic Approach and break the question into bite-sized pieces. Start with the easiest information. Since the question is asking for the total cost and gives the number of members who do not belong to the club and the amount they would pay, multiply those numbers, 30 and $15, respectively, to get (30)(15). Eliminate any answers that do not contain (30)(15): (G), (H), (J) and (K). The correct answer is (F).

5. **E** The question asks *by what percent did the computer's price increase*. This is a percent change question, so write down the formula for percent change: $\dfrac{difference}{original} \times 100$. The change in the price is $650 − $500 = $150, and the question is asking for a percent increase, so the original will be the smaller number, $500. Therefore, percent change $= \dfrac{150}{500} \times 100 = 30$. The correct answer is (E).

6. **G** The question asks for *the measure of* $\angle Y$. Use the Geometry Basic Approach and draw and label parallelogram *WXYZ*, where $\angle W$ and $\angle Y$ are opposite one another and congruent. Label $\angle X$ as 112°. Recall that the rules of parallelograms state that adjacent angles of a parallelogram are supplementary (add up to 180°). Because $\angle Y$ is adjacent to $\angle X$, find the measure of $\angle Y$ by subtracting the measure of $\angle X$, 112°, from 180° to get 180° − 112° = 68°. The correct answer is (G).

7. **D** The question asks for *the probability that Nathan will choose a tan or maroon marble*. Probability is defined as $\frac{want}{total}$. Read the table carefully to find the numbers to make the probability. Since the question asks for *the probability that Nathan will draw a tan <u>or</u> maroon marble*, add the number of available tan marbles to the number of available maroon marbles: $10 + 6 = 16$. This is the *want*. The question states that there are 32 total marbles, so that is the *total*. Set up the expression as $\frac{16}{32}$ and simplify to get $\frac{1}{2}$. The correct answer is (D).

8. **H** The question asks for *the speedboat's average speed, in miles per hour*. The question also provides the distance the boat has traveled, 100 miles, and the amount of time it took to travel that distance, $1\frac{1}{3}$ hours. Note that the question is asking about a shorter period of time than $1\frac{1}{3}$ hours indicated in the question, which means that the boat would travel a shorter distance than 100 miles, so eliminate any answer greater than or equal to 100: (J) and (K). Next, set up a proportion to find the number of miles the speedboat covers in 1 hour: $\frac{100}{1\frac{1}{3}} = \frac{x}{1}$. Since $\frac{x}{1} = x$, calculate $\frac{100}{1\frac{1}{3}} = x$ to get $x = 75$ miles per hour. The correct answer is (H).

9. **E** The question asks for *Shawna's overall performance review value* when *the lowest value* is removed, and the average of the remaining value is calculated. Use the Word Problem Basic Approach and work in bite-sized pieces. The question provides the six evaluation values: 22, 23, 26, 31, 35, and 43. First, remove the lowest value from the list to get 23, 26, 31, 35, 43. To find the average, use the formula $T = AN$, in which T is the total, A is the average, and N is the number of things. The total is $23 + 26 + 31 + 35 + 43 = 158$, and the number of things is 5. The formula becomes $158 = A(5)$, so divide both sides by 5 to get $31.6 = A$. The correct answer is (E).

10. **H** The question asks for the value of *x given the equation* $\frac{3x}{p} = q$. There are variables in the question and answers, so plugging in numbers is a viable option, but it will likely be more time consuming than solving for x in this equation. To solve for x, first multiply both sides by p to get $3x = pq$; then divide both sides by 3 to get $x = \frac{pq}{3}$. The correct answer is (H).

11. **C** The question asks for *the value of 5x*, given $3x - 16 = 5$. Since the question asks for a specific value and the answers contain numbers in increasing order, plugging in the answers is a viable option, but it is likely more time-consuming than solving for x because it would be necessary to set the answers equal to $5x$ and then find x before plugging in to the original equation. Instead, solve for x in the equation by first adding 16 to each side of the equation to get $3x = 21$; then divide both sides by 3 to get $x = 7$. Now multiply by 5 to get $5x = 35$. The correct answer is (C).

12. **H**   The question asks for *the perimeter of the square, in feet, if the area of* the *square is 25 square feet*. Using the Geometry Basic Approach, draw a square and write down the formulas for the area and perimeter of a square: $A = s^2$ and $P = 4s$, respectively. Now use the provided area to solve for the length of the side: $25 = s^2$. Take the square root of each side to find $s = 5$. Now calculate the perimeter: $P = 4(5) = 20$. The correct answer is (H).

13. **B**   The question asks for a percent of a number. Use percent translation to translate the words into math. "Percent" means divide by 100 so 11% equals $\dfrac{11}{100}$ or 0.11. "Of" means multiply, so 11% of the expression equals $0.11(3.22 \times 10^4)$. Use the calculator to solve, remembering to close any open parentheses to ensure proper order of operations. The result is $0.11(3.22 \times 10^4) = 3{,}542$. The correct answer is (B).

14. **H**   The question asks for a *factor of the expression $x^2 + 3x - 18$*. To find the factors of a quadratic in standard form, which is $ax^2 + bx + c$, look at the first term and determine what values would multiply together to get x^2. In this case the factors of x^2 are x and x. Put them in the first positions of the binomials that are the factors of the expression: $(x \quad)(x \quad)$. Now determine the factors of -18 that will add up to $+3$. They are $+6$ and -3. Put these into the second position of each binomial factor to get $(x + 6)(x - 3)$. One of these factors, $(x + 6)$, is an answer choice. The correct answer is (H).

15. **C**   The question asks for *which of the number is the smallest*. Use the Word Problem Basic Approach to work this question in bite-sized pieces. Since $v < w$, w cannot be the smallest. Eliminate (B). Since $y > x$, y cannot be the smallest. Eliminate (D). Since $y < v$, v cannot be the smallest. Eliminate (A). Finally, since $z > w$, z cannot be the smallest. Eliminate (E). Since all other answers have been eliminated. The correct answer is (C).

16. **G**   The question asks for *the value of (3,2) ♣ (5,0)* given that function *♣ is defined as (w,x) ♣ $(y,z) = (wz - yx)(wx - yz)$*. When a strange symbol appears on the ACT it works just like a function. Plug the given numbers into the expression presented and solve. For this question, plugging in the given numbers will result in $(3,2)$ ♣ $(5,0) = [(3)(0) - (5)(2)][(3)(2) - (5)(0)] = (0 - 10)(6 - 0) = (-10)(6) = -60$. The correct answer is (G).

17. **B**   The question asks for the number of *5-inch squares of wood* that *Jamilica needs to create her structure*. Use the Word Problem Basic Approach and break the question into bite-sized pieces. The table shows that Jamilica will be making 10 spheres and 5 pyramids, and that to do that she will need 10 squares of wood for each sphere and 5 squares of wood for each pyramid. Since Jamilica is making 10 spheres that each require 10 squares of wood multiply: $(10)(10) = 100$. Now calculate the number of squares needed to make the 5 pyramids: each pyramid requires 5 squares, so this becomes $(5)(5) = 25$. The total number of squares of wood needed are $100 + 25 = 125$. The correct answer is (B).

18. **H**   The question asks for *the least common multiple of 100, 60, and 20*. The least common multiple is the smallest multiple common to the given numbers. Since the question asks for a specific value and the answers contain numbers in increasing order, plug in the answers. Start with (F) since the question asks for the smallest value. The answers need to be a multiple of all three numbers so start by eliminating any answers that are not a multiple of 100. Eliminate (F) and (G). Because the next smallest answer, (H) 300, is a multiple of 100, determine whether it is also a multiple of 60. Because 300 = 60 × 5, 300 is also a multiple of 60. Finally, because 60 itself is a multiple of 20, any multiple of 60 is also a multiple of 20. Stop here. The correct answer is (H).

19. **B**   The question asks *how many miles shorter is* the trip taken by the first customer along Coles St. than the trip taken by the second customer along Monmouth St. and Brunswick Ave. The customers travel along the legs and hypotenuse of the given triangle. The hypotenuse and one leg of the triangle are labeled with distances of 10 and 6, respectively. Use the Geometry Basic Approach and the Pythagorean Theorem, $a^2 + b^2 = c^2$, to solve for the length of Brunswick Ave or recognize the common Pythagorean triple 6:8:10 to determine that the length of the side of the triangle representing Brunswick Ave. is 8 units. To determine the difference in the length of the trips, add the lengths of Monmouth St. and Brunswick Ave. to get 6 + 8 = 14; then subtract the length of Coles St. to get 14 − 10 = 4. The correct answer is (B).

20. **J**   The question asks *which of the expressions is equivalent to* $\left(y^6\right)^{12}$. When dealing with questions about exponents, remember the MADSPM rules. The PM part of the acronym indicates that raising a base with an exponent to another Power means to Multiply the exponents: 6 × 12 = 72. Therefore, the equivalent expression is y^{72}. The correct answer is (J).

21. **E**   The question asks for the *value of f(−2)*, given $f(x) = 2x^3 + x^2$. The number inside the parentheses is the *x*-value that goes into the function, and the value that comes out of the function is the *y*-value, $f(x)$. Plug $x = -2$ into the f function to get $f(-2) = 2(-2)^3 + (-2)^2 = 2(-8) + 4 = -16 + 4 = -12$. When using the calculator to solve, remember to include the negative sign inside the parentheses and to close any open parentheses to ensure accuracy and proper order of operations. The correct answer is (E).

22. **G**   The question asks which answer *gives the price, in dollars, of any repair with price r*. There are variables in the answer choice, so plug in. Since the question is asking about percents, 100 is a good number to plug in: $r = \$100$. The new price of the repairs will be 20% more than 100. When working with percent increase first multiply the original price by the percent: $100\left(\dfrac{20}{100}\right) = \$20$. Then add that value to the original: $\$100 + \$20 = \$120$. This is the target value; circle it. Choice (F) becomes 0.2(100) = 20. Eliminate (F) because it does not match the target value. Choice (G) becomes 100 + (0.2)(100) = 100 + 20 = 120. Keep (G), but check the remaining answers just in case. Choice (H) becomes 100 − (0.2)(100) = 100 − 20 = 80. Eliminate (H). Choice (J) become 100 + 0.2 = 100.2. Eliminate (J). Choice (K) becomes 100 + (20)(100) = 100 + 2,000 = 2,100. Eliminate (K). The correct answer is (G).

23. **E** The question asks for *the cost to purchase 5 pairs of shoes*, given that 3 pairs of shoes cost \$30.97. Recognize that the question gives the price of 3 pairs of shoes and asks for the cost of 5 pairs of shoes. Use POE to eliminate any answer less than or equal to \$30.97 because the price of 5 pairs of shoes will be more than the price of 3 pairs of shoes; eliminate (A), (B), and (C). Set up a proportion to solve for the cost of 5 pairs of shoes: $\frac{30.97}{3} = \frac{x}{5}$. Cross-multiply to get $(5)(30.97) = 3x$. Simplify to $154.85 = 3x$ and divide each side by 3 to get $x = 51.61666667$. This is the cost of 5 pairs of shoes; round to the nearest hundredth to get 51.62. The correct answer is (E).

24. **G** The question asks *which graph represents* Terra's *profit as a function of the number of days* her business is open. Use the Word Problem Basic Approach and break the question into bite-sized pieces. The question states that Terra's monthly expenses are \$500. If the business is open 0 days, she would have made no money, so the total profit for day 0 would be \$0 – \$500 = \$ –500. Eliminate (F), (H), (J), and (K) since they do not contain this point. The correct answer is (G).

25. **E** The question asks for *the value of the expression* $\frac{6!4!}{5!}$ given that *x*! (*x* factorial) is *defined as the product of all the positive integers less than or equal to x*. Expand the factorial notation to get $\frac{(6)(5)(4)(3)(2)(1) \times (4)(3)(2)(1)}{(5)(4)(3)(2)(1)}$ and cancel to get $\frac{(6)(\cancel{5})(\cancel{4})(\cancel{3})(\cancel{2})(\cancel{1}) \times (4)(3)(2)(1)}{(\cancel{5})(\cancel{4})(\cancel{3})(\cancel{2})(\cancel{1})} = \frac{(6)(4)(3)(2)(1)}{1} = 144$. The correct answer is (E).

26. **G** The question asks for the number of *the more expensive stamps* that Alfred purchased. Since the question asks for a specific value and the answers contain numbers in increasing order, plug in the answers. Begin by labeling the answers as "more expensive stamps." Start by eliminating (K), since there are only 65 stamps total. Start with (G) or (H) since they are the middle of the remaining answers. Starting with (G), if there are 48 "more expensive stamps," then there are 65 – 48 = 17 cheaper stamps. The total cost of 48 "more expensive stamps" is 48 × \$0.45 = \$21.60, and the cost for the 17 cheaper stamps is 17 × \$0.20 = \$3.40. The total cost for all the stamps is \$21.60 + \$3.40 = \$25, which matches the value given in the question, so stop here. The correct answer is (G).

27. **E** The question asks for *the area of the shaded region* given a square with *side length of 2 feet is circumscribed* in a circle. Use the Geometry Basic Approach and label the square with the side length of 2. The area of the shaded region can be found by subtracting the area of the square from the area of the circle, so write both formulas: $A = s^2$ and $A = \pi r^2$, respectively. Calculate the area of the square: $A = 2^2 = 4$. The correct answer must include a subtraction of 4, so eliminate (A), (C), and (D). No measurements are given for the circle, but the diagonal of the square is the same as the diameter of the circle. Draw a diagonal in the square which creates a 45°-45°-90° triangle. Use the Pythagorean Theorem, $a^2 + b^2 = c^2$,

or the special right triangle rules to find that a 45°-45°-90° triangle with side length 2 will have a hypotenuse of $2\sqrt{2}$. To calculate the area of the circle, take half of the diameter to get the radius: $\frac{1}{2}\left(2\sqrt{2}\right)=\sqrt{2}$. Now, calculate the area of the circle: $A=\left(\sqrt{2}\right)^2\pi=2\pi$. Finally, find the area of the shaded region by subtracting the area of the square from the area of the circle: $2\pi-4$. The correct answer is (E).

28. **H** The question asks for the length, in feet, of one side of the smaller triangle when the triangles are similar. Corresponding sides of similar triangles are proportional, and this question gives the ratio of the smaller triangle to the larger triangle as 3:4 or $\frac{3}{4}$. To find the corresponding side of the smaller triangle, use the given measurement of 12 from the larger triangle and set up a proportion: $\frac{3}{4}=\frac{x}{12}$. Cross-multiply to get $4x=36$; then divide both sides by 4 to get $x=9$. The correct answer is (H).

29. **B** The question asks for *the length, in inches, of* $\overline{VZ}$ given the polygon with measures and angles labeled in the figure. Use the Geometry Basic Approach and notice that quadrilateral *WXYZ* is a parallelogram because its opposite angles are equal. Label $\overline{WZ}$ as 10 and $\overline{WX}$ as 15 since opposite sides of parallelograms are also equal. There are trigonometric expressions in the answer choices, so write out SOHCAHTOA to remember the trig functions. The CAH part of SOHCAHTOA defines cosine as $\frac{adjacent}{hypotenuse}$. For triangle *VWZ*, $\overline{VZ}$ is adjacent to $\angle VZW$, and $\overline{WZ}$ is the hypotenuse. Note that $\angle VZW$ and $\angle WZY$ create a straight line. Calculate the measure of $\angle VZW$ by subtracting the measure of $\angle WZY$ from 180° to get 180° − 145° = 35°. Use the definition of cosine to get $\cos 35° = \frac{VZ}{10}$. Multiply both sides by 10 to get 10 cos 35° = *VZ*. The correct answer is (B).

30. **F** The question asks for *the length, in feet, of the other three sides* of the rectangle that are not given in the question. The question provides the perimeter of the rectangle; use the Geometry Basic Approach to draw a rectangle with one side labeled 32 feet and write the formula for the perimeter of a rectangle: $P=s_1+s_2+s_3+s_4$. Since opposite sides of a rectangle are equal, label the side opposite the 32 foot side as 32 feet and label the remaining two sides as *x*. Plug the length of the perimeter, 144, and the side lengths into the perimeter formula to get 144 = 32 + 32 + *x* + *x*; combine like terms to get 144 = 64 + 2*x*. Subtract 64 from both sides to get 80 = 2*x*. Then divide both sides by 2 to get 40 = *x*. Therefore, the sides of the rectangle not given in the question are 32, 40, 40. The correct answer is (F).

31. **C** The question asks for the solution to the provided inequality. Although there are variables in the answer choices, plugging in on this question would be difficult. Instead solve for *x*. To isolate *x*, begin by subtracting 9 from both sides of the inequality to get $4x<2x-16$. Subtract 2*x* from both sides of the inequality to get $2x<-16$. Finally divide both sides of the inequality by 2 to get $x<-8$. The correct answer is (C).

32. **G**   The question asks for the answer that *is closest to the area, in square feet, of the* triangular *advertisement* given in the question. Use the Geometry Basic Approach. Start by drawing a triangle and label the base 2.25 feet. Draw a line to represent the height and label it 3.5 feet. Write down the formula for the area of a triangle: $A = \frac{1}{2}bh$. Plug the values of the base and height into the formula and solve for the area: $A = \frac{1}{2}(2.25)(3.5) = 3.9375 \approx 3.9$. The correct answer is (G).

33. **C**   The question asks for the value of an expression with an absolute value. Taking the absolute value of an expression will yield a positive result, and multiplying a positive by a negative will yield a negative result, so eliminate (D) and (E). When working with absolute values, do the calculations inside the absolute value symbols as if they are parentheses and then take the absolute value. The expression becomes $-8|-2 - 7| = -8|-9| = -8(9) = -72$. The correct answer is (C).

34. **H**   The question asks for the number of sandwiches that *have roast beef only*. Use the Word Problem Basic Approach and work in bite-sized pieces. Start by noting that the first row of the chart says 8 sandwiches contain *at least roast beef*. Eliminate (A) since 8 is the most sandwiches that contain roast beef. Next see that row 5 says that 1 sandwich has *both roast beef and turkey, but no chicken*. Subtract this sandwich from the total sandwiches that have *at least roast beef* since the answer will be sandwiches with *roast beef only*: $8 - 1 = 7$. Now note that column 7, says that 2 sandwiches have *roast beef, chicken, and turkey*. Subtract 2 from the 7 remaining sandwiches to find the number of sandwiches with *roast beef only*: $7 - 2 = 5$. The correct answer is (H).

35. **D**   The question asks how many *5-animal groups of rabbits are in the stockyard*. Since the question asks for a specific value and the answers contain numbers in increasing order, plug in the answers. Begin by labeling the answers as "# of 5-animal groups of rabbits" and start with (C), 35 groups. Find the total number of rabbits by multiplying the number of rabbits in each group by the number of groups in that category and adding those products. Plug in 35 for the number of 5-animal groups of rabbits to get a total of $(5)(1) + (35)(5) + (20)(10) = 5 + 175 + 200 = 380$ rabbits. The question states that *the number of rabbits is equal to the number of chickens*, so calculate the total number of chickens in the same way to get $(0)(1) + (20)(5) + (30)(10) = 0 + 100 + 300 = 400$ chickens. Since these values are not equal, eliminate (C). There needs to be more rabbits for the number of rabbits and chickens to be equal, so eliminate (A) and (B) since having fewer groups will mean there are fewer rabbits. The number of rabbits when there are 35 5-animal groups, 380 rabbits, is close to the number of chickens, 400 chickens, it would not make sense to increase the number of 5-animal groups of rabbits by a large amount. Eliminate (E), because it is too big. The correct answer is (D).

36. **G**   The question asks for *the price of 1 chicken*. Use the Word Problem Basic Approach and break this question into bite-sized pieces. The question states that *Mrs. Bradshaw purchased $\frac{1}{5}$ of the chickens for $1,200.00*. Start by identifying the number of total chickens. The chart shows that there are 0 groups of 1 chicken, 20 groups of 5 chickens, and 30 groups of 10 chickens. To find the total number of chickens, multiply the number of chickens in each group by the number of groups and sum those totals to get $(0)(1) + (20)(5) + (30)(10) = 0 + 100 + 300 = 400$ chickens. Now multiply the total number of chickens by $\frac{1}{5}$ to find the number of chickens Mrs. Bradshaw purchased: $(400)\left(\frac{1}{5}\right) = 80$ chickens. To find the price of each chicken, divide the total amount paid by Mrs. Bradshaw, $1,200.00, by the number of chickens she purchased, 80. This gives a price per chicken of $\frac{\$1,200.00}{80} = \$15.00$. The correct answer is (G).

37. **E**   The question asks *how many complete 5-animal groups of goats* Bethany can create from the goats in the 1-animal group. Use the Word Problem Basic Approach and work in bite-sized pieces. First use the chart to identify the number of animals in the 1-animal groups of goats. Since there are 22 animals in groups of 1, there are $(22)(1) = 22$ goats total for Bethany to group into groups of 5. Divide the number of goats available, 22, by the number of goats needed to make a 5-animal group, 5, to get $\frac{22}{5} = 4.4$. Since the question asks for complete 5-animal groups, round down. Bethany can make 4 complete 5-animal groups of goats with the 22 available goats. The correct answer is (E).

38. **G**   The question asks for the coordinates of point *F* on the given isosceles triangle *DEF*. Start by ballparking. Note that point *F* lies on the *x*-axis. Any point on the *x*-axis has a *y*-coordinate of 0. Eliminate (F), (J), and (K) as they do not have a *y*-coordinate of 0. Now use the Geometry Basic Approach to label the figure. The triangle is isosceles, which means that side *DE* and side *EF* are congruent. This also means that the *x*-coordinate of point *E* is halfway between the *x*-coordinates of point *D* and point *F*. Since the *x*-coordinate of *E* is *c*, and point *D* has an *x*-coordinate of 0, the *x*-coordinate of *F* is twice the *x*-coordinate of *E*, or 2*c*. Eliminate (H). The coordinates of *F* are (2*c*, 0). The correct answer is (G).

39. **E**   The question asks for the measure of the angle on a figure. Use the Geometry Basic Approach and label the figure. Triangle *DEF* is isosceles, so label sides *DE* and *EF* as congruent and $\angle EDF$ and $\angle EFD$ as congruent. There are 180° in a triangle, so the measure of $\angle EDF$ and $\angle EFD$ together is $180° - 135° = 45°$. Since $\angle EDF$ and $\angle EFD$ are congruent, divide that measurement by 2 to get the measure of $\angle EDF$: $\frac{45°}{2} = 22.5$. The question asks for the measure of the angle *formed by DE and the y-axis*. Since the *x*- and *y*-axes form a right angle, subtract the measure of $\angle EDF$ from 90° to get $90° - 22.5° = 67.5°$. The correct answer is (E).

40. **J**   The question asks for the *ordered pair* of point E', which is formed when the *isosceles triangle DEF is rotated clockwise by 180° about the origin*. Use the Geometry Basic Approach. Draw the rotated version of triangle *DEF* in Quadrant III, where the side *DF* is on the negative x-axis and point E' is below the x-axis. In this position, point E' has x- and y-coordinates that are negative. Eliminate (F), (G), and (K), which all have at least one positive coordinate. Point E' will be as far below the x-axis in the new position as it was above the x-axis in the original position. That means that the y-coordinate is $-d$. If that is not easy to see, draw the approximate coordinates of (H) and (J) on the figure. Eliminate (H) because it has the wrong y-coordinate. The correct answer is (J).

41. **A**   The question asks for the answer that is the *closest to the area of the base, in square inches*, of a pyramid shaped container with height of 15 inches and volume of 2 gallons. Use the Word Problem Basic Approach and work in bite-sized pieces. The question asks for the volume of a pyramid, so use the Geometry Basic Approach. Write down the given formula: $V = \frac{1}{3}Bh$. Next, note that the question is asking for the answer in square inches, but it is providing the volume in gallons. Use the conversion given in the question, *a gallon is 231 cubic inches,* to convert the volume to cubic inches: $(2)(231) = 462$ cubic inches. Now plug the volume and height into the volume formula and solve for the area of the base: $462 = \frac{1}{3}B(15)$. Simplify to get $462 = 5B$, and divide both sides by 5 to get $92.4 = B$. The question asks for the closest value, so round to get 92 square inches. The correct answer is (A).

42. **F**   The question asks *what portion of the book, on average, must Aaron read per month for the remaining 4 months*. Use the Word Problem Basic Approach and work in bite-sized pieces. First determine how much of the book Aaron has read at the end of the first 2 months. The question states he reads $\frac{1}{8}$ of the book each month, so add: $\frac{1}{8} + \frac{1}{8} = \frac{2}{8} = \frac{1}{4}$. The portion of the book that remains to be read is $1 - \frac{1}{4} = \frac{3}{4}$. There is $\frac{3}{4}$ of the book left to read in the remaining 4 months, so divide $\frac{3}{4}$ by 4, which is the same as multiplying by $\frac{1}{4}$: $\left(\frac{3}{4}\right)\left(\frac{1}{4}\right) = \frac{3}{16}$. The correct answer is (F).

43. **D**   The question asks for the correct application of the quadratic formula to a quadratic equation. When a quadratic equation is in standard form, $ax^2 + bx + c = 0$, the quadratic formula is $\frac{-b \pm \sqrt{b^2 - 4ac}}{2a}$. In the given equation $2x^2 + 3x - 10 = 0$; $a = 2$, $b = 3$, and $c = -10$. Work in bite-sized pieces and let the answers help. The $-b$ portion of the quadratic formula will be -3, so eliminate (A) and (B). The first term under the radical is 9 in all of the remaining answers, so skip it. The $-4ac$ portion of the quadratic equation becomes $-4(2)(-10)$. Eliminate (C) and (E) since they do not match. The correct answer is (D).

44. **K** The question asks for the coordinates of an end point of a line given the other end point and the midpoint. Use the Geometry Basic Approach. Write down the formula for the midpoint of a line: $\left(\dfrac{x_1 + x_2}{2}, \dfrac{y_1 + y_2}{2}\right)$, where (x_1, y_1) and (x_2, y_2) are end points. Create an equation for each coordinate, and plug in the end points, $(-7, 3)$ and (c, d), and the midpoint, $(-2, 5)$. Working in bite-sized pieces, first solve for c. Start with the x-coordinate: $\dfrac{-7 + c}{2} = -2$. Multiply both sides by 2 to get $-7 + c = 2(-2)$; then simplify to $-7 + c = -4$. Finally add 7 to both sides to get $c = 3$. Eliminate (F), (G), and (H) since their x-coordinate is not 3. Now solve for d by following the same steps for the y-coordinate: $\dfrac{3 + d}{2} = 5$. Multiply both sides by 2 to get $3 + d = 10$. Subtract 3 from both sides to get $d = 7$. Eliminate (J). The correct answer is (K).

45. **A** The question asks for *the length, in meters, of the shadow along the level ground.* Use the Geometry Basic Approach and label this side as x. There are trigonometric expressions in the answer choices, so write out SOHCAHTOA to remember the trig functions. In relation to the angle that is 55°, the side labeled 4 is the opposite side, and the side labeled x is the adjacent side. The TOA part of SOHCAHTOA defines tangent as $\dfrac{opposite}{adjacent}$, so $\tan 55° = \dfrac{4}{x}$. Multiply both sides by x to get $x \tan 55° = 4$; then divide both sides by $\tan 55°$ to get $x = \dfrac{4}{\tan 55°}$. The correct answer is (A).

46. **J** The question asks for the equation that represents a graph. To find the best equation, compare features of the graph to the answer choices. The answer choices are already in $y = mx + b$ form, in which m is the slope and b is the y-intercept. The graph for this question has a y-intercept about halfway between 0 and 4 and a negative slope. Eliminate answer choices that do not match this information. Choices (G) and (K) have the wrong y-intercept; eliminate them. Choice (F) has a positive slope, so eliminate it. The difference between (H) and (J) is the slope. The figure gives an approximate location for the x-intercept, so plug in $y = 0$ and solve for x to see if the points match. Start with (H) to get $0 = -\dfrac{1}{2}(x) + 2$. Subtract 2 from both sides to get $-2 = -\dfrac{1}{2}(x)$; then multiply each side by -2 to get $4 = x$. It is clear that 4 is not the x-intercept for the graph so eliminate (H). The correct answer is (J).

47. **C** The question asks for *the area, in square coordinate units, of ABCD*. Notice that the question provides the quadrilateral *ABCD* as it appears on the coordinate plane and the coordinates of the vertices. Further note that a line can be drawn from point *D* horizontally to side *BC* to divide the quadrilateral into a rectangle and a right triangle that share a side. Find the area of the rectangle and the triangle and add them to find the area of the entire quadrilateral. Use the Geometry Basic Approach and write the formulas for the area of a rectangle and the area of a triangle, which are $A = lw$ and $A = \frac{1}{2}bh$, respectively. Find the width of the rectangle, side *AB*, by using the distance formula, or noting that both points *A* and *B* both lie on the line $y = -3$ and the distance is the difference in the *x*-coordinates: $2 - (-3) = 2 + 3 = 5$. Similarly, the length of the rectangle can be found by subtracting the *y*-coordinates of points *A* and *D* since both lie on the line $x = -3$. This becomes $4 - (-3) = 4 + 3 = 7$. The area of the rectangle is therefore $A = (5)(7) = 35$. Eliminate (A) and (B) since they are smaller than the area of a portion of *ABCD*. Also eliminate (E); 81 is too large because it is more than twice the area of the rectangle. Finally, find the base and height of the triangle so that the area can be calculated. The base of the triangle is the same as side *AB*, which is 5. The height of the triangle will be the difference between the *y*-coordinate of point *C* and the *y*-coordinate of the point at which the horizontal line drawn from point *D* intersects side *BC*. Because the line drawn from point *D* is horizontal, it will have the same *y*-coordinate as point *D*, which is 4. The *y*-coordinate of point *C* is 6. The difference between the two is $6 - 4 = 2$, so the height of the triangle is 2. Substitute the base and height into the formula for the area of a triangle to get $A = \frac{1}{2}(5)(2) = 5$. Add this to the area of the rectangle, 35, to get the total area of figure *ABCD*: $35 + 5 = 40$. The correct answer is (C).

48. **J** The question asks for *the slope between any 2 points on the graph* of *total expenditures*. The question asks for a relationship between 2 values, but there are no values given in the question for *E* or *p*. Plug in values to find 2 points on the graph; then calculate the slope. Use the Geometry Basic Approach and write down the formula for the slope given two points: $\frac{y_2 - y_1}{x_2 - x_1}$. Drawing a coordinate plane and plotting the points can also be helpful, so do that if necessary. Now plug in a value for *p*, the number of products, and calculate *E* to find the coordinate point. Make $p = 1$. The value of *E* equals *p* times the cost of each product, 45¢, so $E = (1)(\$0.45) = \$0.45$. The first point (p, E) is $(1, 0.45)$. Now repeat

with a different number for p to find a second point: $p = 2$, $E = (2)(\$0.45) = \$0.90$. The second point is (2, 0.90). Use the slope formula to find the slope of this line: $\dfrac{0.90 - 0.45}{2 - 1} = 0.45$. Eliminate (F), (H) and (K) since the slope is neither 2 nor negative. Comparing the remaining answers shows that the slope could either be one positive value or several positive values. A slope between any two points on a line is always a constant number, so eliminate (G). The correct answer is (J).

49. **B**   The question asks for *the fifth term in a geometric sequence* given the *first four terms are* 10, 15, 22.5, and 33.75. A geometric sequence is a list of numbers with a constant ratio between terms. This means that each term is multiplied or divided by the same number to produce the next term. Since the question provides the first four terms, use two of them to determine the ratio between terms. Divide the second term by the first to get $\dfrac{15}{10} = 1.5$. To produce the fifth term in this sequence, multiply the fourth term by 1.5: (33.75)(1.5) = 50.625. The correct answer is (B).

50. **H**   The question asks for *the volume, in cubic inches, of a cube*, given the surface area. Use the Geometry Basic Approach and write down the necessary formulas. The formula for the volume of a cube is $V = s^3$. The formula for the surface area of a solid is the sum of the areas of the faces. For a cube this is $S = 6s^2$. Plug in the value for the surface area given in the question and solve for s: $54 = 6s^2$. Divide both sides by 6 to get $9 = s^2$. Take the square root of each side to get $s = 3$. Now plug that value into the volume formula: $V = 3^3 = 27$. The correct answer is (H).

51. **D**   The question asks for *the measure of the central angle of a shaded region* of a circle. Use the Geometry Basic Approach and write out the necessary formulas. The parts of a circle have a proportional relationship. In a circle, the fraction of the degrees in the shaded region to the total degrees in the circle, 360°, is the same as the fraction of the area of the shaded sector to the total area. Set up the proportion $\dfrac{\text{degrees}}{360°} = \dfrac{\text{sector area}}{\text{total area}}$. The total area of the circle isn't given, but since the radius is provided, the area can be calculated. Write down the formula for the area of a circle: $A = \pi r^2$. Substitute in the value for the radius and solve for the area of the circle: $A = 5^2\pi = 25\pi$. Now plug this value and the area of the sector given in the question into the proportion, letting x stand for the number of degrees in the central angle: $\dfrac{x}{360°} = \dfrac{15\pi}{25\pi}$. Cross-multiply to get $25\pi x = (360°)15\pi$. Divide both sides by 25π and simplify to get $x = 216°$. The correct answer is (D).

52. J The question asks for the *equation* that *represents the graph of a circle*. The equation of a circle in standard form is $(x - h)^2 + (y - k)^2 = r^2$, where (h, k) is the center and r is the radius. Since $r = 4$ in this question and $r^2 = 16$, the right side of the equation must be 16. Eliminate (F) and (G) since they do not have 16 on the right side of the equation. The center is at $(2, -6)$, so the value of k in this question is -6. Therefore, the binomial containing y in the equation of this circle will be $(y - (-6))^2$, which simplifies to $(y + 6)^2$. Eliminate (H) and (K). The correct answer is (J).

53. E The question asks for *the expression for the length, in inches, of* $\overline{XZ}$. Use the Geometry Basic Approach.

Draw triangle XYZ and label angle $X = 53°$, angle $Y = 88°$, and the length of side $\overline{YZ}$ is 11. The

note gives the Law of Sines, which relates sines of angles and lengths of sides in a triangle. Set up a

proportion using the sines of the known angles and the lengths of their opposite sides. This would

be $\dfrac{\sin Y}{XZ} = \dfrac{\sin X}{YZ}$. Plug in the given values and solve for XZ: $\dfrac{\sin 88°}{XZ} = \dfrac{\sin 53°}{11}$. Cross-multiply to get

$XZ \sin 53° = 11 \sin 88°$. Divide both sides by $\sin 53°$ to get $XZ = \dfrac{11 \sin 88°}{\sin 53°}$. The correct answer is (E).

54. K The question asks for the difference of the length, in feet, of the circumferences of two circles. Use the Geometry Basic Approach. Draw two circles, the first smaller than the second. Write down the formula for the circumference of a circle: $C = 2\pi r$. There are variables in the answer choices and the question asks for a relationship between variables, so plug in. Make the radius of the second circle 10, and label it. Make $p = 6$. According to the question the radius of the first circle is the radius of the second one minus p. So the radius of the first circle is $10 - 6 = 4$. Label these values on the appropriate circles. Now calculate the circumference of each circle. The circumference of the smaller circle is $C = 2\pi(4) = 8\pi$, and the circumference of the larger circle is $C = 2\pi(10) = 20\pi$. The difference is $20\pi - 8\pi = 12\pi$. This is the target value; circle it. Plug $p = 6$ into the answer choices to see which one matches the target value. Choice (F) becomes $\sqrt{6}$. This does not match the target value, so eliminate (F). It is also possible to eliminate (G) and (J) at this point since neither of those answers include π, which is part of the target value. Choice (H) becomes $\pi 6 = 6\pi$. Eliminate (H) because it does not match the target value. Choice (K) becomes $2\pi 6 = 12\pi$. This does match the target, and all other answers have been eliminated. The correct answer is (K).

55. C The question asks for an expression equivalent to $|y + 3|$ when $y \leq -3$. When working with absolute values, do the calculations inside the absolute value symbols as if they were parentheses, and then take the absolute value. There are variables in the answer choices, so plug in. Make y a value that fulfills the requirements of the question that $y \leq -3$. Make $y = -4$; the expression becomes $|-4 + 3| = |-1| = 1$. This is the target value; circle it. Choice (E) is 0; it does not match the target, so eliminate it. Now plug $y = -4$ into the remaining choices to see which one matches the target value. Choice (A) becomes $-4 - 3 = -7$. Eliminate (A). Choice (B) becomes $-4 + 3 = -1$. Eliminate (B). Choice (C) becomes $-(-4) - 3 = 4 - 3 = 1$. Keep (C) but check (D) just in case. Choice (D) becomes $-(-4) + 3 = 4 + 3 = 7$. Eliminate (D). The correct answer is (C).

56. **H** The question asks for *the total number of countries in the trade union that have 20, 21, or 22 cities*. Use the Word Problem Basic Approach and work in bite-sized pieces. The question states that there are 18 countries total in the trade union and that 7 of those countries have fewer than 20 cities. Subtract 7 from 18 to get 11 countries with 20 or more cities. The question also states that there are 2 countries with more than 22 cities. Subtract these 2 countries from the remaining 11 to get 9 countries with 20, 21, or 22 cities. The remaining information in the question is extraneous and does not help answer the question. The correct answer is (H).

57. **C** The question asks for the value of $\cos 2x$ given that $\sin x = -\dfrac{3}{4}$. The question also provides a note that $(\sin x)^2 = \dfrac{1 - \cos 2x}{2}$. Since both $\sin x$ and $\cos 2x$ are present in this formula, plug in the provided value of $\sin x$ and solve for $\cos 2x$: $\left(-\dfrac{3}{4}\right)^2 = \dfrac{1 - \cos 2x}{2}$. Simplify the left side of the equation to get $\dfrac{9}{16} = \dfrac{1 - \cos 2x}{2}$. Cross-multiply to get $16(1 - \cos 2x) = 18$. Divide both sides by 16 and simplify the fraction to get $1 - \cos 2x = \dfrac{9}{8}$. Subtract 1 from both sides to get $-\cos 2x = \dfrac{1}{8}$. Finally, multiply both sides by -1 to get $\cos 2x = -\dfrac{1}{8}$. The correct answer is (C).

58. **H** The question asks for *the value of k*. In function notation, the number inside the parentheses is the x-value that goes into the function, and the value that comes out of the function is the y-value. This is a compound function question, but the notation still works the same way. Therefore, $y = f(g(x))$ becomes $y = f\left(\dfrac{x}{2} - k\right)$. Plug the point $(-2, 8)$ into the equation to get $8 = f\left(\dfrac{-2}{2} - k\right)$, which simplifies to $8 = f(-1 - k)$. Now plug these values into the f function to get $8 = (-1 - k)^3$. Take the cube root of both sides to get $2 = -1 - k$. Add 1 to both sides to get $3 = -k$. Multiply both sides by -1 to get $k = -3$. The correct answer is (H).

59. **D** The question asks for the number of *disjoint regions* that *have a finite, nonzero area* in a particular situation. Disjoint regions are non-overlapping regions. Note that the question asks specifically for regions that have a *finite area*, meaning the regions are bounded on all sides. Use the Geometry Basic Approach. Draw 7 vertical lines and 7 horizontal lines. This will create a 6 × 6 grid of areas bounded on all sides: 36 disjoint regions with finite areas. The areas on the outside of this grid are all unbounded on at least one side; the area of each one is infinite, and they do not fit the parameters of the question. The correct answer is (D).

60. **G**   The question asks which of the answers *must be less than 0*. There are variables in the answer choices, so plug in. Note that the inequality states that $x^3y^4z^6 < 0$, which means that one of the parts of this inequality must be negative. Exponent rules say that any number raised to an even power will be positive, so the only variable in this inequality that must be negative is x; y and z can be either positive or negative. Plug in numbers for x, y, and z accordingly. Make $x = -2$, $y = 3$, and $z = 4$. Plug these numbers into the original inequality to check that they work: $(-2)^3(3)^4(4)^6 = (-8)(81)(4,096) = -2,654,208$. This is true, so plug in $x = -2$, $y = 3$, and $z = 4$ into the answer choices to see which one matches the requirement: a number that is always negative. Choice (F) becomes $(-2)(3) = -6$. Keep (F) because it is negative, but check the remaining answers just in case. Choice (G) becomes $(-2)(3)^2 = (-2)(9) = -18$. Keep (G). Choice (H) becomes $(3)(4) = 12$. Eliminate (H). Choice (J) becomes $(-2)(3)(4) = -24$. Keep (J). Choice (K) becomes $(-2)^2(3)^2(4)^3 = (4)(9)(64) = 2,304$. Eliminate (K). Choices (F), (G) and (J) work, so pick new numbers and try again. Since this question deals with positives and negatives, try changing one of the signs for y or z. This time plug in $x = -2$, $y = -3$, and $z = 4$. Choice (F) becomes $(-2)(-3) = 6$. Eliminate (F). Choice (G) becomes $(-2)(-3)^2 = (-2)(9) = -18$. Keep (G). Choice (J) becomes $(-2)(-3)(4) = 24$. Eliminate (J). The correct answer is (G).